In Defense Of Liberal Democracy

Walter Berns

GATEWAY EDITIONS

Chicago

Published by Regnery Gateway
940-950 North Shore Drive
Lake Bluff, Illinois 60044

Manufactured in The United States of America

Library of Congress Cataloging in Publication Data

Berns, Walter, 1919-
  In defense of liberal democracy.

  Includes bibliographical references.
  1. United States—Politics and government—Addresses, essays, lectures.   2. Democracy—Addresses, essays, lectures.   3. Liberty—Addresses, essays, lectures.
I. Title.
JK21.B47   1984   321.8'0973   84-17779
ISBN 0-89526-831-0

To my children,
Elizabeth, Emily, and Christopher

CONTENTS

Preface

PART V: RELIGION AND POLITICS

PREFACE

Some of these essays originated in scholarly curiosity; a conspicuous example of this is the *Yale Law Journal* article on the migration of slaves, which began in genuine puzzlement about the meaning of an obsolete constitutional provision, one that had long been *functus officio*, as the lawyers used to say. Others—such as the reply to the Soviets before the UN Human Rights Commission or the *Commentary* article on racial quotas—were responses to current but recurring political events or developments and were intended to influence those developments. Still others, I readily confess, arose out of moral indignation—in this category belong the piece on the Jesuit priest Dan Berrigan and that on the Catholic bishops—and their inclusion here, as well as their original publication, can be justified only if my indignation is not and was not idiosyncratic. Yet, despite their different origins and dissimilar appearance (some scholarly, some journalistic), these various essays are informed by a common and enduring concern. Like Molière's Monsieur Jourdan who had to be reminded that he had been speaking prose all his life, it became apparent to me only lately that, throughout my academic and professional career and in one way or another, I had been doing nothing so much as defending liberal democracy and the institutions embodying it here in the United States.

First among these institutions is the Constitution whose bicentennial we shall soon mark but which not many in public life or the academy are truly prepared or even disposed to celebrate. It is not taken seriously by the typical judge or Supreme Court justice. He treats his commission as a kind of letter of marque authorizing him to keep the Constitution in tune with the times, as the saying goes, which in practice means *his* view of the times and what *he* thinks they require. For this he is likely to be praised by the professors who share his opinions. Thus, the late Justice Douglas was praised for daring to raise the question of what is good for the country and to translate his answer into constitutional law. It seldom occurs to professor or judge that, properly understood, the judge's office is, in part and to the extent possible, to keep the times in tune with the Constitution.

This may explain why the Constitution itself is rarely the object of study in our schools. As I wrote a few years ago, in an essay not reprinted here, there is probably not a law school in the country that does not offer a course in constitutional law or many that do not make it a part of the required curriculum. "One wonders, however, how many offer a course on the Constitution." So far as I have been able to learn, the answer to that question is none. Yet, as I went on to say, "the difference between a course on constitutional law and a course on the Constitution is the difference between a course on the Supreme Court and a course on the principles of free government."

Free government is an endangered species in our world—anyone who doubts this should be sentenced to a term at the UN—and it is not exactly thriving here at home. It is not easy government; it requires obedience to constitutional rules and forms, and political passion is inclined to rebel against rules and forms. When these passions are powerful, free government may become unpopular government, which may explain the inability or (and perhaps it amounts to the same thing) the unwillingness to defend it in our time.

Washington, D.C.
January 1984

PART I

THE CONSTITUTION

CHAPTER 1

THE CONSTITUTION AS BILL OF RIGHTS

I

At a time when so much attention is being paid to the subject of human rights and being focused especially on those countries that do not recognize them, it is only to be expected that Americans would be conscious of their exceptional fortune in this respect. Nor is it remarkable that they should attribute this to the Bill of Rights, in our day probably the most visible part of the Constitution, and to a judiciary with the power to enforce its provisions. Soviet citizens are not permitted freely to express their political opinions, but Americans have the First Amendment; Argentinians are brutally tortured, but Americans are protected by the Fifth Amendment's provision against self-incrimination; Cubans are held in jail without trial, but thanks to habeas corpus and the Sixth Amendment's right to a speedy and public trial, that sort of thing cannot happen to Americans. The list could be extended until it comprised all the privileges, immunities, and rights specified in the Constitution and the literally hundreds of corresponding cases where they have been upheld or enforced by the courts. How does the Constitution secure rights? By delineating them in its text and empowering the courts to enforce them. That is the usual answer to our question.

3

It is, for example, the answer given in the *Citizens' Guide to Individual Rights under the Constitution of the United States of America*, an official government publication prepared by the Subcommittee on the Constitution of the Senate Judiciary Committee.[1] After a brief (three-page) introduction of the sort appropriate to guidebooks and where, for example, the point is made that the original Constitution specified only a few privileges or rights and that still others have their bases not in the Constitution but in various statues, the *Citizens' Guide* proceeds to list and then to elaborate the various constitutional provisions, most of them to be found in the first ten amendments. As then-Senator Birch Bayh said in his preface to the volume, the "guarantees of individual rights found in our Constitution's Bill of Rights are the very foundation of America's free and democratic society."[2] My purpose here is not so much to argue against this contention as to show its inadequacies.

I am aware that most Americans would find Bayh's statement unexceptionable, but it is, nevertheless, an unusual contention, at least in the sense of being one that demands an explanation; after all, it is not usual for an appendage to serve as the foundation of a structure. Of course, Bayh may be right in suggesting that while we owe our system of government to the body of the Constitution, we owe our liberty or our rights to its amendments. But if Bayh is right, the Framers were wrong. They expected the Constitution, even without amendments, to "secure the blessings of liberty," or, they could just as well have said, to secure the rights with which all men are by nature endowed.

What is beyond dispute is the purpose of the original amendments; they were adopted in order to limit the powers of the national government, not of the states. The Supreme Court so held in *Barron* v. *Baltimore* in 1833,[3] and anyone familiar with the debates in the First Congress, which formally proposed the amendments, or with the political agitation that had led Congress to propose and the states to ratify them, would have to agree that the Court was correct in so holding. It was Congress that was forbidden to make laws respecting an establishment of religion or prohibiting the free exercise thereof, Congress that was not to abridge the freedom of speech and press or infringe the right to keep and bear arms; the national executive that was not to quarter troops in a house without the owner's consent, or engage in unreasonable searches and seizures; the national judiciary that, to confine myself to the single example of the Eighth Amendment, was forbidden to require excessive bail, impose excessive fines, or inflict cruel and unusual punishments. Leaving aside the few provisions in Article I, section 10, it was not until after the Civil War that the Constitution was amended to contain specific limitations on the powers of the states.

What is also beyond dispute, although very little attention has been paid to it, is that during what is still the greater part of our history (1789–1925), the Bill of Rights played almost no role in the securing of rights. Prior to the *Gitlow* case in 1925,[4] which began the process of incorporation or absorption of the Bill of Rights into or by the Fourteenth Amendment (thereby making them applicable to the states), there were few cases involving the first ten amendments and fewer still—in fact, only fifteen—in which a governmental action was held to be in conflict with one of them. There were only nine such cases during all of the nineteenth century, one of these being *Dred Scott* v. *Sandford* (scarcely a monument to liberty) and another being *Hepburn* v. *Griswold*, which was promptly overruled.[5] The religious liberty enjoyed by Americans owed nothing to judicial enforcement of the First Amendment, and the same is true respecting the freedom of speech and press; not once during these first 136 years did the Supreme Court invalidate an act of Congress on First Amendment grounds. (This did not occur, in a speech case, until 1967 and, in a religion case, until 1971.[6]) On one occasion, the Court invalidated a federal search and seizure,[7] but most of the pre-*Gitlow* cases involved one or another aspect of the Fifth Amendment.[8] The fact is, the Bill of Rights has served (and continues to serve) mainly to secure rights from abridgment by the states and not the federal government, the very opposite of the role the amendments were intended to play (or the role the Anti-Federalists expected them to have to play).

On the whole, then, history has vindicated the Federalists who insisted that, so far as the federal government was the object of concern, a bill of rights was unnecessary. As they saw it, the threat to rights would be posed by popular majorities, and against such majorities bills of specified rights would prove (as in the states they had already proved) to be mere "parchment barriers."[9] It is, therefore, not surprising that as it came from the Philadelphia convention the Constitution did not contain a bill of rights, or that the word right (or rights) appears only once in its text.[10] Yet, as Publius insisted in *Federalist* 84, "the Constitution is itself, in every rational sense, and to every useful purpose, A BILL OF RIGHTS." We can learn something of importance about the securing of human rights by understanding what Publius meant by this statement.

II

In Article I, section 9, the Constitution contains a statement of what might be called privileges and immunities, but this did not satisfy the Anti-Federalists, such as Patrick Henry. In his view, the Constitution ought to have begun with a statement of general principles, or of "admirable maxims," such as that to be found in the Virginia Declaration of Rights.[11] That statement reads as follows: "That all men are by nature equally free and independent, and have certain inherent rights, of which, when they enter a state of society, they cannot by any compact deprive or divest their posterity; namely, the enjoyment of life and liberty, with the means of acquiring and possessing property, and pursuing and obtaining happiness and safety."[12] In short, a bill of rights ought to be affixed to the Constitution containing a statement of natural rights.

The Federalists disagreed. They were forced to concede that the Constitution might properly contain a statement of *civil* rights, and they were instrumental in the adoption of the first ten amendments which we know as the Bill of Rights, but they were opposed to a statement of first principles in the text of the Constitution. However true, such a statement might serve to undermine or destabilize government, even government established on those principles.[13] And the Constitution was indeed an embodiment of those principles; this is what Publius meant by insisting that it was itself a bill of rights.

It is a bill of *natural* rights, not because it contains a statement or compendium of those rights—it does not—but because it is an expression of the natural right of everyone to govern himself and to specify the terms according to which he agrees to give up his natural freedom by submitting to the rules of civil government. The Constitution emanates from us, "THE PEOPLE of the United States," and here in its first sentence, said Publius, "is a better recognition of popular rights than volumes of those aphorisms which make the principal figure in several of our State bills of rights and which would sound much better in a treatise of ethics than in a constitution of government."[14] It is not usually appreciated that natural rights point or lead to government, a government with the *power* to secure rights, and only secondarily to limitations on govermental power. We tend to think of government as the enemy of rights, as, of course, it can be; but, according to the principles on the basis of which the United States was founded, goverment is first of all the necessary condition of the enjoyment of rights.*

To say this is not to deny the revolutionary character of natural rights, or perhaps more precisely, of the natural rights teaching. The United States began in a revolution accompanied by an appeal to the natural and unalienable rights of life, liberty, and the pursuit of happiness. But these words of Declaration of Independence are followed immediately by the statement that "to secure these rights,

---

*In this section, I have relied heavily on my article, "Natural Rights and the American Constitution," written for the forthcoming *Encyclopedia of the American Constitution*, Leonard W. Levy, editor.

Governments are instituted among Men." Natural rights point or lead to government in the same way that the Declaration of Independence points or leads to the Constitution: the rights, which are possessed by all men equally by nature (or in the state of nature), require a well-governed civil society for their security.

The link between the state of nature and civil society, or between natural rights and government, is supplied by the laws of nature. The laws of nature in this (modern) sense must be distinguished from the natural law as understood in the Christian tradition, for example. According to the Christian teaching, the natural law consists of commands and prohibitions derived from the inclinations (or the natural ordering of the passions and desires), and is enforced, ultimately, by the sanction of divine punishment. Here, for example, in *Calvin's Case* (1609), is Sir Edward Coke on the law of nature understood in the traditional sense:

> The law of nature is that which God at the time of creation of the nature of man infused into his heart, for his preservation and direction; and this is Lex *aeterna*, the moral law, called also the law of nature. And by this law, written with the finger of God in the heart of man, were the people of God a long time governed before the law was written by Moses, who was the first reporter or writer of the law in the world. . . . [15]

The point has been made by leading constitutional scholars—for example, Edward S. Corwin[16] and more recently Thomas C. Grey[17]—that not only did Americans understand natural law in this sense (and to support this they are inclined to cite pre-revolutionary cases in which Coke is quoted or accepted as authority), but that it was this understanding of a natural law that was embodied in the founding principles. But they are mistaken. What they fail to understand is that natural rights and traditional natural law are, to put it simply yet altogether accurately, incompatible; to espouse the one teaching is to make it impossible reasonably to espouse the other, and in 1776 Americans espoused natural rights. Natural law according to the tradition constituted a kind of higher law (which is how

Corwin refers to it) by which one judges the justice or goodness of the positive law. But here is Thomas Hobbes on that subject: "by a good law I mean not a just law: for no law can be unjust."[18] And here is John Locke: "Can the law of nature be known from man's natural inclinations? No."[19]

In the teachings of Hobbes and Locke, the laws of nature are merely deductions from the rights of nature and ultimately from the right of self-preservation. Rather than being a "higher law" as Corwin and Gray use that term, these newly discovered laws of nature are no more than prescriptions, or better, directions, showing men how to escape from the state of nature, or, how to escape the condition that nature put them in; this must be escaped because it is unbearable—which is to say, unmodified nature is unbearable.

It is unbearable precisely because everyone has a right to preserve his own life and there is nothing to prevent him from doing whatever he thinks is necessary to secure it. The consequence is that the state of nature is indistinguishable from the state of war, where in Hobbes's famous formulation, life is "solitary, poor, nasty, brutish, and short." Even in Locke's more benign version, and for the same reason, life in the state of nature is characterized by many unendurable "inconveniences."[20] In short, while men have rights by nature, or in the state of nature, these rights are insecure in the state of nature; in fact, human life itself becomes insufferable.

What is required for self-preservation, the fundamental right of nature, is peace, and, as rational beings, men can come to understand "the fundamental law of nature" which is, as Hobbes formulates it, *"to seek peace, and follow it."* From this is derived the second law of nature, that men should enter in a contract with one another according to which they surrender their natural rights to an absolute sovereign who is instituted by the contract and who, from that time forward, represents their rights. More briefly stated, each person must consent to be governed, which he does by *laying down* his natural right to govern himself.[21]

Locke agrees that the state of nature has a law of nature to govern the relations among men. This law obliges everyone, "when his own preservation comes not in competition . . . to preserve the rest of mankind."[22] The law of nature, therefore, dictates the preservation of everyone as well as the condition of this preservation, peace. The trouble is, although there is a degree of difference between Locke and Hobbes on this question, at a certain point peace becomes virtually impossible in the state of nature: the law of nature dictates peace but, because everyone must be concerned first of all with himself, the law cannot be obeyed.[23] In another of its aspects, the law instructs men as to how to achieve peace, but the provisions of this law can be understood only by a "studier of that law,"[24] someone like Locke and those who study and master his text. What that text teaches is that men must leave that state of nature and enter a political society, which is possible only "where every one of the members has quitted his natural power [to enforce the law of nature], resigned it up into the hands of the community. . . ."[25]

In the same way, Americans of 1776 were guided by "the Laws of Nature and of Nature's God" when they declared their independence and constituted themselves a new political community. Commanding nothing, for these are not laws in the proper sense of commands that must be obeyed, the laws of nature (for Hobbes, for Locke, and for the Americans of 1776) point to government as the way to secure natural rights, government that derives its "just powers from the consent of the governed."

It must be emphasized that in the natural rights teaching neither civil society nor government exists by nature or in nature. By nature everyone is sovereign with respect to himself, free to do whatever in his judgment is necessary to preserve his own life. Civil society is an artificial person to which this real person, acting in concert with others, surrenders his natural and sovereign powers, and upon this agreement civil society becomes the sovereign with respect to those who consented to the surrender.[26] It is civil society, in the exercise of this sovereign power, that institutes and empowers government.

So it was that Americans became "the People of the United States" in 1776 and in 1787–8, ordained and established "this CONSTITUTION for the United States of America." The Constitution is the product of the "will" of the sovereign people of the United States,[27] the civil society to which the individual and formerly sovereign persons surrendered their natural rights. They agreed to the surrender because they were persuaded that only by surrendering their rights to defend themselves could there be peace, and with peace, security for their rights.

Peace and security for rights require first of all a government with powers. "In framing a government which is to be administered by men over men," Publius said in *Federalist* 51, "the great difficuty lies in this: you must first enable the government to control the governed. . . ." What will be required to effect this control will vary from place to place and from time to time, and the powers to be exercised by government will vary accordingly. This is the burden of John Marshall's frequently quoted (and almost as frequently misunderstood) statement in his opinion for the Court in *McCulloch* v. *Maryland*. Congress's powers are given in a Constitution "intended to endure for ages to come, and consequently, [those powers are] to be adapted to the various crises of human affairs." It is not the Constitution that is adaptable—its meaning is fixed—but the powers must be adaptable, for, as Marshall says,

> To have prescribed the means by which government should, in all future time, execute its powers, would have been to change, entirely, the character of the instrument, and give it the properties of a legal code. It would have been an unwise attempt to provide, by immutable rules, for exigencies which, if foreseen at all, must have been seen dimly, and which can be best provided for as they occur.[28]

Men surrendered their sovereign power to defend themselves only with the understanding that government would provide them with a more effective defense. As in the state of nature so in civil society, rights are threatened most of all by other men, and by other nations, and it is the primary function of government to protect men from other men and other nations. It is not for no reason that Hobbes, the first natural rights philosopher, created a sovereign—a Leviathan—who resembled nothing so much as a chief of police.

By way of summary: the fundamental human right (or in the original and correct parlance, the right with which all men are endowed by nature) is the right of self-preservation. Men enter civil society as the first step in the process by which this right can be secured. Since all are equal in respect of this right (and, on this occasion, this is the only relevant respect), each member of that civil society is entitled to one vote on the question of the form, organization, and powers of the government instituted to secure the rights of all; and since these votes must be weighted equally, it follows that the majority rules and that each must agree to be bound by the majority. (By so agreeing, each shows his respect for the rights of others.) The right to share equally in this decision is the most important human right because government is the means by which all other rights are secured. Of necessity, this government must possess the strength or the powers required to protect those rights against the forces that threaten them.

III

The power exercised by civil society, that artificial sovereign created by men upon contracting to leave the state of nature, is, in principle, almost unlimited. Its single function is to institute government; acting through its majority, it is free to determine the form of government (for, as I indicated, the Declaration of Independence says indirectly and Locke says explicitly,[29] that any one of several forms of government—democratic, republican, or even monarchical—may serve to secure rights) as well as the organization of that government and the powers given and withheld from it.[30] It will make these decisions in the light of its purpose, which is to secure the rights of the persons authorizing it and, guided by theory and experience alike, it will recognize that government, too, can pose a threat to the rights of man, even a government intended to secure them. This is why the doctrine of natural rights, if only secondarily, leads or points to limitations on government; government, as Publius said in his *Federalist* 51 statement of the problem, must not only control the governed, but must be obliged "to control itself." So it was that in 1787, "the people of the United States" decided to withhold some powers from government and, guided by what Publius referred to as an improved "science of politics,"[31] sought to insure that the powers granted would not be abused.

How does the Constitution secure rights? Not, as Publius understood the problem, by a bill of rights. Historically, bills of rights have been "stipulations between kings and their subjects, abridgments of prerogative in favor of privilege," such as Magna Charta and the English Bill of Rights of 1689,[32] and their terms have been enforced, if at all, by the political power that has been brought to bear by popular assemblies. But in the United States there will be no king to guard against; what must be feared is precisely the power of the majorities that, under republican conditions, will gain control of those popular assemblies. Everything will turn on the character of those majorities. If they are "actuated by some common impulse of passion, or of interest," they will not respect the rights of other citizens; nor will they be readily restrained by the judiciary. A Moral Majority that is allowed to become a political majority will strip the judiciary of its powers—for example, by depriving the judiciary of its jurisdiction to decide certain kinds of cases. (And it is easy to see, Publius said in *Federalist* 78, "that it would require an uncommon portion of fortitude in the judges to do their duty as faithful guardians of the Constitution, where legislative invasions of it had been instigated by the major voice of the community.") Appropriately, the problem is best stated in the most famous paper of *The Federalist*: "to secure the public good and private rights against the dangers of [a majority] faction, and at the same time to preserve the spirit and form of popular government, is the great object to which our inquiries are directed."[33] This statement reminds us that our question—how does the Constitution secure rights?—is essentially the same question raised and answered in *The Federalist*: By what means will government be prevented from abusing the powers that, of necessity, are vested in it?

Under a popular form, and especially in democratic times, those powers will be exercised by a majority. As explained by Publius, the problem can be solved, it at all, only by preventing the formation and thereby the rule of a factious majority. This can be accomplished, and on the whole has been accomplished, by means of the institutional arrangements familiar to any student of *The Federalist*: a regular distribution of power into distinct departments, a system of legislative balances and checks, an independent judiciary, a system of representation, and an enlargement of the orbit "within which such systems are to revolve."[34] Together these institutions constitute a structure designed to ensure that the country will be governed not by simple majorities but by constitutional majorities, majorities that respect constitutional limitations which are defined by private rights.

A simple majority may be defined in the terms used by Publius to define a faction; politically, it is one assembled— by a populist or a demagogue, for example—directly in and from the people. A constitutional majority is one that is assembled in the legislature and its constituent elements are representatives of the people. The possibility of assembling or building such a majority depends, first, on a system of representation (whose virtues and American characteristics are described in *Federalist* 10, as well as elsewhere), and secondly on the "enlargement of the orbit."

> The smaller the society, the fewer probably will be the distinct parties and interests composing it; the fewer the distinct parties and interests, the more frequently will a majority be found of the same party; and the smaller the number of individuals composing a majority, and the smaller the compass within which they are placed, the more easily will they concert and execute their plans of oppression. Extend the sphere and you

take in a greater variety of parties and interests; you make it less probable that a majority of the whole will have a common motive to invade the rights of other citizens. . . . [35]

Republican government requires the forming of majorities, and what is done by government—whether or not it abuses its powers—depends on the character of the majorities formed. Publius's argument is that a majority formed in a system of separated powers and a bicameral legislature is more likely to respect the rights of all the people than a majority formed in and from the people directly, especially if the members of the legislature represent a wide variety of interests and parties, and especially—hence the decision in favor of fewer representatives and larger districts—if each representative himself represents more than one interest or party. Security for rights, as the Framers saw it, would depend on the ability of these institutions, or this structure, to prevent divisions in which the majority and minority are divided on a single issue, and especially on a moral issue.

The fundamental soundness of this constitutional plan has been demonstrated in and by our history, and nowhere more dramatically than on those occasions when it has failed. The single-issue division in 1798 between "Francophiles" and "Monocrats" produced the Alien and Sedition Laws, the latter of which especially is commonly held to be one of the most egregious denials of the freedom of speech and press ever enacted by Congress. The fact is that Congress's speech and press record is not so good as the absence of Supreme Court decisions might suggest. In 1835, President Jackson called upon Congress to enact a criminal statute prohibiting "the circulation in Southern States, through the main, of incendiary publications intended to instigate the slaves to insurrection."[36] After a long and acrimonious debate, Congress refused to enact the bill, or the even more objectionable substitute measure introduced by John C. Calhoun, but this proved to be only a nominal victory for First Amendment rights. Postmasters in southern states simply refused to deliver antislavery newspapers, and no action was taken against them.[37] Then in the Civil War, when the division on the slavery issue threatened permanently to divide the country, newspapers were shut down, persons were held in jail without being brought to trial, civilians were tried by military courts, and, to mention one more example of a right abridged, property was confiscated.

These systemic failures have a common cause. The denial at the beginning of the black man's fundamental right not to be governed without his consent made it almost inevitable that he would later be denied his other rights, including his right to be represented in constitutional majorities. The consequence was that he remained a slave, and, as time passed, what was required to keep him a slave was the formation of a single-issue party. The consequences of this were felt by everyone.

All this might have been and could have been anticipated. In *Federalist* 53, Publius expressed his confidence that an increased intercourse among the different states would lead to "a general assimilation of their manners and laws," but it is only in our time that Georgia has come to resemble Pennsylvania, or the Sun Belt, in essential respects, New England. Again, in *Federalist* 56, he predicted that the changes of time on the comparative situation of the different states "will have an assimilating effect."

> The changes of time on the internal affairs of the States, taken singly, will be just the contrary. At present some of the States are little more than a society of husbandmen. Few of them have made much progress in those branches of industry which give a variety and complexity to the affairs of the nation. These, however, will in all of them be the fruits of a more advanced population; and will require, on the part of each State, a fuller representation.

That is, the states will, in time, come to resemble each other insofar as each state becomes economically more diverse. And when that happens, its representatives in Congress will each represent more than a single interest. What was required for the Framer's system to work was industrialization, and especially the industrialization of the southern states. Only then might they escape the curse of single-interest, or factional politics.

Security for rights depended on diversity of interests. Publius's most famous statement of this proposition is to be found in *Federalist* 51:

> In a free government the security for civil rights must be the same as that for religious rights. It consists in the one case in the multiplicity of interests, and in the other in the multiplicity of sects. The degree of security in both cases will depend on the number of interests and sects; and this may be presumed to depend on the extent of country and number of people comprehended under the same government.

What Publius does not say here explicitly is that while a multiplicity of interests comes with diversity, diversity does not necessarily come with greater size. An agrarian society, even one built on a continental scale, would not be characterized by a diversity or multiplicity of interests. As Martin Diamond used to say, a large Saharan republic would be divided by the Marxist-like class struggle between date-pickers and oasis-landholders. Diversity comes with commercialization or industrialization, and to promote this was Hamilton's purpose in the great state papers written during his term as Secretary of the Treasury.

What informed the Framers' constitutionalism was their knowledge, acquired from Hobbes, Locke, and Montesquieu, that security for rights would depend on their ability to devise a system in which moral differences would not become political issues. Their initial plan to foster a commercial society, with its multiplicity of economic interests, should be seen as a major element in their effort to achieve this end. In the event, as I have explained elsewhere,[38] it was James Madison (the Publius of *Federalist* 10, 51, 53, and 56) who, as much as anyone, blocked the efforts to industrialize the south and thereby diversify its interests. Thus, the national government, rather than being allowed to make the effort to control events, allowed the country to drift until the passage of time brought with it not diversity within each section and thereby a similarity of manners and laws, north and south, but the most dangerous of dissimilarities. Each section came to regard the other as a moral abomination, and a house so divided cannot stand.

But the Framers' intention was to prevent divisions along moral lines and, on the whole, their effort was successful. To this end, church was separated from state, with a view, as I once put it,[39] to subordinating religion, consigning it to the private sphere where differences could be tolerated.

To the same end, the equal right to property was secured and the "different and unequal faculties of acquiring property" were protected. This, Publius said, was "the first object of government."[40] Not only would this cause a proliferation of the kinds of property and interests connected with them, but it would serve to channel the passions and energies of Americans into safe activities. America's business would be business. In the large commercial or business republic, the animosities of moral factions would be replaced by the competition of economic interests, and, properly organized, this competition would be peaceful. As Adam Smith and before him John Locke promised, it would promote material growth and the prosperity in which all interests could share.

Before the foundation of this constitutional policy could be laid, however, men would have to be persuaded to pursue material ends above or before spiritual ones. To persuade them of this was part of the great modern project fostered by the new political philosophy of natural rights. Macaulay, writing 150 to 200 years after Locke and Hobbes, understood this as well as anyone of his time. The aim of the old philosophy, he pointed out, was to raise us far above vulgar wants, whereas the aim of the new philosophy was to satisfy our vulgar wants. "The former aim was noble," he said, "but the latter was attainable."[41] What Macaulay did not mention was that this latter aim was connected to a project that was not ignoble: the securing of rights, or to say the same thing, the achievement of human liberty. The American Constitution should be seen as an institutionalization of this modern project.

The Framers' plan for the securing of rights had still another aspect that, while closely related to industrialization and diversification, is sufficiently distinct as to deserve separate treatment. The principal political decisions would have to be made at the national rather than at the state level. In *Federalist* 51, immediately after saying that security of civil and religious rights would depend on a multiplicity of interests and sects, which, in turn, would depend on the extent of the country, Publius addresses himself to the subject of a "proper federal system." In this context he scores telling points against the Anti-Federalists and their latter-day descendants who, through the years, have advanced the cause of states' rights. To the extent that the interests of each state are not diversified and, in addition, the Union is divided into "more circumscribed confederacies, or States," he says, "oppressive combinations of a majority will be facilitated [and] the best security, under the republican forms, for the rights of every class of citizen, will be diminished." What he is contending against here is not the mere existence of the states, but the existence of "more circumscribed" states, states cut off or separated from each other by legal boundaries behind which they exercise great political powers. The political decisions that affect "the rights of every class of citizen," should, to the extent possible and feasible, be made at the national level. If such a system is not established, and local majorities are thereby left free to deprive minorities of their rights, the solution will be found only "by creating a will in the community independent of the majority."

There is no evidence showing that Publius here had in mind the Supreme Court, but the example he provides of such a "will"—"an hereditary or self-appointed authority"— is a fairly accurate description of the Court as it now exists; and it is altogether accurate to say that the country had initially to rely on the Court to secure the rights of minorities (beginning with the rights of the principal racial minority) from hostile state legislation. The unnoted consequences of this will be discussed in the following section.

By way of summary: In *Federalist* 9, Publius explains why the Framers were confident that, unlike governments in the past and in other places, free government could now be established in America. Recent improvements in the science of politics, he says, or newly discovered principles, make it possible to devise "models of a more perfect structure." The Constitution was seen as such a structure. An expression of the people's natural right to be governed only with their consent, it granted powers in order to enable the government to control the governed and, by its structure, it prevented those who controlled the government from abusing these powers. A significant aspect of this structure was the size of the country: with the "enlargement of the orbit" and industrialization would come diversity of the sort of interests that can be safely represented; with industrialization (or the commercial way of life) would also come a weakening of those interests—those moral or passionate interests—that cannot be safely represented. In these ways, Americans hoped to secure their rights and those of their posterity.

IV

Among the newly-discovered principles made part of the structure of the Constitution was a judiciary "composed of judges holding their offices during good behavior." Clearly the federal judiciary was expected to play a significant role in American constitutionalism; equally clearly, at least in Publius's account,[42] it was expected to exercise what we have come to call judicial review. What was not expected was the scope of this power or the manner in which it is now being exercised.

The federal judiciary was established independent of the other branches government in order that judges might better be able "to do their duty as faithful guardians of the Constitution"; in this capacity they were to enforce constitutional limitations against the other branches and especially the branch from which the Framers feared encroachments were most likely to issue, the legislative. When acting in this capacity, they represent the people of the

United States in their sovereign or constituting capacity; or, stated differently, the power they exercise belongs by natural right to the people, who wrote and ratified the Constitution and who can amend it. (This power is exercised by the judiciary rather than directly by the people for the reasons given by Publius in *Federalist* 49.) The authority to enforce constitutional limitations does not "by any means" suppose a superiority of the judicial to the legislative power; it only supposes that the will of the people, "declared in the Constitution," is superior to the will of the legislature. "Until the people have, by some solemn and authoritative act, annulled or changed the established form, it is binding upon themselves collectively, as well as individually; and no presumption, or even knowledge of their sentiments, can warrant their representatives in a departure from it prior to such an act."[43] And if the representatives of the people in their legislative capactiy are bound to such limits, it ought not require an argument to say that the representatives of the people in their sovereign capacity—i.e., the judges—are bound to the same strict limits. The judges are independent, but they owe this independence to the Framer's judgment that only with it would they be able effectively to exercise the power that by natural right belongs to someone else, the constituting people. To the people of the United States belonged the power to ordain and establish the Constitution with its specified rights, and to them alone—which means only the people in their sovereign capacity—belongs the power to amend the Constitution and add to or subtract from the number of these rights. The Framers would have regarded it as contrary to natural right to endow the judges with authority to "create" rights, and sheer usurpation for the judges to exercise such a power without authorization.

Yet, not only do the judges now create rights, and do so openly and avowedly—indeed, it was in the course of dissenting from a creative judgment that Justice Byron White said that although "the Court has ample precedent for the creation of new constitutional rights [that] should not lead it to repeat the process at will"[44]—but they do so with the support of major figures in the legal fraternity, especially those who teach constitutional law and jurisprudence. The process is known as taking rights seriously, to use the title of Ronald Dworkin's influential book.[45] Unfortunately, this way of taking rights "seriously" treats the Constitution frivolously and ultimately will undermine its structure.

Almost all of the judicially-created constitutional rights have been fashioned out of the language of the Fourteenth Amendment or in Fourteenth Amendment cases, at any rate, cases coming to the Court from the states. It is sufficient to mention the right of privacy and the right to substantially equal election districts.[46] This is instructive because it indicates the extent to which judicial creativity is an outgrowth of, or, some would say, is made necessary by, that amendment's presumed vagueness. It is, as I have said, "an amendment seemingly worded in so general a fashion that the judges are invited to provide it with a substance fashioned from their own 'values.'"[47] But the vagueness derives from judicial interpretation, not from the text of the amendment itself.

As Michael Zuckert has demonstrated,[48] each of the three troublesome clauses of the first section of the amendment is precisely drafted and is addressed, as it were, to a separate branch of the state governments. The first forbids state legislatures to legislate in a manner that "shall abridge the privileges or immunities of citizens of the United States." And in section 5 of the amendment Congress is given the authority to define these privileges and immunities.

The second forbids state courts, whenever a "person" is brought before them, to "deprive [him] of life, liberty, or property, without due process of law"; this means that state courts are forbidden to sentence any person to be executed, imprisoned, or fined, or otherwise to be divested of property, except according to the processes of law and after a fair trial.

The third is addressed to the state executives who are enjoined not to "deny"—meaning withhold from—any and every person within the jurisdiction of the state the protection of the laws. The beneficiaries of this clause are described with greater specificity ("any person within its jurisdiction") because what is required of the state here is affirmative action—it must act to protect anyone who is threatened by private parties—whereas it will have already acted against and, therefore, will have identified, the persons entitled to due process.[49]

If the amendment is read in this way, the only substantive clause is the first, and, if Zuckert is correct in his reading of the legislative history, it was Congress, not the Court, that was authorized to provide the substance, which it would do by defining privileges and immunities.[50] Without dwelling on the point, fidelity to the text as written would have spared us the era of "substantive due process" and its surviving progeny, "substantive equal protection"; and we would not have reason today to complain about an "activist" judiciary. Policy would have been made, and would be made, in the Congress where, under the Constitution, policy-making belongs.

Unfortunately, the amendment has never been read as it is written; and the consequence of this has been that we have come to expect the Supreme Court to provide the rules by which the country is governed in essential respects. Perhaps the best evidence of this is contained in the text of the proposed but unratified Equal Rights Amendment: "Equality of rights under the law shall not be denied or abridged by the United States or by any state on account of sex." For the first time in what is now almost 200 years, a constitutional provision would not specify the substance of the right or rights being secured.

In proposing this language, the congress simply but abjectly abdicated in favor of the judiciary, as if the judges had demonstrated their ability to serve as "faithful guardians of the Constitution." But, in fact, they have demonstrated no such thing and considering the education they receive as undergraduates and especially in the law schools, it would be extraordinary if they had. What school today offers instruction in constitutionalism or, even more important, in the American Constitution? Some, surely, but not many, and, so far as I know, not any law school. Courses in constitutional law are to be found everywhere, but these are courses on the Supreme Court, the judicial process, or the judicial power, and are as likely as not to be devoted to defenses of the Court's policy-making powers. It is no wonder that the judges fancy themselves authorized (and, what is more, qualified) to create constitutional rights or that they do so without regard either to the text of the Constitution—for which, in the case of the Fourteenth Amendment, our contemporary judges cannot be blamed— or for the conditions of constitutional government, and for this they can be blamed.

We are told by a famous judge writing in a prestigious law journal that the Warren Court especially should be praised for demonstrating to law students that there is "no theoretical gulf between law and morality,"[51] which means, between the law of the Constitution and the judges' morality. This is surely heady stuff for law students who may one day be judges themselves. For, to allow the judges to "create" constitutional rights means to endow them with the authority to impose their "values" on the country; in practice, of course, what they will impose will be the currently fashionable "values." This, and the contempt or disdain for the Constitution that accompanies it, is nowhere better seen than in Justice Brennan's work in *Frontiero* v. *Richardson*,[52] where the issue on which the judges found themselves divided was whether sex, like race, should be treated as a suspect classification.

> Brennan circulated a draft opinion on the limited grounds, and then he sent around an alternative section that proposed a broad constitutional ban, declaring classification by sex virtually impermissible. He knew that his alternative would have the effect of enacting the Equal Rights Amendment, which had already passed Congress and was pending before the state legislatures. But Brennan was accustomed to having the Court out in front, leading any civil rights movement.[53]

The authors of this account conclude by quoting Brennan as being of the opinion that there "was no reason to wait several years for the states to ratify the amendment"—no reason other than the fact, which implicitly Brennan acknowledged, that the Constitution *as then written* would not support the law he wanted to write.

This sort of constitutional law-making is given what purports to be its philosophical underpinning by Ronald Dworkin who argues that rights cannot be taken seriously until there has been "a fusion of constitutional law and moral theory." To make it clear that he is not referring to any moral theory that may have informed the Constitution as written, he finishes that sentence by saying that that fusion "has yet to take place."[54] The moral theory he propounds, and which he hopes to fuse with constitutional law, is that of John Rawls, which, in turn (or, at least, as Dworkin would have it), proves to justify precisely those positions that a typical liberal academician of the 1970s finds it comfortable publicly to adopt: radical egalitarianism, reverse discrimination, a narrowing if not an elimination of property rights, civil disobedience, and the like. I am not concerned here with the validity of these positions or the cogency of the arguments he uses to support them;[55] I want only to make it clear that to take rights seriously in the Dworkian sense requires the judge to ignore whatever instruction he might receive from the men who ordained and established the Constitution. This is what the Court has been doing.

In the apportionment cases, for example, and especially in those involving the second chambers of state legislatures, the Court was given the opportunity to reflect on the nature of representative government. Instead of being guided by the Constitution as elucidated by the Framers, the justices proceeded to misstate some American history, utter some platitudes about representing people rather than trees or acres, and then to advance the cause, which the Framers repudiated, of government by simple majorities. "Logically [as if logic were the determining factor], in a society grounded on representative government, it would seem reasonable that a majority of the people of a State could elect a majority of that State's legislators."[56]*

But there is a good deal more to representative government than seeing to it that everyone has a vote and that votes are equally weighed. The purpose of representative government as the Framers understood it was to permit government by constitutional rather than simple majorities, majorities assembled not from among the people but, as I said earlier, from among their representatives. These will represent a variety of interests, which means that the majority required to legislate will have to be assembled, and there are rules governing this process, rules of behavior as well as of procedure. These rules encourage accommodation. For example, they require debate, which implies on the part of those participating in it a capacity and willingness to be persuaded, persuaded by another with an equal right to form the majority or to be part of it, with an equally legitimate interest, and perhaps, with a superior argument. And it implies, and even encourages, the willingness to abide by the vote of the majority assembled. The importance of this cannot be exaggerated. Those who participate in this process are not permitted to overlook, because the rules require them to recognize, the right of every representative to be part of the majority, or to overlook the fact that the purpose of

---

*If one is to judge from the holdings in these cases, and even more from the opinions written to support them, it would appear that the Court sees itself as the only legitimate antimajoritarian institution or influence in our system of government. If this is so, the justices owe it to themselves, and beyond that to the country, to ponder the Framers' warnings against a reliance on "parchment barriers." Especially in the face of some of the forces unleashed by the Court's creation of additional constitutional rights—I'm thinking of the self-styled Moral Majority, for example—these barriers might prove to be very fragile indeed. Even as this is being written the Congress is considering bills to reverse, in effect, the abortion decisions, to amend the Constitution so as to permit the states to forbid abortions, and to deprive the Court of jurisdiction in a variety of kinds of cases.

forming a majority is to govern. Free government especially is not a simple business, as representatives will come to realize as they seek the consent of those with different interests. This is calculated to affect the speeches they make. Thus, representative government is characterized by speech whose purpose is to gain the consent of others, and the right to speak with a view to gaining consent is given constitutional protection in Article I.

It is also given constitutional protection by the First Amendment. But from this amendment (and, in some cases, the due process clause) the Supreme Court has created an additional right: the right to self-expression. This new right has nothing to do with representative government in general or the gaining of consent in particular. By this right one may express himself by wearing obscene jackets in courthouse corridors,[57] uttering the foulest of language in school board meetings[58] or publishing it in student newspapers,[59] hanging the American flag upside down[60] or wearing it on the seat of one's trousers[61] or, under some circumstances, by burning it.[62] All forms of political expression, no doubt, but not the sort of speech that is calculated to elicit consent, nor, for that matter, is it expressed with that intention. On the contrary, it is a way of expressing contempt: for fellow citizens, for the country (Amerika), and for the very idea of representative government. By creating this constitutional right, the Supreme Court has, on its part, demonstrated its ignorance of the natural rights of Americans to be governed by constitutional majorities. A people that exercises a right to express it*self* cannot form or be part of such majorities.[63]

The Court was surely not thinking of representative government or the conditions of constitutional democracy when it created the right of self-expression, or the right to disobey a *valid* criminal statute,[64] or the right, on ill-defined moral grounds, to refuse to serve in the armed forces,[65] or, to mention one more example, the right to abortion on demand, a right fashioned out of constitutional language the Court did not bother to specify.[66] It is doubtful that it was thinking of anything other than its reputation as a court accustomed to being "out in front" of the other branches of government.

The Court has done more than its share to generate the host of single-interest groups that characterize our politics even as they make our politics more difficult. They make demands, typically moral demands, they fill the streets with their agitating, they confront each other, but they do not talk with each other with a view to gaining mutual consent. Because they do not, they tend to lose in the representative assemblies; whereupon they take their demands to the courts, eventually to the "out-in-front" Supreme court. Here they are likely to win.

It is as if the Court is of the opinion that taking rights seriously requires it to accord to demands or wants the status of rights, as if, by natural right, a person consents to be governed on the condition that his wants be satisfied. But this is absurd because it is impossible, and it is impossible because not all wants can be satisfied. (For example, the wants of the pro- and anti-abortion groups cannot both be satisfied.) What government can promise, if it is organized properly, is that rights can be secured, by which I mean the natural right to be governed only with one's consent. Under the Constitution's system of representative government, this becomes the right to be part of a governing majority.

To repeat: while rights, properly understood, can be secured, not all wants can be satisfied. As our history attests, however, when those rights are secured, many wants are satisfied. Their satisfaction depends on their not being seen as rights.

CHAPTER 2

JUDICIAL REVIEW AND THE RIGHTS AND LAWS OF NATURE

The current controversy over the proper role of the judiciary can be said to have begun twenty years ago with Herbert Wechsler's appeal for Supreme Court decisions resting on "neutral principles of constitutional law."[1] More recently, Alexander Bickel and Philip Kurland charged that the Court had become brazenly political yet lacked political competence.[2] This provoked one well-known federal judge not only to defend the Court but contemptuously to dismiss its critics—Wechsler as well as Bickel and Kurland—as "self-appointed scholastic mandarins."[3] Since then there has been a further "explosion of judicial power."[4]

The controversy provoked by this explosion is over the proper role of the judiciary in constitutional cases. In a recent paper, Judge (then Professor) Ralph Winter, while acknowledging the differences within each of the two schools, divided the profession of constitutional lawyers into those who argued that the judges are limited to finding the law in the constitutional text and those who argued that they are empowered to go beyond the text and make constitutional law out of history or natural law or fundamental "values." He referred to these as the "interpretive" and "judicial power" models of judicial review, and, although treating them as if they were equal contenders for acceptance by courts and commentators, he had to concede that the judicial power model had become the dominant.[5]

The critics of the courts are faced with a difficult task. To make the case that judges are misusing judicial power and to urge a return to the "interpretive model," or "pure interpretive model," has implications that not many critics and probably no judges would be willing to accept. Professor Thomas C. Grey has provided a list of examples of judicial creativity, and, with some exceptions that I think could be shown not to be exceptions, they all involve Fourteenth Amendment adjudication—for example, state cases involving freedom of speech and religion or cruel and unusual punishment.[6] This list is instructive because it indicates the extent to which the growth of judicial power is related to—or even limited to—this one Amendment, an Amendment seemingly worded in so general a fashion that the judges are invited to provide it with a substance fashioned from their own "values."

It is of little use to complain that the alleged vagueness of the Amendment is, in fact, a product or a consequence of judicial misinterpretation of its terms.[7] There is no feasible way open to us now to restore its intended meaning. Yet, it deserves mention that fidelity to the original text would have avoided the era of "substantive due process" and its progeny, "substantive equal protection." It would have spared us the embarrassments of Raoul Berger's disclosure of the cat that many of us wanted, for political reasons, to keep in the bag of our history, namely, that the Equal Protection Clause was not intended to forbid segregated schooling or require public busing to effect desegregated schooling.[8] It would have spared us a generation of constitutional lawyers who feel obligated to spin out elegant (but obviously absurd) theories in the vain attempt to provide some valid textual basis for the Court's Fourteenth Amendment decisions.[9] Best of all, it would have made it easier to preserve the public's esteem for the Constitution as fundamental law.

As Dean John Hart Ely has recently demonstrated, the friends of judicial power are faced with an equally difficult task when they attempt to justify what the Court is doing.[10] Some of them do not even make the attempt. Here are the words of Lynn D. Compton, a California appeals court judge:

> Let's be honest with the public. Those courts are policymaking bodies. The policies they set have the effect of law because of the power those courts are given by the Constitution. The so-called "landmark decisions" of both the U.S. Supreme Court and the California Supreme Court were not compelled by legal precedent. Those decisions are the law and are considered "right" simply because the court had the power to decree the result. The result in any of those cases could have been exactly the opposite and by the same criteria been correct and binding precedent.
>
> In short, these precedent-setting policy decisions were the product of the social, economic and political philosophy of the majority of the justices who made up the court at a given time in history. . . .[11]

This means that the Constitution cannot be misinterpreted; that it is a thing without form or substance, except that it authorizes the judges to give it substance. In providing that substance, the judges need consult only their own "social, economic and political philosophy."

Such candor on the part of the judges is unusual, and, despite this desire to "be honest with the public," it may be doubted that we shall ever encounter it in the official reports. Even Justice William O. Douglas, who earned the praise of Professor Kenneth L. Karst for his unsurpassed willingness to ask what is best for the country and to "translate his answers to that question into constitutional law,"[12] always claimed to be expounding the Constitution, if not its explicit provisions then, at least, its emanations, penumbras, or lacunae.

Some friends of judicial power attempt to justify it by claiming the authority of the most venerable of our judges, John Marshall. To live under a constitution, the argument goes, means to live under a living constitution, and this, of necessity, requires the judges to adapt it to the times and circumstances. C. Herman Pritchett argued that this idea of a "'living Constitution'... can trace its lineage back to John Marshall's celebrated advice in *McCulloch* v. *Maryland* (1819): 'We must never forget that it is a Constitution we are expounding... intended to endure for ages to come, and consequently to be adapted to the various crises of human affairs.'"[13] The opinion attributed here to Marshall is at odds with his well-known statements that, for example, the "principles" of the Constitution "are deemed fundamental [and] permanent" and, except by means of formal amendment, "unchangeable."[14] But the discrepancy is not Marshall's; it is largely the consequence of the manner in which Pritchett renders Marshall's opinion in *McCulloch*: Pritchett employs ellipses to join two statements separated by some eight pages in the original. Marshall's meaning is not that the Constitution may be adapted to "the various crises of human affairs," but that the legislative powers granted by the Constitution are adaptable to meet these crises. The first statement, in which Marshall admonishes us to remember that we are expounding a constitution, is part of his argument that a constitution cannot specify "all the subdivisions of which its great powers will admit"; if it attempted to do that it would "partake of the prolixity of a legal code."[15] In the second statement, Marshall's subject is the necessary and proper provision which, he says, "is made in a constitution intended to endure for ages to come, and consequently, to be adapted to the various crises of human affairs."[16] The immediate sequel makes it even clearer that he is talking of legislative powers, not the Constitution itself: "To have prescribed the means by which the government should, in all future time, execute its powers, would have been to change, entirely, the character of the instrument, and give it the properties of a legal code." His meaning is put beyond any doubt in an essay he published in the *Alexandria Gazette* in which, with specific reference to his *McCulloch* statement concerning adaptation, Marshall says this: "Its [the statement's] sole object is to remind us that a constitution cannot possibly enumerate the means by which the powers of government are to be carried into execution."[17] It was not Marshall's view that the Constitution must be kept in tune with the times; on the contrary, his view was that the times, to the extent possible, must be kept in tune with the Constitution. Marshall cannot be counted among the friends of judicial power as the term is currently understood.

The difficulties of reconciling an expansive judicial power—indeed, judicial review itself—with majoritarian democracy are explored in two recent and important books. If, as Jesse H. Choper says in the first of these, "majority rule has been considered [by Madison, Jefferson, and Lincoln, as well as in "this nation's constitutional development"] the keystone of a democratic political system in both theory and practice,"[18] then, of course, judicial review has no place whatever. But, to say nothing here of Madison and Jefferson, Lincoln led this nation into the Civil War rather than submit to the proposition, known as popular sovereignty, that the issue of slavery in the territories ought to be determined by majority vote of the people in the territories. Fortunately, this initial misstatement plays no part in Choper's subsequent analysis of the issue. The Supreme Court is not democratic, but, as he proceeds to show in detail, neither are the political branches simply majoritarian. They were not intended to be, as any reader of *Federalist* No. 10 alone must know. Simple majoritarinism was likely to lead to rule by majority faction, and, as Publius shows, the Constitution's elaborate and complex structure was designed to prevent such majorities. "In the extent and proper structure of the Union," he concludes, "we behold a republican remedy for the diseases most incident to republican government."[19]

As I shall shortly argue at some length, the Constitution was intended "to secure these rights" (not to enable a majority of the people to rule), so the question becomes whether the judiciary has a legitimate role to play in the securing of rights, either by protecting the structure or by intervening when, through some structural or systemic failure, rights have been violated by or in the political branches. Since the victims of such violations are more likely to be members of minority groups, it is, Choper argues, primarily on their behalf that the judiciary should exercise its powers.[20] But which minorities? And, in addition to those "specifically designated" in the constitutional text, which rights? Choper recognizes the problem—". . . each time any group loses any political battle . . . it may lay claim to the label of . . . 'submerged and beaten minority,'"[21]—but he has no principled way to resolve it. Like John Hart Ely, he says the critical question facing constitutional scholarship is the development of a principled approach to judicial enforcement of the Constitution's open-ended provisions that secure individual rights; unlike Ely, however, Choper "does not attempt to resolve [it]."[22]

Like Choper, Ely is no friend of unguided or unprincipled judicial power, largely because he denies that the Constitution, on the whole, embodies the "substantive values" on the basis of which the courts may invalidate the actions of the other branches of government. In his view, the Constitution as written is "overwhelmingly concerned, on the one hand, with procedural fairness in the resolution of individual disputes (process writ small), and on the other, with what might capaciously be designated process writ large, with ensuring broad participation in the processes and distributions of government."[23] There is more truth in this statement than some of his critics have allowed. Ely, of course, recognizes that the Constitution embodies some "substantive values"; for example, the government it establishes is popular in form (not monarchic or aristocratic), and that form will affect the way justice is distributed (or, in Harold Lasswell's phrase, who gets what) in the political process. It obviously promotes a commercial society, which will affect how we live and, indeed, what we are; and, as Laurence Tribe points out, "in many of its parts, the Constitution also evinces a substantive commitment to the institution of private property and to the contractual expectations that surround it."[24] Nevertheless, the

Constitution as it came from the Philadelphia convention was, as Ely says, mainly concerned with "process writ large." What he fails to appreciate, however, is that the process—or, as I should prefer to say, the structure governing the process—was designed with a view to a particular and substantive end. It was designed to secure the rights with which all men by nature are equally endowed.

Ely cannot acknowledge this "substantive value" because he denies the existence of natural rights and natural law. What was self-evident to the authors of the Declaration of Independence is not at all evident to Ely. Jefferson and his colleagues may have appealed to "the Laws of Nature and of Nature's God," but Ely cannot credit them with being serious. The Declaration is a mere lawyer's brief, he maintains ("with certain features of an indictment"), and like those who write briefs, the authors of the Declaration threw in "arguments of every hue." Some "broadly accepted natural law philosophy surely could have found a place within [the Constitution], presumably in the Bill of Rights [but] such philosophies were not that broadly accepted."[25]

Because he cannot take seriously the idea that the Founders were persuaded of the fact of natural rights, he does not recognize that the gravest fault in our history as a people was a fault precisely because it was a violation of natural right. By natural right no man may be governed without his consent, yet black Americans (or the overwhelming majority of them) were denied the opportunity to vote for or against the Constitution. Denied that fundamental right, they were also denied the constitutional right to be represented in the majorities assembled in the legislative process, the majorities that made the laws.

The Founders recognized their treatment of blacks to be contrary to natural right.[26] Ely, however, even though he justifies judicial review on behalf of those groups that are not represented in the governing process, or do not fare well in it, has no principled basis on which to distinguish groups that are mistreated from those that are not mistreated, or those deserving of judicial solicitude from those not deserving of it.[27] He cannot provide a principled basis for judicial review, and he cannot do so because he does not recognize that the Constitution was and is designed to secure rights and, in that respect, is informed by moral principle.[28]

Thomas C. Grey's work, still in progress, promises to provide the judicial power school with what it has always lacked, a sound theoretical and historical basis. For him, the issue whether the judiciary should exercise a sweeping policymaking power does not turn mainly on "how one evaluates the practical results" of the decisions—whether, for example, one favors or opposes a liberal abortion policy—but on the legitimacy of what the judiciary is doing. As he states it, the decisive question is whether in writing the Constitution we left "in the hands of [the] judges the considerable power to define and enforce fundamental human rights without substantial guidance from constitutional text and history."[29] His answer is yes.

> For the generation that framed the Constitution, the concept of a "higher law," protecting "natural rights," and taking precedence over ordinary positive law as a matter of political obligation, was widely shared and deeply felt. An essential element of American constitutionalism was the reduction to written form—and hence to positive law—of some of the principles of natural rights. But at the same time, it was generally recognized that written constitutions could not completely codify the higher law. Thus in the framing of the original American constitutions it was widely accepted that there remained unwritten but still binding principles of higher law The [N]inth Amendment is the textual expression of this idea in the federal Constitution.
>
> As it came to be accepted that the judiciary had the power to enforce the commands of the written Constitution when these conflicted with ordinary law, it was also widely assumed that judges would enforce as constitutional restraints the unwritten natural rights as well.[30]

The issues he raises in this essay, and which he begins to answer in a subsequent essay,[31] are of the first importance and their resolution does indeed require "lengthy and detailed historical documentation." It also requires an inquiry—more extensive than I can hope to provide here—into the doctrine of modern natural right and its connection to American constitutionalism. Grey does not essay such an inquiry here because, although he recognizes the role of modern natural rights in the revolutionary break with England, he denies the role "in the disputes that led up to the break."[33] His argument is that Americans clung to the traditional understanding of natural law, the natural law (perhaps) first taught by Cicero, put into Christian terms by Thomas Aquinas, and made known to Americans in the opinions of a famous English judge, Sir Edward Coke. Here are Coke's words in *Calvin's Case* (1609):

> The law of nature is that which God at the time of creation of the nature of man infused into his heart, for his preservation and direction; and this is *Lex aeterna*, the moral law, called also the law of nature. And by this law, written with the finger of God in the heart of man, were the people of god a long time governed before the law was written by Moses, who was the first reporter or writer of law in the world....[34]

This, Grey argues, was "the dominant view of natural or fundamental law among revolutionary Americans."[35] But with due respect for his scholarship, which is formidable, I must say that in the essential respects he is mistaken. Like every American constitutional lawyer and judge who has written on this subject and whose work I have read, from Corwin[36]—considered the authority by several generations of Americans—to Justice Hugo L. Black and others still living and writing, Grey does not understand the doctrine of modern natural rights and natural law from which, as I hope to show, we derive our understanding of constitutionalism.

II

The modern natural rights teaching begins with the assertion, which its authors regarded as no more than a recognition of the fact, that men are by nature adversaries. Being hostile one to another, and living naturally without government, their lives were, in Hobbes's famous formulation, "solitary, poor, nasty, brutish, and short,"[37] and even under government their lives too frequently resembled this natural condition. The problem thus posed was to find a way that these naturally hostile men could live, or could be made to live, in peace. The solution to this problem consisted in organizing politics on the basis of something as to which all men can agree, and, second, excluding from politics those subjects that traditionally give rise to strife and disorder. One can say that nature is the problem, or the cause of the problem, and the escape from nature the solution. This means, stated here only provisionally, that the laws of nature, instead of constituting a body of "higher law" as Grey uses the term— meaning, a model or a set of principles by which one judges the goodness of the positive law—are a set of directions enabling men to escape from their natural condition, which is unbearable.

They are, these laws of nature in the modern sense, all derivative from and, as it were, made necessary by, the rights of nature, or, men's natural rights, the rights that all men possess equally. Nature is the problem precisely because all men possess natural rights, the right to self-preservation and the right to use whatever means are required, or are thought by each man to be required, to preserve himself. As Hobbes makes explicit, if his own preservation requires it, or is thought to require it, every man has a natural right not only to take from another but to kill the other.[38] Locke, whom we are more inclined to acknowledge as the founder of our modern politics, taught the same lesson but less explicitly.[39] Again, the fact that, according to nature, "every man has a right to everything,"[40] is that which gives rise to the problem. It is because men have natural rights of this description and are only too inclined to exercise them that the state of nature is a state of war "of every man, against every man."[41] The rights of nature give rise to war; the laws of nature point the way to peace. As Hobbes put it, "as long as this natural right of every man to every thing endureth, there can be no security to any man.... [C]onsequently, it is a precept, or general rule of reason, *that every man, ought to endeavour peace....*" The first branch of which rule "containeth the first, and fundamental law of nature; which is, *to seek peace, and follow it.*" The second is derived from the first: "*that a man be willing, when others are so too, as far-forth, as for peace, and defence of himself he shall think it necessary, to lay down this right to all things; and be contented with so much liberty against other men, as he would allow men against himself.*"[42] Except that no man can give up the right to resist them "that assault him by force, or take away his life," the laws of nature require men mutually to lay down their natural rights by entering into a covenant one with another. By the third of these natural laws, men are enjoined to perform this covenant, this mutual divesting of rights, but Hobbes knew that men, tempted by "avarice, ambition, lust, or other strong desire," cannot be held to performance by mere words; they must be made to fear the consequences of breaking their word. ("The passion to be reckoned upon is fear.") Hence, if the first aspect of the covenant, or social contact, is the agreement to lay down their natural rights, the second aspect is the agreement to recognize the sovereign, to whom these rights are transferred, and, by means of this transfer, to endow him (or it) with an absolute power to require performance. The threat of terror or punishment must overcome the temptation to break the covenant;[43] and the covenant is the foundation of peace and of all justice. (There is no justice in the state of nature.) The sovereign preserves the peace among beings who are by nature enemies.

Hobbes's political science is built on these propositions: that there is no basis in nature for opinions of good and bad, that men are certain to disagree about good and bad, but that men can agree on the need for peace.[44] It is the only thing they can agree on, but, precisely because of that, civil society is possible. The peace of this civil society would be jeopardized, however, if men were permitted to dispute questions of good and bad, or, say the same thing, if men in their capacity as citizens were permitted to raise questions concerning the end or ends of civil society. Such questions must be suppressed in the modern liberal state. (Whether they can be suppressed is another matter.) In principle, by contracting with each other to yield their rights to the sovereign in exchange for the peace which will provide the only real security for their rights, men agree not to raise such questions. Each man agrees that his opinions of good and bad, right and wrong, justice and injustice are just that—private opinions—and the principle of equality requires him to acknowledge that other opinions, even if they are contrary to his own, have as much (or as little) dignity as his own. What this means is that each man agrees to forgo his private judgment of the goodness or badness of the sovereign's laws; he agrees to obey the sovereign in exchange for similar promises on the part of his co-covenantors. The sovereign enforces those promises. Hobbes summarizes all this, or encapsulates it, in his famous revision of the Golden Rule: *"Do not that to another, which thou wouldest not have done to thyself."*[45] Not: *do* unto others, for to do means to act on the basis of some idea of the good, and every idea of the good is mere opinion, without foundation; so to act implies a right to impose one's own idea of the good on others and this gives rise to dispute. Hence, the revised rule: do *not* do as you would *not* have done to you. Leave other men alone in exchange for their promise, which the sovereign will enforce, to leave you alone. The happy consequence of this sovereign's peace is liberty, which is why some have given the name liberalism to this kind of politics.

Harvey C. Mansfield, Jr., whose formulations I have adopted, provides a convenient statement of the conclusion to be drawn from much of what I have said thus far about the origin of modern natural right:

> If men could stop disputing the ends of politics and agree on the condition of all ends, they could follow privately those ends whose pursuit is consistent with the same allowance to other ends. Under Hobbes's golden rule, the universe of tolerated ends is defined by the condition of all ends, including the intolerable, and that is civil peace. The end of government thus becomes security for those ends that can be represented.[46]

To recapitulate: men are created equal in the sense that everyone by nature has a right to rule himself, which means that no one by nature has a right to rule anyone other than himself. Hobbes's sovereign is an artificial ruler because no real person is a ruler of anyone but himself. This artificial ruler represents all the real persons insofar as he is the representative of all the private rights that had to be renounced to make civil society (and peace) possible. He is an absolute ruler because he represents all the absolute rulers who entered into the covenant and because only an absolute ruler can guarantee the achievement of the end of sovereign power, peace.[47] It may seem paradoxical, but Hobbes, whose reputation is simply that of a teacher of absolutism, is the founder of self-government in the modern sense. We govern ourselves through the sovereign who is ourselves, and, in Hobbes's scheme, this government is made possible only because we renounce our natural rights. With the exception of the right to defend ourselves against physical attack, we transfer our rights to the sovereign; it is our rights that he exercises. It goes without saying that this doctrine of natural rights has no room for judicial review.

In fact, judicial review is likely to prove a threat to the civil society built on natural rights, for, as Hobbes makes clear in a number of places in his writings, the greatest threat to civil peace comes from men who, in violation of the covenant and moved by their vanity, claim the right to pass judgment—which necessarily means "private judgment"— on the laws or the sovereign's commands. "[H]ow many rebellions hath this opinion been the cause of, which teacheth that the knowledge whether the commands of kings be just or unjust, belongs to private men, and that before they yield obedience, they not only may, but ought to dispute them."[48] He was concerned mostly with priests because in his day—and our own time is not without its examples of this class of potentially dangerous men[49]—it was primarily the various denominations of priests who taught the right of private judgment and, by so doing, represented a constant threat to the civil peace. But next on his list of potential public enemies were the lawyers.[50] Lawyers cannot claim to be "the Lord's anointed," but their possession of the Latin and the other strange tongues of the law feeds their vanity until it becomes overweening. As Mansfield says, by way of explaining Hobbes's attitude toward lawyers, "expertise in law implies a standard of law external to the will of the sovereign, such as the common law or the traditional natural law of 'right reason.'"[51] It is not judicial review but rather Justice Black's complaints of his "natural-law-due-process" colleagues that find their origin in Hobbes's natural right teaching. Hobbes could have predicted that, unless we take steps to protect ourselves, the day would come in which lawyers, when "called" to the bench, will decide what is best for the country and then "translate [their] answers to that question into constitutional law."[52]

I indicated above that Hobbes the absolutist is the founder of self-government in the modern sense and acknowledged that this would be seen as a paradox. This is so because his teaching has come down to us—in the sense of being installed among us—in a form that is, outwardly at least, much more benign, and therefore more acceptable to us, and in one important respect is in fact more benign. We know it, and Grey knows it, in the form it assumes in the teaching of John Locke, "America's philosopher," as someone called him. Locke made two significant changes that greatly contributed to the practical success of the new natural rights teaching: he found a way to conceal the absolutist character of sovereignty and he discovered the principles of the modern commercial society which we call capitalism.

Locke's civil society is a Hobbesian society with a difference, but not so great a difference as is sometimes thought. Corwin, for example, says that where "Hobbes and Locke part company is in their view of the state of nature, that is to say, in their view of human nature when not subjected to political control." Locke, he says, in contrast to Hobbes, "depicts the state of nature as in the main an era of 'peace, goodwill, mutual assistance, and preservation'."[53] Corwin is mistaken. Locke, in the section of the *second treatise* from which Corwin quotes, does not say that the state of nature is peaceful, or even in the main peaceful. What he says is that the state of nature and the state of war are distinguishable; they are "as far distant . . . one from another" as are a state of peace and a state of enmity, or as are a state of "good will" and a state of "malice."[54] Well, what is the distance between the state of peace and the state of enmity and, therefore, the state of nature and the state of war? Locke's answer is given almost immediately in the beginning sentence of section 21: "To avoid this state of war . . . is one great reason of men's putting themselves into society, and quitting the state of nature." Men quit the state of nature in order to avoid the state of war. Thus, for Locke too, civil society comes into being with a contract made by self-interested men who, if not enemies to the extent of Hobbesian men, are nevertheless compelled by the conditions of nature to be adversaries.[55] He, too, requires men to renounce their natural rights (except, again, what he calls the natural power to preserve themselves) and specifically the right of "private judgment [respecting] any matter of right."[56] And he, too, faces the problem of how to ensure that men will perform the terms of the contract. He does not, however, follow Hobbes to the extent to endowing a person with sovereignty and teaching that that person must rely on fear as a means of controlling men. In his teaching no person is the embodiment or representative of the people. Instead, "political power" is first of all the "right of making laws."[57] It follows that sovereignty, or as he puts it, the supreme power, is in the hands of those who share in the legislative power.[58] Locke succeeds in institutionalizing sovereignty, which is to have great consequences in and for America. His sovereign speaks not in commands but in laws, and the laws apply to everyone, even to those who share in the making of them.[59] In this way Locke makes it less likely that absolute rule would be arbitrary or tyrannical rule. But this rule by law or by means of law is not the rule by lawyers. There is no room for judicial review in Locke's system. Locke, who emphasizes the legislative power and, however reluctantly, concedes the need of what we call the executive power,[60] makes no provision for—he does not even recognize—the judicial power. Thus, while it remains to be seen whether Grey is correct in saying that Americans "assumed that judges would enforce as constitutional restraints the unwritten natural rights,"[61] it is absolutely clear that this view of the role of the judiciary was not shared by Locke or Hobbes, the first philosophers of natural rights.

Locke's second contribution to the success of the new natural rights teaching was his discovery of the principles of the new commercial society. With these principles Locke could promise not merely self-preservation but comfortable preservation, in fact, a very commodious life. The "wise" and "godlike" prince who establishes laws of liberty respecting the acquisition, use, and disposition of property, and by doing so promotes "the honest industry of mankind," is the greatest of mankind's benefactors. Under his laws, Locke predicts the wealth with which nature endowed mankind will increase a thousandfold. Indeed, compared with what is possible under this new—that is, capitalist—prince, nature's providence is "almost worthless."[62] Men will perform the terms of the contract—which is to say, they will obey this sovereign's laws and forgo the right they had in the state of nature to pass private judgment "concerning any matter of right"—because it will be so profitable for them to perform and obey. The new commercial society promises a larger and ever larger gross national product, and this product can be shared more readily than the scarce wealth of the past. There will be a steady improvement in the material conditions of all men. As a consequence, the passions of men will be redirected from great causes to the small, from the poetic to the prosaic, from dreams of heaven and glory to dreams of money, from the subjects as to which they disagree to the one subject as to which they can agree. In Mansfield's terms, Locke found a better way to achieve the Hobbesian end. In the new commercial society men would "stop disputing the ends of politics and agree on the condition of all ends"—civil peace—because they would devote themselves to making money and they would succeed. They would become tolerant, being content to live and let live, because they would cease to care about the things that men tend to be intolerant about. Hobbes promised peace if men would transfer their rights to a heavily armed policeman. Locke promised peace if men would pursue wealth, in exchange for which Locke promised to conceal the policeman. In the Lockean regime, men are still adversaries, but their hostility is channeled into the safest of all forms, that of free economic competition. This competition is safe because it is productive of the things Lockean men want: material goods. James Madison, America's Founder, revealed his debt to Locke when, in the famous *Federalist* No. 10, he said that "the chief object of government [is] the protection of different and unequal faculties of acquiring property. . . ." The goverment's duty to protect unequal faculties (or talents) derives from its duty to secure equal rights.

According to a most authoritative statement on the subject, governments are instituted to secure the rights with which all men are naturally endowed. America's Founders learned from Hobbes and Locke, and others, that these rights cannot be secured except under government, which is why the Constitution they wrote in Philadelphia was essentially one of powers. It did not even contain a bill of rights because, as Hamilton said, "the Constitution is itself, in every rational sense, and to every useful purpose, A BILL OF RIGHTS."[63] They also learned that to secure these rights the power of governemnt must be limited, and that the most efficient way to limit power was not to withhold powers—although they did that too—but to organize power in a particular way.

In sum, the doctrine of natural rights as expounded by Hobbes and Locke, and the natural laws to which the rights give rise, is not a "higher law" doctrine as understood by Grey. He means by it what Coke meant in *Calvin's Case,* a law that was part of the law of England and, as Grey puts it, taking precedence over earthly law because "it was of Divine origin, eternal and unchanging."[64] This understanding of natural law derives from the Stoics and Thomas Aquinas. But the new natural law merely commanded men to seek peace, in Hobbes's case, or, in Locke's, to find the arrangement under which men might preserve both themselves and others. Natural law in this modern sense is not a legal discipline. Lawyers, simply as lawyers or even as judges, have no competence in it, and courts have no jurisdiction over it. As for natural rights themselves, or the powers that men enjoyed in the state of nature, with the exception of the right of self-defense, they had to be renounced or transferred to the sovereign.

III

The issue is whether the Founders endowed judges with the authority to "define and enforce fundamental human rights without substantial guidance from constitutional text and history."[65] Grey contends that they did, but he implies that he can find no support for his answer in the writings of Hobbes and Locke when he says he can find none in Locke and Blackstone. Natural rights "rhetoric" played a role in the break with England, he concedes, and is embodied in the Declaration of Independence and in Tom Paine's *Common Sense*, but the "dominant view of natural or fundamental law among revolutionry Americans" derived from a different source.[66] "While Americans drew on the natural rights rhetoric of Locke and Blackstone, they found the best contemporary support for their own more traditional constitutional views in those curious products of the Age of Reason, the systematic treatises on the law of nature and nations [written by Pufendorf, Burlamaqui, Vattel, and Rutherforth]."[67] But, even assuming that revolutionary Americans continued to understand natural law in the old sense, a subject the investigation of which would be an enterprise in itself, they could not have found support for this understanding in these treatises—unless, of course, they misread them—because these treatises propound a natural law teaching that is Hobbesian in every essential respect.

That these treatise writers sought to conceal their indebtedness to Hobbes can, I think, be demonstrated, especially in Pufendorf's case, and that they would have reason to want to do so is known to students of the history of political philosophy. Hobbes's name was, as Locke said, "justly decried," and a writer's reputation—in those circles where it was decried—depended in part on the distance, or the seeming distance, he put between himself and Thomas Hobbes. (Locke owed his popular success to his seeming distance from Hobbes.) Thus, we find in Pufendorf[68] countless references to the Bible and the other approved books, and to God as "the author of natural law," from which it is easy to conclude that we are in the presence of a writer steeped in the Christian tradition and propounding a Christian natural law teaching. That God is the author of natural law, he says, is a "fact which no sane man can question." He then goes on to say, however, that it is "uncertain *how* the divine will can be discovered, and on what evidence we can be certain that God wished to include this thing or that under the natural law."[69] This, he admits, is an "inconvenience," a problem. What is instructive is how he solves that problem. He solves it by following Hobbes's method of examining man's natural condition and propensities, discovering that man is most of all consumed by love for himself and the "desire to preserve himself by any and all means," that man is weak and therefore unable to "live and enjoy the good things that in this world attend his condition," and that the reasonable thing for men to do—the dictate of right reason working from the new premises—is to seek peace by becoming sociable and to become sociable by entering into a covenant one with another to form civil society. This Pufendorf describes as the fundamental law of nature. And this Hobbesian method is, he says, patently the "way of eliciting the law of nature."[70]

There are, as I said, numerous passages in which Pufendorf seems to refer to the "natural and divine laws" in a traditional sense. These, he says, are of universal obligation, and those who transgress against these laws can expect to be punished. But punished by whom? Not, it turns out, by any civil authority, unless natural offenses have been made civil crimes. And what is the principle to be followed by the civil authority in deciding what offenses against "natural and divine laws" should be made civil offenses and which should "be left to the vengeance of God"? Pufendorf's answer is taken straight from Hobbes: "[T]he force of civil law [will be accorded to] those precepts of nature, the observance of which is absolutely necessary for the conitnuance of internal peace."[71]

He appears to differ from Hobbes, who argues[72] that whereas murder, for example, is contrary to natural law, there is no way of knowing what murder is until the civil law defines it. Pufendorf replies that "we who venerate Sacred Scripture" can know what murder is from "the laws which God gave the Jews, and from other revelations."[73] But he had earlier said that is was "uncertain . . . on what evidence we can be certain that God wished to include this thing or that under the natural law."[74] The careful reader is obliged to wonder, therefore, whether Pufendorf included himself among those who "venerate Sacred Scripture."[75] (The following passage is instructive on this issue. The context is his "method of deducing the natural law," and he is responding to the objection that given this method, there can be no demonstration of the validity of the precepts it yields, that, on the contrary, the virtuousness of what is called virtue can be proved only by assuming divine punishment which, in turn, depends on the soul being immortal. Pufendorf says, "the view of a certain scholar, that upon our principle the virtue of fortitude [for example] cannot be proved unless a basis is laid for it in the immortality of the soul, since otherwise no reward could fall to the lot of the man who sacrifices his life for a worthy cause, his view, I say, offers little difficulty. Although it is impious to deny or to cast doubt upon such a belief, still it is possible to show that even without it a soldier can be commanded to do battle to the death for his country. For . . . it is certainly agreed that it lies within the power of the supreme authority to arm citizens, and to proclaim upon pain of death that no one flee from his appointed place. Now of two evils a man cannot avoid choosing the lesser. But it is the lesser evil to fight with peril to one's life, and even to one's least breath, than to face certain death.")[76]

Varous conclusions can be drawn from this interesting passage, one of them being—although it may be "impious" to say so—men can be made to do what they should do without any catechism from the churches and without any instruction in, or guidance by, the traditional law of nature. Fear, as Hobbes also pointed out, is the passion to be reckoned on, fear not of eternal damnation but of a sovereign armed with a "sting."[77])

Despite these pieties, anyone who reads him with a modicum of care should be able to recognize his disagreements with the tradition and his agreement with Hobbes on the essential issues. Like Hobbes, he argues that sociality is not natural, but that men can be forced to be social, or forced to observe the rights of others, and that by nature man is the fiercest and most uncontrolled of beings whose situation makes peaceful coexistence impossible in the state of nature. Man is totally dependent on his own strength and judgment as to when, and by what means, it is necessary to defend himself. Thus, when "sane reason suggests that he is threatened" by another man, he may kill him, and do so without violating any of nature's laws. This, Pufendorf boldly says, is Hobbes's meaning too. Sociality comes with civil society, and civil society is founded when men, anxious to escape "the infinite miseries of a state of nature"—strong Hobbesian language that—covenant one with another to transfer their natural powers to a sovereign. Civil society arises out of fear and it is ultimately fear that the sovereign relies on to get men to obey the terms of the covenant: "divine vengeance moves with slow foot and often unfolds itself in hidden ways."[78]

His differences with Hobbes are, however, significant. To a greater extent than did Locke, Pufendorf delineates an institutional arrangement designed to deal with the problem that Hobbes acknowledged but left unsolved, that of a tyrannical sovereign. Men are "endowed with natural liberty and equality" and when they covenant to enter civil society they may do so either absolutely or, unlike Hobbes's men, conditionally. The agreement is absolute if they agree to remain subject to the sovereign authority no matter what form of government the majority of them subsequently decide on, or conditional on the part of a man who "stipulates that the form of government be such as he approves of." What is more important, and was to prove decisive to the future of constitutional government, Pufendorf requires another covenant, this one between the members of the civil society so formed and the sovereign, or "rulers," a covenant by which the former agree to obey and the latter agree to care for "the common security and safety."[79] On the basis of Hobbes's principles, Pufendorf moves beyond Hobbes to state the necessity of a written constitution. The supreme sovereign is not "accountable." In fact, he (or it) is "superior" to the civil laws and "to raise any question regarding divine and natural laws would be folly."[80] But he is bound by the "express convention" he made with the people. The limits to the sovereign's powers, like the powers themselves, derive from the will of the people and not from God or the laws that, according to Coke and others of his time and before, God wrote in the heart of man. Because the people transfer to him their natural rights, they may themselves, at the time of the transfer, limit sovereignty. Specifically, they may prescribe "certain institutions and a particular manner of conducting affairs."[81] Here is one of the sources in modern political philosophy of the idea of a written constitution; but there is nothing here to support Grey's suggestion that Pufendorf endowed judges with the authority to enforce the terms of this constitution, to say nothing of an "unwritten" constitution.

Pufendorf, he writes, "made clear that acts by a ruler violating either natural law or the constitution were not merely wrongful or unjust but were void—without legal effect."[82] The passage he cites in support of this statement, and the only passage he cites, is as follows:

The sovereignty of a king is more strictly limited, if, at its transfer, an *express* convention is entered into between king and citizens that he will exercise it in accordance with certain basic laws, and on affairs, over the disposal of which he has not been accorded absolute power, he will consult with an assembly of the people or council of nobles, and that without the consent of one of the last two he will make no decision; and if he does otherwise, the citizens will not be bound by his commands on such affairs. The people that has set a king over them in this way is not understood to have promised to obey him absolutely and in all things, but in so far as his sovereignty accords with their bargain and the fundamental laws, while whatever acts of his deviate from them, are thereby void and without force to obligate citizens.[83]

This is his authority for saying that Pufendorf supports those revolutionary Americans who (he says) insisted that judges have the power to enforce fundamental human rights or an unwritten constitution. But the passage says no such thing. It says nothing about a judiciary, nothing about natural law, and the context makes it clear that by "fundamental laws" Pufendorf is referring to the terms of the "express convention."

Because men are anxious to escape the "infinite miseries of a state of nature," they are willing to give up a portion of their natural liberty and powers to the sovereign whom they endow by their covenant. They will do so because they think their condition will be improved in civil society. To make it more certain that it will be improved, they will transfer to the sovereign "no more power . . . than what a man of reason may judge" to be necessary to "the common peace and defence." The next question is obvious: Who decides whether the sovereign has violated the covenant by exceeding the limits of his lawful powers? Pufendorf answers this question in a continuation of the sentence last quoted: "What may at any particular moment work to that end [that is, will conduce to the common peace and defense] is a matter for decision, not by those who do the transferring, but by him on whom that power was transferred."[84] If, despite the institutional checks that are written in the "express covenant," the sovereign abuses his power, Pufendorf, like Hobbes, can only counsel the people to endure these crimes with the same patience with which they endure "drought, floods, and all other acts of nature."[85] If the crimes become unendurable, they can exercise their natural right to rebel.

Pufendorf might have advocated judicial review—that is, he might have constituted a body of judicial guardians of the "express convention"—but his principles would not permit judicial enforcement of the terms of an unwritten constitution. This can be demonstrated by reflecting on what it means to say that the decisive political fact is that all men are by nature free and equal.

To hold this view is to hold that there are no natural differences among men that qualify anyone to rule anyone other than himself: no right by grace of God and no entitlement by virtue of a quality possessed unequally. If the decisive political fact is that men are naturally free and equal, then no one possesses a valid claim to rule, whether he be wise, good, godly, beautiful, strong, experienced, or whatever. In Mansfield's terms, the only legitimate ruler is an artificial ruler. Stated otherwise, the only legitimate government is man-made, an artifact fashioned out of the wills of men anxious to escape their natural condition, which is characterized by the absence of rule and unendurable. "We the people" make government. Pufendorf's view is wholly in accord with this:

> Now a union of wills cannot possibly be encompassed by the wills of all being naturally lumped into one, or by only one person willing, and all the rest ceasing to do so, or by removing in some way the natural variation of wills and their tendency to oppose each other, and combining them into an abiding harmony. But the only final way in which many wills are understood to be united is for every individual to subordinate his will to that of one man, or of a single council, so that whatever that man or council shall decree on matters necessary to the common security, must be regarded as the will of each and every person.[86]

According to the traditional natural law teaching, however, men are not equal in every relevant respect. In principle, the illuminations of reason are available to all men, but they are clearer to virtuous men and, because they are clearer to them, these men can acquire an expertise in the natural law and may rightly claim political authority. Men in general can have only a "superficial" knowledge of this law of nature, said one English authority. Even the king's knowledge is, compared with that of his judges, "superficial."[87] Indeed, the esteemed Sir Edward Coke dared to make this very point in his famous confrontation with King James at Hampton Court in 1608.[88] Thus, if it were the case that Pufendorf held to this older understanding of natural law, he would have had to recognize that it was a legal discipline and that those who were schooled in that discipline would be entitled to exercise authority—even if only a judicial authority—over other men. But he did not do this. He could not consistently do this so long as he subscribed to the principles of the new natural law with respect to which no one can claim to be an expert or so long as he held to the view that all men are, in decisive respects, naturally free and equal.

On the basis of these new principles, legitimate government can arise only from a "union of wills," all wills being equal. For every man to "subordinate his will to that of another, or of a single council," requires him to acknowledge that his opinions of good and bad or justice and injustice have no status in this process, that they are merely private opinions. He will acknowledge this only when other men, his co-covenantors, also acknowledge it, which is to say that everyone must agree that nobody is wise, good, or otherwise naturally qualified to rule. It is consistent with Pufendorf's principles if men, upon entering civil society, agree to withhold certain powers from the sovereign they "will" into being, and to do so in an "express convention." It would not be inconsistent if he were to counsel them to take the next step and endow a body of judicial guardians with the authority to represent their collective will and enforce it against the sovereign. But it would be inconsistent if Pufendorf were to permit men to endow anyone with the authority to enforce the terms of an unexpressed convention or an "unwritten constitution." Government built on the principle of the natural freedom and equality of all men is absolute government except—Pufendorf's contribution—insofar as certain powers are withheld. But when government is built entirely out of materials supplied by the will—or a union of wills—that will must be expressed. In a world where all opinions of justice and injustice are understood to be merely private opinions, no man can rationally agree to an arrangement where another man is authorized to convert his opinion into fundamental law.

Contrary, then, to what is said by Grey, Pufendorf lends no support for the view that the judiciary should enjoy a jurisdiction over an "unwritten constitution." There can only be private opinions of what is unwritten. This is also true of the treatises of Burlamaqui, Vattel, and Rutherforth.[89]

IV

One would have had reason to believe that the successful outcome of the Civil War would set to rest all doubt concerning the principles on the basis of which our country was founded. Chief Justice Roger Taney's depreciation of the Declaration of Independence in his *Dred Scott* opinion was answered not only on the battlefield of Gettysburg but, a few months later, by Lincoln's address on the site of that battlefield. Lincoln insisted there, as he had in many other places and on many other occasions, that the nation was born in 1776 when the men in Philadelphia set it down as a self-evident truth that all men are created equal and are endowed by their Creator with certain unalienable rights, and that government is instituted to secure these rights. Taney, and the South in general, had denied this—John C. Calhoun and Alexander Stephens said it was a self-evident lie and went so far as to denounce Jefferson for asserting it—but what the South then lost to the arbitrament of battle it seems now to have won back in the groves of contemporary journalism and academe. Garry Wills, for example, has recently been praised in many important places for telling us that Lincoln was wrong about the Declaration of Independence,[90] and many a scholar has asserted that it was mere propaganda, a convenient weapon to use against the British and no more. Americans may have said that "the laws of nature and of Nature's God" entitled them to rebel against one government and to found a new one, but, we are now solemnly told, they did not mean it. They "never intended" that the "natural law" be used as a measure of "rights and wrongs of colonial life."[91] As for self-evident truths, "our society does not, rightly does not, accept the notion of a discoverable and objectively valid set of moral principles."[92] So say some scholars. In our official documents, however, now as in the past, in what are described as "The Organic Laws of the United States," the Declaration of Independence occupies first place: in the Statutes at Large, in the Revised Statutes, in the United States Code, and in a volume entitled, *The Federal and State Constitutions, Colonial Charters, and Other Organic Laws of the United States.*[93] Whatever place it holds in the hearts and minds of today's scholars, in the Organic Laws it is first and it is listed first. First, the Declaration of Independence; second, the Articles of Confederation; third, the Northwest Ordinance of 1787; and fourth, the Constitution and its amendments. And there, one should like to think, it will continue to be, an obstacle, as Lincoln rightly said, to anyone who "might seek to turn a free people back into the hateful paths of despotism." Its authors knew "the proneness of prosperity to breed tyrants, and they meant when such should re-appear in this fair land and commence their vocation they should find left for them at least one hard nut to crack."[94]

Of course, there was in the beginning, as there is now and, as Ely shows,[95] as there has been throughout the course of our history, a good deal of confusion as to what is meant by natural right and natural law. But what matters is the Founders' understanding and not that of Thomas

Hutchinson, John C. Calhoun, or the host of modern writers quoted by Ely. And the Founders were not confused.

They referred to man's natural condition as a "state of nature."[96] They said that men were created free and equal, and that government was instituted by men to secure their equal rights—it was even proposed in the first Congress that the Bill of Rights contain as its first provision one stating not that power derives from God, but "that all power is originally vested in, and consequently derived from the people," which was rejected only on the grounds of its redundancy (the Constitution's Preamble already made that point when it began with the words, "We the People").[97] In declaring their *right* to self-government, they invoked not the God of the Old Testament (who, of course, says nothing about that right and whose grace—*Dei gratia rex* or *Dei gratia regina*—has traditionally been claimed by kings and queens), but "Nature's God"; and not the laws of nature that a providential God writes in the hearts of men and which only the judges can read, but the self-evident "laws of nature" that direct men to seek peace and security for their rights by contracting one with another to form society. They then, being authorized by those natural laws, ordained and established a Constitution in which they granted power, divided power, and, especially in the ninth and tenth sections of the first article, withheld powers. Modern natural law culminates in a government of powers. Anyone who argues that the Founders intended the courts to exercise a natural rights-natural laws jurisdiction must come to terms with the fact that the original and unamended Constitution contains precious few provisions for such courts to work with. Among the powers granted, however, was the "judicial power of the United States," which was vested in an independent judiciary. The importance of this cannot be exaggerated.

The idea of a constitutionally independent judiciary did not make its appearance in modern natural rights theory until the publication in 1748 of Montesquieu's *Spirit of the Laws*, a work that had an enormous influence in America.[98]

To the Founders, Montesquieu—the "celebrated Montesquieu"[99]—was the man who, more than anyone else, showed
them how to solve what they understood to be the problem
of modern republican government. If Locke and Pufendorf
feared a tyrannical monarch, the Founders had greater reason
to fear a tyrannical people who would rule by right and
misrule by inclination unless somehow prevented from
doing so. Montesquieu's system of separated powers
provided the key to the solution of this problem. There is,
however, a significant difference between his system and the
American, and that difference has to do with the role of the
judiciary. The American situation required a more powerful
judiciary; unlike Montesquieu's judiciary, the American
must have the power of judicial review.

Montesquieu presented his teaching respecting the
separation of powers in the context of a discussion of what he
saw, or pretended to see, as the English constitution. I
recently explained this as follows:

> In England not only was the legislative power separated from
> and thereby independent of the executive, and the judiciary
> separated from each of the other branches, but the legislative—
> in modern times the most dangerous branch—was itself
> divided into two houses, one popular and the other
> representing the hereditary nobility. Thus, the separation of
> the legislative power corresponded to a division of power
> between the traditional factions, the rich and the poor, or the
> few and the many. It would be an unstable balance ... were it
> not for the fortuitous presence of the hereditary monarch who
> belonged to neither faction and whose interests could be said
> to correspond more or less to those of the country as a whole.
> The monarch used his absolute veto to maintain this balance
> between the factions and, thereby, to prevent each from
> oppressing the other. The judiciary was not involved in this
> balancing of factions; its roles was to enforce the rule of law.
> What emerges from the legislature takes the form of law
> applicable to everyone, and the balance achieved in its
> formation guarantees its nonoppressive character. It is the
> function of the executive, separated from the legislature, to
> apply this law to everyone; and it is the function of the

independent judiciary to see to it that it is the law, and the only law, that is being applied.... The *balance* of power, in which the judiciary plays no role, prevents class oppression; the *separation* of powers, in which the judiciary plays the indispensable role, prevents the oppression of any individual. This is how the separation of powers preserves liberty understood as security under the rule of law.[100]

This was the judicial power described by Montesquieu as "in some measure next to nothing,"[101] and to which Hamilton referred in *Federalist* No. 78 as "next to nothing." It was not, and of course is not, the judicial power of the United States. In addition to the powers described by Montesquieu, the American judiciary was intended to exercise powers accorded by Montesquieu to the English monarch and the English House of Lords. The existence in England of these two institutions made possible the separation of powers in England. "If these hereditary institutions had not existed in England," I wrote, "it would have been necessary for [Montesquieu] to invent them; their absence in America made it necessary for the Founders to invent a substitute for them."[102] What they invented was a written constitution and judicial review, an approximation of the English monarch's absolute veto and the House of Lord's power to mitigate the severity of the laws.

> What Montesquieu sought to accomplish by dividing the legislative power between two factions—the people and the nobility—the American Constitution seeks to accomplish by means of a written document that limits the legislative power by specifying "exceptions to the legislative authority; such, for instance, as that it shall pass no bills of attainder, no *ex post facto* laws, and the like." By enforcing these limitations, the Supreme Court will, in its way, maintain a balance between the factions that will arise in America, not between nobles and the people, but between few and many or creditors and debtors. What we have in America is a constitutional balance in the form of a limited Constitution, and the Court is very much a part of that balance.[103]

In principle, either faction—the few or the many—might threaten the constitutional balance by seeking to promote its interests at the expense of the interests of others, but, clearly, the Founders expected the many to pose the greater danger.[104] They invented judicial review in order to preserve the written Constitution and its balance of power. The judges were to be, Hamilton said, "faithful guardians of the Constitution." Hence, when the Court first declared an act of Congress unconstitutional, Marshall justified this action, in part, by pointing to the requirement that public officials take an oath to support the Constitution and said that this applies "in an especial manner" to the judges.[105] What he meant is that their relation to the Constitution is unique. Unlike other officials, the judges have no constituents in the usual sense of that term, and, this being so, they represent the Constitution and derive all their authority from it. And by preserving the Constitution, the judges will secure rights, for the Constitution was adopted "to secure these [natural] rights."

V

More, of course, than the principles of modern natural right and law went into the founding of the United States. In theory, the country was founded by men claiming rights against each other; in fact, they were men closely associated in families, churches, and a host of other institutions. In their books, government is created by men living in a state of nature and seeking to escape its miseries; in fact, the American government was created by men whose characters had been formed under the laws of an older and civilized politics.

Moreover, although they knew that their principles forbade the use of the laws directly to generate virtuous habits—the First Amendment, which embodies those principles, forbids religion to be established—they understood the need to preserve such habits, and they did not regard it as improper for the laws to support the private institutions (for example, the churches) in which they were generated and were to be generated.[106] And they apparently took it for granted that the laws would support the institution of the family; even the Supreme Court recognized its political importance. Here is John Marshall writing for the Court in 1823:

> All know and feel . . . the sacredness of the connection between husband and wife. All know that the sweetness of social intercourse, the harmony of society, the happiness of families, depend on that mutual partiality which they feel, or that delicate forbearance which they manifest towards each other.[107]

The family may have had no place in liberal theory, or the theory of modern natural rights,[108] but it was indispensable to the perpetuation of the liberal state. So said Alexis de Tocqueville,[109] and the Founders would surely have agreed.

It is not sufficient to say that the Founders looked only to the principles of modern natural right and law when they established and empowered the major political institutions. More than the teachings of Locke, Pufendorf, and Montesquieu went into their design for the Senate, for instance. This can be understood, I think, by asking what Alexander Hamilton meant when, in *Federalist* No. 9, he described representation as one of the "wholly new discoveries [made by] the science of politics." There had been representative bodies for thousands of years, so one must wonder what is new about American representation. James Madison provides a clue to the answer in *Federalist* No. 63 when he says that in America there is no representation of the people *"in their collective capacity."* Whereas previously representation was used as a means of drawing people into government and administration, now, as Herbert Storing used to point out, it is meant to exclude the people as such from direct participation in government and administration. The Senate best illustrates representation in this modern sense. There was no noble class in America, and the Founders did not expect one, or want one, to develop. Thus, unlike in Montesquieu's system, there would be no noble class to balance against the people, and the separation of the legislative power would not in itself produce a balance of power. Furthermore, Madison, unlike John Adams, had no confidence that the American society would in time produce a natural aristocracy. Time, he anticipated, would produce distinctions in the society, but these would be along the lines of rich and poor, and the rich, merely as rich, would bring nothing of value to the Senate. But what Senators did not themselves bring into the Senate, they might nevertheless acquire in the Senate by being given long tenure, special powers, and being restricted in number. Combined, these constitutional elements might produce a substitute for a natural aristocracy. Madison's words in the Constitutional Convention are instructive on this point (he is speaking against the proposal to enlarge the number of Senators):

> The more the representatives of the people [are] multiplied, the more they [partake] of the infirmities of their constituents, the more liable they [become] to be divided among themselves either from their own indiscretions or the artifices of the opposite factions, and of course the less capable of fulfilling their trust. *When the weight of a set of men depends merely on their personal characters; the greater the number the greater the weight. When it depends on the degree of political authority lodged in them the smaller the number the greater the weight.*[110]

Thus, with the institutions they devised, as well as with those private institutions they inherited from a preliberal past, the Founders sought to ensure the success of a country founded on the new principles of natural right and law. A country so founded—which is to say, a country founded on the principle of self-interest—could not be expected to flourish if it consisted only, or mainly, of self-interested men.

Nowhere is this better recognized than in the case of the federal judiciary. Only a few men, said Hamilton, "will have sufficient skill in the laws to qualify them for the stations of judges," and, even more to be regretted, fewer still who will unite "the requisite integrity with the requisite knowledge." It was, therefore, essential that these few be persuaded to forgo self-interest in favor of public service, or, as Hamilton puts it, to quit "a lucrative line of practice to accept a seat on the bench."[111] They must be promised life tenure and, if not a high salary, then at least one that may not be diminished during their continuance in office; this will guarantee their independence of the electors as well as of the persons they elect. Beyond that, the judges can expect to be honored for their services as "faithful guardians of the Constitution."[112]

This is the source of the problem of our time. Recipients of honors are not independent; they are dependent on those who bestow the honors. Hamilton does not acknowledge this problem, but he must have known that this method of perpetuating constitutional government will depend ultimately on the continued presence of a disposition among the Court's most attentive public—in our day, the legal profession and especially the professors of law—to honor judges who do indeed "guard the Constitution"[113] and its "fundamental [and] permanent" principles.[114] Instead of being dependent on the electors, either directly or indirectly, there is always the possibility that the judges will seek the approval of the law professors who, like Kenneth Karst, tell them to translate their ideas of what is good for the country into constitutional law.[115] But, as we know from Ronald Dworkin,[116] what the professors hold to be good for the country, or even what they hold to be fundamental rights, will be indistinguishable from what Hobbes and Locke called "private judgment." Modern constitutionalism began when, for very good reasons indeed, they sought a way to deny private judgment any role in politics.

PART II

FOREIGN POLITICS

CHAPTER 3

THE NEW PACIFISM AND WORLD GOVERNMENT

There have always been pacifists in this country. As early as 1789, during the debates on the proposed Bill of Rights, Congress found it necessary to decide whether Quakers, Mennonites, and Schwenkfelders should be constitutionally exempted from any requirement to bear arms in defense of the country. As members of traditional peace churches, these "religiously scrupulous"—Madison's term for them—were firmly of the opinion that the willful taking of human life was expressly forbidden under any and all circumstances, and, therefore, that war, even the American War of Independence, was contrary to the principles of the Gospel. For a variety of reasons, not the least of them being the fear that exemption might be exploited by "those who are of no religion," it was decided to leave the question of exemption to legislative discretion. Subsequent Congresses, while insisting that "no man can claim this indulgence by right," have accorded a measure of respect to this religious opinion by permitting those who honestly hold it to register as conscientious objectors. They have always amounted to an insignificant proportion of the population.

Now, under what is said to be the threat of imminent nuclear war, the number of pacifists has increased dramatically. They fill our streets and parks with their banners and placards demanding a freeze on the production and development of nuclear weapons. Hundreds of thousands of young men—some of them sounding like the Oxford Unionists who in the 1930s resolved not to fight for king or country—refuse to register for a draft that has not yet been called up, and one older man, weary of demonstrating at the gates of the White House, threatened to blow up the Washington Monument unless we immediately engaged in a nationwide debate on nuclear disarmament. (Shot dead by the police, he is buried among the nation's honored dead at Arlington.) Some Catholic bishops refuse to pay their defense taxes and, what is more, the National Conference of Catholic Bishops has issued a pastoral letter calling upon us to disarm, to forgo reliance upon weapons now discovered to be "immoral" in favor of a newly acclaimed policy of nonviolent resistance.

We are certain to hear a good deal more about non-violent resistance. That was Gandhi's tactic, and the recently released film of his life has been described by *Newsweek* as one of the "very few movies that absolutely must be seen." Gandhi employed his form of resistance with great success against the British, which makes it somewhat ironic that it should now be a British film that celebrates his life and times. After all, Churchill once referred to Gandhi as a "half-naked, seditious fakir." But the world has changed a lot since Churchill said he had no intention of presiding over the liquidation of the British Empire, and the British have changed at least as much as the world. They may fight the Argentinians in the Falklands, but at home they seem more inclined to join hands and bodies around American missile bases or, a more serious problem in its implications, to heed their Labor Party's call for unilateral nuclear disarmament.

If they were to be put to the test, however, if these legions of peace demonstrators—British, Dutch, German, and American—were to be confronted not with a squadron of British cavalry or a convoy of American jeeps but with a line of Soviet tanks, there would likely be much nonviolence but precious little resistance. Some demonstrators may protest that martyrdom is preferable to surrender of principle or violation of conscience, and a few of them may mean it, but what characterizes their brand of pacifism is not religious faith but fear. It is out of fear that they call for nonviolent resistance or no resistance, out of fear that they demand a freeze on the production of nuclear weapons, out of fear that some of them call for unilateral disarmament and (they presume) peace, and out of a fear fed by Jonathan Schell's *The Fate of the Earth* that many of them join in his call for the abolition of sovereign states and their replacement by a world government.

Peace, and especially in our time, is of course the fervent wish or prayer of all rational beings, and only someone wholly oblivious of the political situation can fail to appreciate how tenuous is our hold on it. There is good reason to be afraid. Yet it is somewhat unfair that these fears, and the radical proposals they have inspired, should have multiplied or have been intensified during a Republican Administration. The world has lived under the threat of nuclear war for a third of a century, and I intend no criticism when I point out that it was a Democratic President, not a Republican, who authorized the development of the first atomic bomb, a Democratic President who first authorized its use as a weapon of war, and a Democratic President who, during the Cuban missile crisis, came closest to authorizing its use against an enemy similarly armed. It is, in fact, only a slight exaggeration to say that Republicans would prefer to have nothing to do with foreign powers (except to trade with them). This may explain why, since McKinley's presidency, it has been easier for the Democrats to take the country into war and for the Republicans to make peace; for the Democrats to want to take the country into a league of nominally united nations (and on one occasion to succeed) and for Republicans to beat a retreat into isolationism; for a Democratic President to impose an embargo on shipments of grain to the Soviet Union and for a Republican President to lift it; for a Democratic President to establish a system of registration of draft-age men and for a Republican President to be reluctant to use it; for a Democratic President to stand at the Berlin Wall and say, *"Ich bin ein Berliner"* and, as his response to the Polish crisis shows, for a Republican President to hang a ceremonial wreath in his White House window and say, in effect, *"Ich bin ein* Kansas wheat farmer."

Nevertheless: it was Jimmy Carter the Democrat who recognized most clearly the politial (as well as the military) reasons for coming to some agreement with the Soviets on nuclear-arms limitation. (Who can forget that picture of him emerging from one negotiating session with his arms around Mr. Brezhnev and planting a kiss on his startled cheek?) Ronald Reagan, by contrast, promised to increase the defense budget, revived the B-1 bomber program, announced the intention of deploying the neutron bomb, proposed the stationing of land-based missiles in Europe and the MX in Wyoming, denounced SALT II, and, until prompted by events, appeared to be reluctant to engage in any negotiations with the Soviets. In the opinion of many, he is the principal cause of this sudden burgeoning of the new pacifism, in Western Europe as well as here at home.

The movement's most prominent spokesman appears to be Jonathan Schell. His book *The Fate of the Earth* has been more than adequately reviewed in these pages, but the implications of his arguments for peace deserve further scrutiny. Others have argued that man's fate on this earth is in jeopardy, and Schell is not the first person to conclude that a full-scale nuclear war would lead to the extinction of the human species, but he claims to be the first to have thought about the meaning of extinction. He thinks about it in (by rough count) some thirty thousand words, and his conclusion is that it would be awful, or appalling, or horrible, perhaps even (figuratively speaking, of course) unthinkable. "Death is only death," he finally pronounces in a stunning formulation, "but extinction is the death of death."

In order to survive, Schell says emphatically, the world must first disarm. "Unless we rid ourselves of our nuclear arsenals," he writes, "a holocaust not only *might* occur but *will* occur—if not today, then tomorrow; if not this year, then the next." He knows that no country is likely to deprive itself of its nuclear weapons if, by doing so, it puts itself in a situation in which it can be overwhelmed by an enemy's conventional forces. It follows that all countries must divest themselves of all weapons, conventional and nuclear alike, for "the present nuclear powers are hardly likely to throw away their conventional arms while non-nuclear powers hold on to theirs."

But how likely are the non-nuclear powers to throw away their arms? So long as they are independent, and see themselves threatened by countries that are also independent, they are only too likely not only to hold on to their arms but to increase the number of them. India, for one, spends more on arms proportionately than either of the two superpowers. Disarmament would thus seem to be impossible so long as the world consists of independent sovereign states, which must therefore be eliminated. Sovereignty "is now to the earth and mankind what a polluting factory is to its local environment."

In this way the argument comes back to the solution advanced by the United World Federalists and others at the dawn of the nuclear age. In the aftermath of Hiroshima and Nagasaki, the argument for world government was held to be "simple and irrefutable." Let us see.

II

The postwar pacifists of thirty-odd years ago—Albert Einstein, Bertrand Russell, Robert M. Hutchins, and others almost equally illustrious—began with the practical question of *how* to exchange a system of sovereign states for a world government, a United Nations with powers; unlike the new pacifists, they did not evade the question. They were concerned with at least the form of the world they would create. Yet none of them ever doubted that if only the means could be found the end would be an unmitigated blessing to mankind. It was on the basis of this assumption that the original one-world conferences were convened and the one-world constitutions drafted. The only debate in those conferences came on the subsidiary issues: Should the government be federal in form, and, if so, who or what would be represented? Should the parliament consist of one or two houses, and, if two houses, should each state have one vote in the second? Should it be a parliamentary system after the British model or one of separated powers, and, if the latter, how would the executive and the judiciary be chosen? Should there be universal suffrage, or some restrictions based on age or literacy? What provisions should be included in the bill of rights? And so on. There was no disagreement as to whether the world should have a government; nor, as should be clear from the list of topics debated, was there disagreement as to the kind of government the world should have. It was to be a liberal democracy. What else?

Well, why not a dictatorship of the proletariat? It had its champions, if not in these constituting conventions, then out there in the world. Stalin, for one; Mao, for another. As for the presumed necessity to secure human rights, that, as Marx had argued in his *Critique of the Gotha Program*, was bourgeois nonsense. And why not a monarchy? Were there not kings and princes (or, in Persia, shahs) who ruled by the Grace of one God or another? And at least one remaining caudillo (in Spain) charged with an historic mission to defend Christianity against the Communists? And a panoply of mullahs, sheiks, muftis, colonels, Oriental despots, tribal chiefs, petty bandits, and just plain thugs?

The conferees spoke confidently of world peace through world law, and they meant the rule of law as taught in the law schools from which so many of them came—Harvard, Yale, and especially Chicago, where Hutchins and his one-world colleagues wrote their world constitution—but anyone with political responsibilities had to have asked whether this would be the rule of Soviet law or American law, British law or South African law. They had to have known that the rule of law is an empty phrase until the substance of that law is defined and someone is appointed to administer it. In short, the world then was in no mind to come to an agreement as to how it should be governed, and in the absence of such agreement there could be no world government—or, at least, no world government based on the freely given consent of the governed.

The United World Federalists had good reason to know as much. According to an account in the *Journal of Politics*, the Federalists were united on the need for a "global government able to enforce law (in the sense of 'domestic law') on individual violators," and united as well in the opinion that, "given a certain amount of good will and political education" (which, of course, they were ready to provide), such a global government was possible. They also agreed that the "only practicable form for such a world government was the federal form." Unfortunately, for them at least, they could not agree as to "how such a world federation was to be brought about, which of the present states should be founding members, and what powers should be constitutionally delegated to it." In the course of trying to resolve their differences on such secondary issues, the members became "enraged," accused each other of "political immaturity," and demanded that the charters of some affiliated groups be revoked. The upshot was a series of schisms that left the parent organization with only half its previous membership. *Setting out to unite the people of the entire world under a single government, they soon learned they could not even unite themselves.* For those members who reflected on it, this ought to have been a sobering experience.

The new pacifists make occasional references to the early champions of world government, but only to express deep regret that their pleas went unheeded. This they attribute to blindness or selfishness on the part of political office-holders who lulled the world into a thirty-year slumber with their unfounded assurances of peace through mutual deterrence. Now, at last, seeing themselves on the very brink of disaster, people will finally realize the necessity to "acquiesce in their own survival," as Hutchins and his colleagues used to say. Whether this acquiescence is forged out of a common fear or a mutual love—and it is in this connection that we encounter the references to Gandhi—is of little concern to the new pacifists. As Schell puts it, by fear or by love, what matters is that both paths "lead to the same destination." He and his fellow enthusiasts are probably right in this: both paths lead to a global tyranny.

III

Tyrants have always appreciated the power of fear; they have always known that human beings can be forced to do all sorts of things out of fear, most of them terrible or despicable. They can be silenced, they can be made to grovel or debase themselves; they can be made to kill their neighbors and betray their friends; if George Orwell was right in 1984, they can even be made to love that which they ought to hate. More to the point here, they can be subjected to monstrous political rule; General Wojciek Jaruzelski of Poland is merely the latest in a long string of tyrants to demonstrate this. "As fear is the principle of despotic government," Montesquieu wrote, "its end is tranquility, but this tranquility cannot be called a peace: no, it is only the silence of those towns which the enemy is ready to invade." This was written some two hundred years ago in a world that knew nothing of nuclear fusion, but technological advances can only enhance its relevance. Is it not still important to ask whether a world built solely on our fears will be a despotism, and even *more* important because its powers would extend far beyond a few silenced towns?

The government of this new and fear-ridden world would be charged with keeping the peace, and, at a time when hydrogen bombs can be designed by Princeton under-graduates, it would have to remain alert; the enemy ready to invade the towns might be armed with atomic weapons. The pacifists are mistaken in their easy assumption that world government will bring disarmament with it. That government would have to be armed. Moreover, it would have to see to it that no one else was armed—or, at a minimum, that no one else was strongly armed—and that no quondam sovereign state had retained its arms. The situation would demand verification, as we say today, and verification would require a police force authorized to search and seize at will. After all, the mycotoxins used today by the Soviets to make yellow rain—which, of course, they deny making—can be concocted in university laboratories, and Molotov cocktails can be manufactured in basements. Considering the extent of the territory to be kept under surveillance and the ease with which our deadly weapons can be concealed (the Berrigan brothers once talked of descending into subterranean Washington and blowing up the government's heating system), the government would have little choice but to employ a huge secret police force, probably modeled after the KGB. Its tasks, made "awesome" and "urgent" by the perils to be avoided, would be to prevent the manufacturing of weapons (nuclear, biological, and "conventional") and to ferret out potential manufacturers of these weapons— anyone of whom there was the *slightest* suspicion. This brave new world would have to be saturated with informers. After all, a snitch in time might save more than nine; it might save the world.

No one should harbor the illusion of a world in which political power would be in the hands of a World Parliament. Plans may call for a parliament, but, even were it to be established, it would quickly become the equivalent of the impotent Supreme Soviet. The real power would be in the hands of the secret police, or the army that is charged with keeping the peace, or the party in control of both.

And who would object to all this? Old-fashioned liberal democrats, of course, but there would be no room for a Committee for the Free World in this new and "safe" world, and no space for a Freedom House. The secret police would see to that; that would be its job, among other things. Besides, anyone who thinks the world today is teeming with lovers of liberal democracy and its institutions, or even that the world is moving in the direction of liberal democracy, has never spent any time at the United Nations.

Except for a few and incredibly brave dissidents such as Andrei Sakharov and Vladimir Bukovsky (and in one world, where would they escape to and who would take up their cause?), we could not expect effective protest from the present citizens of the so-called people's republics. They would be unlikely to notice much, if any, change in the condition of their daily life, except, perhaps, some improvement in its material aspects. The new pacifists would not object, not so long as they held firm in their present views. They would not like it—the typical American would not like it—but anyone who believes that the death of the species is the worst of all fates would prefer universal despotism to our present situation, in which, according to the demonstrating pacifists, that death is inevitable.

So much, then, for this idea of a world government's deriving its powers solely from the fearfully given consent of the governed. It would almost certainly be, it would have to be, a tyranny of global proportions.

IV

We are sometimes assured that the agreement to live under an unarmed global government could also be generated by love, the love we bear for other human beings. This argument, such as it is, begins with the familiar invocation of Gandhi's name and proceeds as follows: Just as Gandhi proved that millions of people could be converted to the way of nonviolence, so millions more can today be converted by the power of love to accept disarmament. The human capacity to love will in fact be enhanced because, having understood that extinction will mean the death of death, people will naturally reach out for and embrace the unborn generations. Once again, Jonathan Schell says it all: "Love, a spiritual energy that the human heart can pit against the physical energy released from the heart of matter, can create, cherish, and safeguard what extinction would destroy and shut up in nothingness."

This, as it turns out, is about all that is ever said on the subject of love as the basis of world government. Had some modern Gandhi wanted to pursue the argument into the realm of politics, he could have shown that people who love each other—unless, of course, they are consumed by jealousy—will tend to trust each other and, as a consequence of that trust, will have no cause to fear each other. This would be decisive, because freedom can flourish, and can only flourish, where men have nothing to fear. It follows that for the first time in modern history, the whole of loving mankind would inhabit a house that is not divided; and a house that is not divided can stand on its own foundation: without despot, without police, without army, without arms, without even a constitutional right to bear arms. For, all sovereign nations having been consigned to the dustbin of history, against whom would anyone want to bear arms?

Meanwhile, back in our world, Britain wars with Argentina, South Africa with SWAPO, Israel with the PLO, Iraq (a Muslim state) with Iran (a Muslim state), Lebanese with Lebanese, Syrians with Syrians, North Yemen with South Yemen, Ethiopia with Somalia, Vietnam with the Cambodians (or some of them), Morocco with the Polisarios supported by Algeria, Nicaragua with its own Miskito Indians (and off and on with Honduras), and, if Colonel Muammar Qaddafi can have his way, Libya with Egypt or, for that matter, almost anyone else. The inventory, of course, is only partial, omitting, as it does, any mention of Soviet activities. Then there is Washington, where people living in sight of the Capitol are afraid to go out at night, and where at the Capitol itself Congress cannot muster the majority needed to enact a gun-control law.

Some dare to say that love will unite and disarm this world, but we cannot even disarm our own citizens. Nor can we or the United Nations unite and disarm the various parties now at war with each other. It is conceivable that the Israelis and Palestinians, for example, might reach an agreement permitting the two nations to live side by side, separate but equal, armed but at peace; but it is inconceivable that they might come together as one people in a United Israbia, not so long as they are Jews and (mostly) Muslims. And there is no prospect whatever that they will disarm themselves.

V

To persuade or frighten us into abolishing the United States in favor of a United Nations with powers, the new pacifists point to what they insist will be the inevitable consequences of the nuclear-arms race. In their treatment of blast effects, ozone layers, and the like, they rely on scientific studies and informed judgments; but for their political prescriptions they rely on pious and sometimes maudlin exhortation. Instead of political analysis, they offer us a bit of new scripture that someone else might in time work up into a polished sermon. But a sermon is of no use to us here.

Christians, for example, have from their beginning been sermonized, exhorted, even commanded, first to love God—"with all thy heart, and with all thy soul, and with all thy mind, and with all thy strength"—and then to love their neighbors *as* themselves. But experience suggests (if it does not in fact prove) that they are more likely to love their neighbors when their neighbors are *like* themselves: when they too, are Christians and not Jews, Muslims, Buddhists, or, most significantly in this context, not a different persuasion of Christian. They pray "for all sorts and conditions of men"—it is a beautiful prayer—but they tend to love and trust only particular sorts of men. And as the Ayatollah Khomeini demonstrates almost daily, this characteristic is not peculiar to Christians. There is no question but that men can be inspired by the love of God to love their fellow men, but there is no reason to believe that they can be so inspired to love all their fellow men. Religious faith seems to unite men but to divide mankind.

In this respect, it resembles the other forms of love. Love expresses itself as a caring for what is one's own, as distinguished from (and often at the price of) what is someone else's. A parent will prefer his own children over others, which is why Plato, in order to build the perfectly just city, had to abolish families. The patriot will prefer his country over others, which is why the new pacifists would abolish countries. The believer will prefer his god over others, which is why the inventor of the new world would have to abolish the gods. He would have to abolish the many gods and, because men need something to love, replace them with one god.

There could, of course, be no separation of church and state under this new dispensation; the state that adopts a policy of indifference to church affairs soon finds itself faced with many churches and many gods, and, so long as the gods are taken seriously, with the same old problem. This means that the ruler of this new Holy World Empire must be head of state and church alike, political ruler and defender of the faith. He will be like a god—Orwell gave him (or it) the name of "Big Brother"—and, like the various gods he replaced, he will love his people and promise to give them what they need, in this case, the peace that will permit the species to be kept "biologically intact." Also like the older gods, he will be jealous and insist that no other gods be put before him. (This will now be a political as well as a theological necessity.) It is, in fact, a desire akin to the erotic that impels someone to want to govern other men, and, as one student of tyranny said, "Erotic desires crave reciprocity." Thus, even more than, say, Lyndon Johnson, and much more, the governor of the world will want to be loved in return; and unlike Lyndon Johnson he would be able to demand love of everyone and, what is more, enforce that demand.

Now, it might be objected that what I have written here is wholly visionary, concocted in total ignorance of prevailing political and theoretical conditions. In my defense, I would point out that it was not I who suggested that world government might be built on love's foundation, and that I have merely looked more closely at the possibility. Had I begun independently, I would have suggested that the universal tyrant will present himself not as a god to be loved but as a philosopher, or scientist, to be respected. There is in fact a powerful body of thought right now whose expositors assure us that the fundamental human problems are in the process of being solved by the dialectics of history. This final solution, so to speak, will take the form of the "universal and homogeneous state," expounded by Hegel with corrections added first by Marx and then by Stalin and his successors. It is wise to assume, I think, that this universal and homogeneous state will have to be ruled (the Marxists to the contrary notwithstanding), and that it will be ruled by the same "philosophers" who, through their understanding of the historical forces that will bring it into being, now rule at the penultimate stage of history in the USSR. These rulers present themselves in turn as the final philosophic authority, and, since their rule depends on it, they can permit no challenge to their doctrine from philosophers of a different school or, for that matter, from priests, novelists, literary critics, or even, as we know, from biologists. This universal and homogeneous state will differ from the Soviet Union in only one important respect: there will be no escape from it. Orwell understood that, too, which is why, when Winston Smith declares his love for Big Brother, the novel, like history, comes to an end.

VI

The new pacifists, pointing to the prospect of calamity, can still insist that it is better to be red than dead, and, although Solzhenitsyn, Sakharov, and Bukovsky might disagree, this argument cannot be dismissed out of hand. Yet there is reason to wonder whether the argument is not usually combined with, or is not dependent on, the hope, or even the expectation, that we would not be red forever, or that, somehow, we can escape into a better world. For example, Schell assures us that "not even the most thorough-going totalitarian regimes have succeeded in wholly shaping the lives of their peoples." But the example he provides is that of Solzhenitsyn, whose soul was formed in an earlier Russia and who now lives in Vermont. And we know from the dissidents themselves that they are sustained not only by the expressions of support they receive from the West but also by the existence of the West. In one way or another, the fact that there remains a world outside the Soviet Union—a world with prisoners to exchange, grain to sell, technology to transfer, and opinions still to be formed or influenced—causes the Soviets to moderate their treatment of the dissidents, if only occasionally, and then only slightly. Anyone who harbors such hopes or expectations is obliged to imagine what would happen when the West disappears or is absorbed by the universal homogeneous state; he is obliged to wonder whether he is not, in fact, harboring illusions. Most of all, he is obliged to consider modern science and the powers it puts into a ruler's hands. Designed originally to provide the means by which man's estate on this earth might be relieved, it can serve as least as well as the means by which he can be enslaved.

It is also not irrelevant to point out that, so far, we—at least, we here—are neither red nor dead; and that there are reputable studies that conclude that even a full-scale nuclear war would not cause the extinction of human life; and, more important, that there is no *necessity* of a nuclear war (the example of the non-use of poison gas in World War II is sufficient to show that); and that, so long as the liberal democracies of the West remain strong, there is good reason to hope and some evidence leading one to believe that there will not be a full-scale nuclear war. In short, contrary to what the pacifists are saying, what might be need not be.

Finally, as we compare our life in this country—giving due weight to all its imperfections—with that of citizens or subjects of the Soviet Union, Poland, Iran, Libya, or, for that matter, of almost any of the countries not touched by the principles of constitutional democracy, are we not obliged to wonder whether they speak for us who say that nothing takes precedence over staying alive? That was not the view of "our fathers" who founded this country or of the "sons" who, at places like Gettysburg, fought and died. Do we now regard them as fools? They, like the others who avoided the battle, are long since dead, as dead as if they had been killed in a nuclear war, but it was they, and not the others, whom Lincoln asked us to remember—and whom we do remember, and whom we can honor only by dedicating ourselves to the cause for which they gave their lives. The new pacifism can only teach us about risks, but life without risk is inconceivable, and the risks we take to preserve an honorable way of life are both necessary and noble.

CHAPTER 4

WHERE THE MAJORITY RULES: A U.N. DIARY

Early June: I am asked whether I would be willing to serve as the American "expert" in a United Nations Seminar on the Relations that exist between Human Rights, Peace, and Development. (Actually, my caller begins by asking whether I would be willing to kill two weeks in New York in early August.) The Seminar, he explains, is one of those U.N. functions whose establishment the United States votes against but, when outvoted, it feels obliged to attend, the principle being that a no-vote is better than no vote. I protest that I hope to be in Maine in August and, in any case, in August I would prefer to be anywhere other than New York; he replies that I should look upon this as a form of national service. Besides, he adds, since the appointment would in fact be made by the U.N. Commission on Human Rights, I would receive the U.N. per diem allowance which is somewhat more generous than the American (even though the money comes from the same source, us). Warming up to his task, he leads me to believe that, if I stay at a modest hotel—he must have had in mind the YMCA—I might break even. Well, with one thing or another, it proves to be an offer I cannot refuse.

June 22: Today I receive from Geneva a formal notice of my appointment. The Director of the U.N.'s Division of

---

Human Rights writes that participants in the seminar are expected to contribute working papers "approximately ten quarto-sized, double spaced typewritten pages in length," which papers will be translated, reproduced, and distributed "in advance of the Seminar, if possible."

July 1: A packet arrives from Geneva containing three working papers: one from the Soviet participant (44 pages) detailing the life-long human rights work of Mr. Brezhnev; one from the Indian (55 pages); and one from the Norwegian (85 pages.) The Norwegian is not a participant, although he will participate; he is a "consultant" employed by the Seminar; reading his paper, I wonder if consultants are reimbursed on a per page rather than on a per diem basis. All three papers indicate that there has been a marked improvement in the "overall global human rights situation" in recent years; proof of this is to be found in the number of U.N. declarations on the subject.

July 15: I finish a ten quarto-sized (actually a ten $8\frac{1}{2} \times 11$ sized) double-spaced typewritten paper and send it off to Geneva. In it, among other things, I point out that I don't think the "overall global human rights situation" is actually so hotsy-totsy. "Billions of the world's peoples," I write, "are being governed without their consent, millions are being systematically and deliberately annihilated, hundreds of thousands are crowding fearfully into the flimsiest of vessels and fleeing the lands of their birth, millions more see their homeland suddenly and viciously occupied by an army launched by a neighboring state, while, across a continent, another people trembles at the prospect of being invaded— because they had committed the horrendous mistake of forming a free trade union!—by troops launched by that same friendly neighbor, and so on." Where, I ask, is the evidence of an improved human rights situation. "Iran? El Salvador?"

August 3: I arrive at the U.S. Mission to the United Nations (otherwise known as USUN), am assigned an office and an "alternate participant," who is a foreign service officer and a U.N. veteran; he will act as a kind of shepherd for me. When leaving the Mission to cross the street for the opening session, we run into one of our U.N. ambassadors, a friend from Washington, who gives me an idea of the importance generally attached to the Seminar by greeting me with the words, "What in the hell are you doing here?" It is a blistering day, so it is a relief to leave USUN, where Jimmy Carter's thermostat rules are still in effect, for the General Assembly Building, where the temperature is kept at a comfortable 72 degrees. My shepherd introduces me to a number of my fellow participants who prove to be not "experts" at all but members of their various countries' U.N. missions; in fact, the only other country that appointed an "expert" is the Soviet Union, which named its "Director of the Institute of State and Law of the Academy of Sciences." He is accompanied by a short chap with dark glasses who, I presume, is the KGB agent. Since under the prevailing alphabetical seating rules, we are placed next to the Soviet delegation, the four of us are soon engaged in an exchange of pleasantries. The same cannot be said of the situation with our neighbors on our right, the PLO, with whom, my shepherd informs me, we do not speak and *must* not be photographed. The PLO, along with SWAPO, the African National Congress, and the Pan African Congress, is present as an observer, one of the "Liberation Movements" recognized by the U.N. My shepherd, who has an eye for such details, notices that the alphabetical rules have been violated in the seating of the observers; a quiet word with some U.N. functionary leads to a rearrangement of the plastic name cards and a reshuffling of the observing delegations. We end up with the African National Congress on our right. The first order of business and, as it turns out, the morning's only business, is the election of the Seminar's officers, all of whom are elected unanimously. The chairman, (or, as the Australian participant, a woman, will insist on saying, the chairperson) is from Sri Lanka, the rapporteur is a charming lawyer from Sierra Leone, and there are three vice-chairmen: one from the Soviet bloc (Bulgaria), one from the Third World (Cuba, formally nominated by Mexico), and one from the WEOG (the Western European and Others Group). By some alchemy that I do not understand, we decide that WEOG's vice-chairman must be the participant from Finland; unfortunately, due to the air controllers' strike, he has not yet arrived. Belgium, speaking on behalf of the WEOG, asks the chair if the election of the third vice-chairman can be delayed pending his arrival. None of this matters so nobody objects. We adjourn for lunch, which I take with a USUN friend in the U.N. cafeteria where prices seem to have been set in the late 1950s and, perhaps in an effort to refute Milton Friedman, not changed since. We reconvene thirty minutes late—every session begins at least thirty minutes late—and spend the afternoon adopting the agenda and deciding, despite the wishes of Kenya who prefers that we be divided into three discussion groups, to do our business in plenary sessions. As France points out, most delegations consist of only two members and some of only one, and neither two nor one is divisible by three. A very sensible observation, but what the decision will mean is that there will be nothing resembling discussion, merely one speech after another.

August 4: The WEOG vice-chairman is elected unanimously. The chairman delivers his opening lecture and sets the tone of the Seminar by saying that it is "cynical to speak of civil rights to a poor and hungry man." The rapporteur follows by reciting a long list of U.N. declarations on human rights, peace, and development, and contradicts the chairman, whether knowingly or not I don't know, by saying that "people living in freedom are likely to work harder and thereby contribute to development." Cyprus is next; after congratulating each of the officers on his election to an important post in this important Seminar, he drones on until 12:10. Since no one else indicated a desire to speak, we adjourn until 3 P.M. During lunch I am informed by a USUN friend that it costs $400 to publish one page of an official U.N. document. This includes the cost of translation and distribution; it also represents more than twice the per capita annual income of some countries. We reconvene shortly after 3:30 and spend a few hours listening to India, the USSR, France, and the Norwegian consultant congratulate the officers on their election and speak of the interrelation of human rights, peace, and development. Everyone speaks of a right to development, so I raise my hand, which, when noted by the secretary, will earn me a place on the list of speakers. In due course, I speak my piece: development is not a right but a necessity. To say that the 780,000,000 people living in absolute pvoerty have a right to development suggests that they are poor because they are not developed (which is true), and that they are not developed because someone—guess who?—is denying their right. And to say (as every other speaker does) that the human right to develop is a right possessed by collectivities as well as individuals is merely to invite the governments of those collectivities to violate individual rights. For example, a government might decide that agricultural development can best take place through collectivization and then seize all private farms. This is likely to be resisted by the dispossessed farmers, who will then be dealt with harshly; in fact, they will be killed. And why not? The right to develop includes a right to the means of development as well as the right to decide on which means are appropriate or necessary. Thus, in this case, the U.N. would be sanctioning the elimination of the farmers. (A half hour later the "distinguished participant from the USSR" will take exception to my remarks, but I will lean over and say, innocently, that I didn't mention the Soviet Union or even utter the word "kulaks.") The Norwegian consultant says he is for human rights and peace and development, urges us to "embrace all three and to rise above them," and says there must be a "comprehensive redistribution" of income, which, of course, is what this seminar is really about.

August 5: Morocco identifies Israel as the world's chief villain. Bulgaria tells us that the "great October Revolution opened up a new epoch for human rights," and that individual rights cannot be separated from collective human rights. He concludes by calling on "some countries" to transfer wealth to the poor. Cuba, who, after Algeria, will prove to be the nastiest participant, says there is no possibility of tension between individual and collective rights; Prime Minister Castro solved this problem when he said the U.N. must recognize the rights of mankind. He spends the next fifteen minutes denouncing me. In my working paper, I had criticized the idea that human rights can be declared into existence by the U.N.; what the U.N. can give, I wrote, the U.N. can take away (which it now proposes to do with freedom of the press). In any case, it is simply foolish to suggest that one can discover his human rights by telephoning the U.N. Secretariat. (Dial a human right?) Cuba's answer to this is that, unlike 1945, the U.N. now represents the majority of the world's people, so it can say what are human rights—and the United States better get used to it. Syria denounces Israel, and we adjourn for lunch. Resuming at 3:40, Czechoslavakia, in the person of a rather attractive young woman, gives its version of the Soviet line, but gives it in English. Ireland, in an eloquent speech, reminds us that this is supposed to be a seminar of experts, and that "we don't come here with instructions in our pockets"; this is followed by a series of speeches—by Algeria, Belgium, Senegal, Kenya, Australia, and then the World Council of Churches which has no instructions because it has no government to issue them. The day ends with a passionate speech by the PLO; it appears that "almost all the miseries in the world, during the past 200 years, have been caused by capitalism."

August 6: The chairman tells us that "fruitful discussion has taken place." In the afternoon, Senegal, the World Council of Churches, and the USSR call for disarmament.

August 7: I put in an appearance at the appointed hour merely to see if anyone else is present; the only person in the chamber is the representative of the African National Congress. He is reading the *New York Times.* In the course of the day, Romania, Morocco, Egypt, Finland, Ireland, Australia ("Thank you, Mr. Chairperson"), Costa Rica, and Kenya deplore the arms race. Kenya also thanks the USSR for the most appropriate gift ever given to the U.N. and the world; it seems that some years ago, the Soviets installed a piece of sculpture in the U.N. garden depicting the beating of a sword into a plowshare. Cuba follows with a vituperative speech calling upon the United States to beat *its* sword into a plowshare. We adjourn one hour and fifteen minutes early, being told by the chairman that it has been an arduous week. That evening my wife calls me from Mount Desert Isle to say that Maine is very pleasant.

I spend the weekend writing my objections to the Seminar's report which, of course, I have not yet seen because it is not yet written.

August 10: The week begins (thirty-seven minutes late) with a long speech by the Soviet Union calling upon the U.N. to ban production of the neutron bomb (which, over the weekend, the United States said it was going to produce and deploy), and calling upon the United States to ratify Salt II. He also says the U.N. should establish the new International Economic Order (a code term for massive redistribution of wealth from us to the developing nations), adopt the resolutions on mass communications (a code term for restrictions on the freedom of the press), and promote research on the relations between human rights and peace; the results of this research are to be given to students. (I note that in addressing the participants he always says "gentlemen," which must make Australia squirm.) Nigeria recommends that we denounce colonialism, neo-colonialism (and I remind him of quasicolonialism), imperialism, and racism. China, in its first utterance of the Seminar, adds hegemonism to the list. Cuba calls for a "massive transfer of resources to the developing countries and complete forgiveness of debts accumulated in the past." This strikes most seminarians as a good idea. The World Jewish Congress speaks on behalf of Israel. We adjourn an hour-and-a-half before the scheduled 6 P.M.

August 11: The Indian participant sweeps in, clad in still another dazzling sari. This reminds me of the story in the *Times* today; it seems that in India, which, of course, has signed the U.N. convention on women's rights, women can still be bought and sold on the open market. I resist the temptation to ask India about this. During the morning session we listen to many speeches, including one from the Baha'i International Community. The Soviet Union leans over to ask, "Vat's Baha'i?" I tell him it's a religious organization and he smiles condescendingly. In the afternoon, I point out that everyone present, even the Soviet Union, is for human rights, although Marx himself had nothing but contempt for the very idea of rights; that it is foolish to think that we can agree on a report because we have incompatible ideas on what these rights are. Some of us, I point out, say human rights are those natural rights delineated by the political philosophers of the 17th and 18th centuries, and those that are reasonably derived from them; others say that a human right is any desired good—development, for example—that the U.N. transforms into a right; still others define as a human right whatever their own governments are prepared to grant, such as free dental care (or as Clifford Orwin and Thomas Pangle put it mischievously in a recent paper, free *bad* dental care). As for what the peoples of the world think about human rights, I suggest we look at the countries people escape from, or try to escape from, and the countries they escape to, or try to escape to. This right to emigrate, I say, is derived from the fundamental natural right not to be governed without one's consent. If this right is secured, the civil rights (the right to speak, to vote governments out of office, to acquire, possess, and pass on to one's heirs the property one earns by the sweat of one's brow or the acuity of one's brain, and to associate in free trade unions, *et cetera*) are likely to be secured. The truth of this was demonstrated in America by an egregious denial of rights: I refer, of course, to the failure to afford black Americans the opportunity to vote for or against the Constitution in 1787–88. The consequence was a denial of their right to be part of the constitutional majorities that governed the country, and it is not surprising that, until after the Civil War, they did not enjoy civil rights. That is why we in the liberal democracies attach so much importance to this right to be governed only with consent. In fact, of course, we all know that human rights properly understood are best secured in liberal democracies, and that liberal democracies are the most developed; as for peace, it is worth pointing out that there has never been a war between two liberal democracies. This ought to form the basis of our report on the relation of human rights, peace, and development; better that than a listing of demands which we call rights and which, as Ambassador Jeane Kirkpatrick said recently [and she picked it up from that Orwin and Pangle paper], may be likened to letters to Santa Claus. I have news for the participants of this Seminar: there ain't no Santa Claus. And if the report is going to contain a condemnation of Israel, honesty requires us to point out that Jordan has killed more Palestinians, that Syria has killed more Palestinians, than has the state of Israel. Finally, although I cannot speak for the government of the United States, I think the record shows that it stands ready to assist any country that demonstrates its willingness to use assistance in a way calculated to foster development. . . . Bulgaria, Australia, India, and Cuba deplore my letters to Santa Claus allusion. Cuba points out (unnecessarily, I think) that property rights are "out of fashion" in the U.N. As for this immigration business, he asks, what is it in fact? "A brains drain." The United States only takes the doctors and scientists educated in the poor countries. As for freedom of the press, why has the American press paid no attention to this seminar? (I could have told him, because they're all in Maine.) At 5:26, the PLO begins a violent speech and suddenly the Seminar becomes interesting. He makes a deprecatory reference to the Camp David accords, and Egypt bangs on the table and shouts, *"Pointe d'ordre! Pointe d'ordre!"* She insists that Camp David is not on the agenda. It seems, however, that points of order are not allowed in a seminar, but, then, what we are engaged in cannot fairly be described as a seminar. The chairman seems to be aware of this because he asks the PLO to confine his remarks to agenda items, and Egypt settles back in her chair. I decide that this is fun, so when the PLO, without referring to Camp David, launches a tirade against Israel, I pull out the plastic name card—"the United States of America"—and begin pounding on the table. Israel, I say, is not on the agenda. This produces some consternation among the participants because most of them are of the opinion that Israel (along with South Africa and American wealth) *is* the agenda. Still, I am sustained by the chair. But this has no effect on the PLO who, of course, has only one speech in his repertory, and when he continues his denunciation of Israel, I bang again with the name card. Under what conditions, I ask, are observers permitted to speak? At the pleasure of the official participants, I am told. Well, if it comes to a vote, I am sure to lose, so I, too, settle back in my chair. When the tirade resumes, I gather up my papers and walk out, which, I confess, gives me some pleasure: the United States walks out (even though, of course, as an independent "expert" I am not representing the United States). Back in the USUN, I report all this to my shepherd (who, wisely, no longer bothers to accompany me to these sessions); he says I must be late to the next day's session in order to make it clear that my departure was not required by the need to attend to one of nature's functions. I point out that it is not easy to be late; one has to be later, and that is not readily accomplished. It is decided that he will take my place for the first hour tomorrow, which has the further advantage of allowing me to be absent when the Soviet Union replies to my speech.

August 12: I arrive at noon and am told by my shepherd
that the time was given over entirely to the U.S.S.R.'s reply
to me. On the table there is a set of draft recommendations,
fifty-odd in number and largely repetitive, since it is largely a
compilation of recommendations made by the various
participants. France makes the reasonable suggestion that
there should be a drafting committee, but Nigeria says there
is no time for that. We adjourn to confer privately on the
question as to whether there is time for a drafting committee.
When reconvened, various participants argue over who
possesses the collective right to development: Algeria insists
it is the states, Australia prefers communities, Cuba agrees
with Algeria but nevertheless fancies the term "peoples."
Aware that we are not making progress and that time is
running out, we agree that the rapporteur should return in
the afternoon with a two- or three-page draft of
recommendations, which, surprisingly, he manages to do.
So, being pressed for time, we reconvene at 3:25, only
twenty-five minutes late, and begin consideration, item by
item, of the recommendations. It appears that U.N. seminars
are expected to achieve consensus on their recommendations, which affords me opportunities to toss a few monkey
wrenches. I cannot agree with any resolution, I say, that
speaks of the right to development. Rights, I say, have
corresponding duties; for example, in the United States we
have a right to speak freely, and the government has the duty
to protect speakers; in the Soviet Union they have a right to
work, and the government has the duty to provide jobs, at
which point the Soviet Union interrupts to say that Soviet
citizens have the right to free speech, too. I say that is nice,
then ask (pretending that I don't know the answer) who has
the duty that corresponds to a country's right to
development? Ireland asks more or less the same question
concerning the so-called right to peace. France asks what the
fifth resolution means. I offer the following new resolution:
"This Seminar appeals to the General Assembly to devise
procedures by which it may be ascertained whether the

peoples of all countries enjoy their fundamental human right of being governed only with their consent." The U.S.S.R. objects to this. On behalf of the PLO, Algeria argues vigorously in favor of the resolution calling upon the U.N. to guarantee the Palestinian people their rights; I offer an amendment adding, "the people of Israel, the people of Afghanistan, and the people of Cambodia." This proves to be a formidable monkey wrench, and haggling continues until 6:15 when the chair announces that the various interpreters (some twenty in number: French into English, into Chinese, into Spanish, into Russian; Russian into....) insist on their right to go home.

August 13: We spend the day haggling, much to the annoyance of the Soviet Union who wants to get on. I ask why the Soviet Union is so anxious; after all, Soviet delegates are renowned for their ability to outlast, or outsit, the delegates of other countries. "Iron-bottom Molotov" was a term of grudging respect in the United States, I add. He is not amused. By the end of the day, we have approved—i.e., gained consensus on—one innocuous resolution.

August 14 (last day): We WEOG's have our customary pre-session meeting to discuss strategy. As usual, the expression most frequently heard is, "We can live with that." That speaks volumes, because it reflects the fact that the West is engaged in a holding operation here, and that the initiative, and the power, here as in the U.N. generally, is in the hands of others. Australia is becoming annoyed with me and, truth to tell, I with her. The morning session is devoted entirely to consideration of the following Algerian resolution: "The Seminar recognizes that racism as a state ideology violently negates the basic humanity of its victims. Apartheid, racism, and racial discrimination, colonialism, neo-colonialism, foreign domination and occupation [the Namibia situation], aggression, and threats against national sovereignty and territorial integrity, and the denial to self-determination of a people are flagrant breaches of human rights, deny the political and social conditions for development, and constitute a threat to international peace. Collaboration with states that have racism as a complement to state ideology endangers peace and international security. The fight of oppressed peoples for self-determination is an inalienable right." That's quite a mouthful, but I indicate my support, provided the following words are added: "The right of a people not to be governed without its consent is also an inalienable right." Algeria makes the reasonable point that my addition is not germane to the subject of her resolution. Cuba, in what he would have me believe is the spirit of conciliation, says I should introduce this as a separate resolution. I say I am quite willing to do this if the two resolutions can be voted on as a package. Cuba and Algeria refuse this, and I refuse to withdraw my amendment unless, as a separate resolution, it is voted on along with the Algerian resolution. Cuba becomes angry, saying that there is no reason why we cannot vote on, first, the Algerian, then the American resolution. Since it is now after one o'clock, the chairman adjourns us, whereupon the Soviet Union says to me, "I agree with you. Package deal, yes?" I thank him for his support and he makes a beeline for the Cuban participant. One minute later the Cuban comes to me, a broad smile on his handsome face. "O.K.," he says in halting English, "a package." I apologize for my inability to speak Spanish and we shake hands. When, after lunch, the package is formally proposed, France offers what I see as an insignificant amendment, saying that, at least in the French version, there is a troubling phrase that he cannot accept. Algeria refuses to accept the French changes and the package deal collapses. We then turn to another resolution championed by Algeria: "This Seminar appeals to the U.N. member states to implement U.N. resolutions and decisions concerning the inalienable rights of the Palestinian people to freely determine their political status and exercise their human rights as a prerequisite to achieving peace and development." I offer the following amendment: after the words, "Palestinian people," add, "the people of Israel, the people of Afghanistan, and the people of Cambodia." To put it mildly, no consensus is reached on this, and the wrangling becomes somewhat nasty. The Soviet Union cannot understand me, he says; Professor Berns is surely not like the American people he has encountered during his very pleasant visit to New York; they are cooperative, friendly. "And Professor Berns? he's not democratic. He's preventing us from doing our business. He talks about democracy. O.K. Why doesn't he go along with the majority." Algeria pipes up, claiming I have not kept a promise I made to her, and proceeds to lecture me on morality. (At this point I half expect to see a blind man grope his way into the chamber and start lecturing me on the colors of the rainbow.) Australia joins in the attack, then Morocco. I haven't felt so uncomfortable in a parliamentary situation since the Cornell faculty meetings of 1969; still, I don't budge. Instead, I remind the participants of what it means to have a right, and that I intend to exercise my right to withhold my consent. They have a corresponding duty to allow me to exercise it. Kenya proposes a recess during which some of us might get together privately. The chairman agrees, and a half dozen of us repair to the adjoining small conference room. Here I am persuaded by Morocco that my amendment is not really germane to the Algerian. O.K., I say, I'll withdraw it and replace it with this one: add, "and the right of Israel to live in peace within secure and recognized boundaries." This, I point out is germane; this is the language of U.N. resolution 242. . . . Of course, this is unacceptable. Senegal complains that no one else supports my amendment, but Ireland immediately says he supports it. Morocco then recalls a precedent; it seems that at least one previous U.N. seminar presented its recommendations in two categories, one for recommendations on which there was consensus, and the other for recommendations on which there was no consensus. We troop back to the main chamber where a new quarrel erupts: Cuba argues that my resolutions don't even belong in the second category because no one else supports them, or almost no one else supports them. He suggests a third category for my resolution but, because there is no precedent for this, and because I threaten to object to all recommendations (even the innocuous ones), I eventually win. In this context, I insist that the chair determine how many participants support my resolution concerning Israel's right to live in peace within "secure and recognized boundaries." There is some confusion and hesitation, but eventually the following raise their hands: Ireland, France, Australia, Portugal, and Belgium. Conspicuously not raising their hands are Cyprus, Egypt, India, Mexico, Finland, and, of course, all the Soviet bloc and Third World countries— this in a Seminar that will adopt resolutions on the sovereign rights of nations, etc.... Eventually, we adopt our two categories of recommendations: consensus (innocuous) and nonconsensus (contentious). But it is now 7:45, and the interpreters have agreed to remain only until 8:30, and we have not yet adopted our report. (Our recommendations constitute only chapter 4 of a four-chapter report.) The chairman suggests we begin immediately to consider the draft submitted by the rapporteur, and that we do so page by page. But the draft numbers some 150 pages, being a compilation of all the various points made during our two weeks. I suggest that we will never finish if we adopt this procedure, that he should merely ask whether there are any objections. (Since we were given the draft only today, I doubt that anyone has had time to read it all; I know that I got through only thirty pages of chapter one.) Australia objects to the uniform use of the masculine pronoun, etc., and suggests that it be redrafted, but when the rapporteur winces, Australia says she is content that her objections be noted somewhere. Most of us sigh in relief. Whereupon Algeria objects to paragraph 39 of chapter one, which reads as follows: "The view was therefore expressed that it would be preferable to speak of development as a necessity rather than a right. ..." Yes, she says, that view was expressed, but only by one participant. Here (and elsewhere) it should be indicated that the view was expressed only by one country. (So saying, she glares at me.) Cuba, Senagal, the Soviet Union, etc. rally to her support. I say, I have no objection to these changes being made, but insist that this be done in every case. That is, we must ascertain the number of participants who agree with each view expressed. The chairman shouts that that would take us another two weeks and it is now almost 8:30. "Distinguished participants, we *must* adopt our report....It would be unprecedented for a seminar not to adopt a report, unprecedented!" (Who, I wonder, will ever read it?) Some thirty minutes are consumed by this dispute; finally, the chairman says he will assume that there are no objections to the draft report as written, and before anyone can open his mouth, he bangs his gavel saying, "the report is adopted." It is, in fact, now a few minutes before 9 P.M., but, so far as I can learn by twisting my dial, the interpreters are still with us. This is fortunate because the chairman must make a closing speech. He thanks us, we thank him—and the rapporteur, and the secretary, and the vice-chairmen, and the various members of the Secretariat who have been so helpful, and the documents custodian. With that we adjourn. As we gather up our papers, Ireland, who is a charming and eloquent man, asks me for my impressions. I say that if asked, I shall recommend that the United States reduce its contribution to the U.N. (We now pick up 25 percent of the tab, and more.) He says he was afraid I would say that, but for us to do that will mean the end of the United Nations. I reply that that might not be the tragedy he implies, but he thinks it will be the prelude to World War III. He then chastises the United States for its attitude: "In one sense, you don't take the U.N. seriously. For example, you are constantly changing your personnel, and as a result you don't establish the relationships that might permit you to work effectively here." We shake hands; in fact, there is a general round of handshaking, and I even receive a friendly slap on the back from Bulgaria. I run for a cab—I am of course late for a dinner engagement—and as I am being driven uptown I reflect that most of the participants will soon be meeting and working together again—in fact, unlike me, they do represent their countries, most of them on the U.N.'s Third Committee (which deals with human rights)—and most of them will regularly vote against the United States. As Cuba said, they are the majority.

August 15: I go to my USUN office and begin discarding part of the mountain of paper that has accumulated on my desk (and to which, I confess, I contributed a few foothills). Then, as I promised, I go up to the eleventh floor to chat with one of our ambassadors. When I report what Ireland had said about our attitude toward the U.N., he says Ireland may be right. And the ambassador may be right, but I wonder what difference it would make if our U.N. representatives served longer and succeeded in establishing closer relations with other delegations.

I suspect this Seminar was typical of U.N. meetings, especially of meetings on human rights, and it was surely not convened with the view that we might learn something from each other. It was not conducted with that purpose in mind. One can argue, as I did, that to know what human rights are requires that we understand what it means to be human, and what it is that distinguishes humans from other classes of beings, but all this falls on deaf ears. Jefferson and Tom Paine, following the political philosophers, could speak of the rights of man and were prepared to explain how these rights were related to and derived from man's nature; but U.N. seminarians are impatient with such talk. What they want is a U.N. declaration saying that the "South" has rights and the "North" (which means the United States) has duties, and it matters not a fig to them that, when challenged, they cannot present a rational argument on behalf of their demand. They have the votes.

Privately, some of them will concede that human rights have been best secured in the liberal democracies, but such concessions are quickly overwhelmed by their resentments toward their "former colonial masters." Privately, some of them will acknowledge that the Soviet Union is acting with gross hypocrisy, but the Soviet Union and its bloc supplies them with votes. A U.S. mission made of scores of Eleanor Roosevelts and Adlai Stevensons, all serving for life, would not, I sadly conclude, change this situation one whit.

CHAPTER 5

HOW TO TALK TO THE RUSSIANS

The following speech was delivered in February, 1983, at the 39th session of the United Nations Human Rights Commission meeting in Geneva. I was serving as the Alternate U.S. Representative to the Commission. The speech concerns Agenda Item 22—"Measures to be taken against all totalitarian or other ideologies and practices including Nazi, Fascist, and neo-Fascist, based on racial or ethnic exclusiveness or intolerance, hatred, terror, systematic denial of human rights and fundamental freedoms, or which have such consequences"—a resolution introduced by perennial advocates of human rights Afghanistan, Bulgaria, the Byelorussian SSR, Cuba, Czechoslovakia, the German Democratic Republic, Hungary, the Libyan Arab Jamahiriya, Mongolia, Mozambique, Nicaragua, Poland, the Ukrainian SSR, and Vietnam.

* * *

Mr. Chairman, it was useful to hear the distinguished representative of Canada remind us of the title of this agenda item. That title is, "Measures to be Taken Against All Totalitarian or Other Ideologies"—that is, Mr. Chairman, ideologies in addition to Nazi, Fascist, and neo-Fascist ideologies—all ideologies that have the consequence of

---

© *The American Spectator*, July 1983. Reprinted with permission.

systematically denying human rights and fundamental freedoms. In their interventions this morning, the distinguished representatives of Bulgaria, the Soviet Union, and Poland concentrated on Fascism and Nazism, and completely overlooked the first and longest-lived totalitarian ideology, namely, Communism. Contrary to what was said this morning Hitler was not the first totalitarian to seize power; Stalin preceded him by a few years. And when it comes to denying human rights, only a judge with the wisdom of Solomon could referee a contest between Hitler and Stalin—although everyone (at least everyone my age) remembers that both Hitler and Stalin killed millions of their own people. Whatever the distinguished representative of the Ukrainian SSR may remember (or forget), his forebears in the Ukraine remember this. That's why, in 1941, they welcomed the German Army with open arms. They thought Hitler was the lesser of the two evils. And who is to say they were wrong? As I suggested, only a Solomon could judge between Hitler and Stalin. Neither one of them believed that human beings have human rights.

In this respect, Stalin was only following Karl Marx. I do not mean that Marx was a gangster or murderer—far from it—I mean that Marx was contemptuous of the very idea of human rights. He always referred to them as the "so-called human rights" or the "so-called rights of man." He said that especially in his essay "On the Jewish Question," which is why anti-Semitism, which used to be a phenomenon of the Right, is now a phenomenon of the Marxist or Communist Left. One should not, then, be surprised when Marxist or Communist regimes treat their people as Hitler treated his. And it is no accident, as the Communists would say, that Hitler admired Stalin; Stalin was a man of iron will, a man who did not hesitate to act (so to speak), a man who did not allow human rights to stand in his way when, in his judgment, things had to be done—even if they were terrible things. They had a lot in common, Hitler and Stalin, and the political systems they established had a lot in common—with this difference: Stalin's system survived World War II.

I was reminded of the similarities between Nazi Germany and the Soviet Union as I listened this morning to the distinguished representative of the USSR. He obviously learned something from Hitler's propaganda minister, Joseph Goebbels. He learned that if you repeat an untruth often enough, passionately enough, and loud enough, it might someday be accepted as the truth. That untruth, which he would have this commission accept as the truth, is that my country, if not yet a Fascist country, is moving in that direction; that it is "soft" on Fascism in the way that Senator Joseph McCarthy used to say it was "soft" on Communism, that it goes out of its way to protect Fascists: the John Birch Society, for example, or the Ku Klux Klan, the various young Fascists, and the various old Nazis. In this connection, he mentioned the trial in Greensboro, North Carolina, where members of the Ku Klux Klan were put on trial for murder and other crimes but were acquitted. He also mentioned the street riots in Washington last fall; and he mentioned the difficulties encountered by the special investigating office in the U.S. Department of Justice which is now attempting to have Nazis deported; these are Nazis who, under false names, have been living in the United States since the end of World War II.

Mr. Chairman, these are familiar charges; the USSR has made them before, here and in the General Assembly. It is not worth our time to reply to them in detail or at length. Quite obviously, the distinguished representative of the USSR has no experience with a legal system that guarantees everyone—Fascist, Communist, or anyone else—a fair trial before a jury of one's peers. Under such a system, even Fascists and Communists are entitled to a fair trial. One might regret this in some cases, but we in the United States believe in due process of law, even if nasty persons are sometimes acquitted. And by due process of law, we mean a public trial, before a jury of one's peers, with the assistance of an independent and vigorous legal counsel. And a trial in which the government is required to prove the defendant guilty beyond a reasonable doubt.

In the same way, the distinguished representative of the USSR obviously has no experience with a legal system that guarantees the human rights of freedom of speech and assembly, even assembly that takes the form of marches and demonstrations in the streets and sometimes leads to riots. Thus, he cannot understand how the police are charged with the responsibility of protecing the demonstrators, even if this means protecting Fascist demonstrators. So long as they are peaceful, they have a right to march, and the police have the duty of protecting them. The distinguished representative of the USSR cannot understand this sort of legal system. It is foreign to him. It doesn't happen in the Soviet Union. The Soviet Union has a different system; here's an example of what I mean.

A few years ago, a handful of men in Lithuania tried to hijack an airplane, intending to fly it to Israel; they failed and were arrested. In due course there appeared in a Soviet legal journal a full account of their trial: the charges, the speeches of the prosecution, the speeches of the defense attorney, the verdict (guilty, of course), and the sentence. In short, here was a full account of what had taken place in that trial. The only thing wrong with this account duly published in the legal journal was that the trial had not taken place. It had been postponed, and someone had failed to inform the editor of the legal journal that it was going to be postponed; either that or the editor forgot to cancel the story. I've often wondered what happened to that editor; perhaps the distinguished representative of the USSR can enlighten us. At any rate, the experience of the Soviet representative is obviously limited to the Soviet legal system and excludes the American system where defendants are *first* tried and *then* sentenced, and sometimes tried and acquitted.

Mr. Chairman, a word now about the Nazis whom the United States is now trying to deport. As the distinguished representative of the USSR knows very well, this too requires a legal trial in the United States, and the government does not always win those trials. Still—and again, the distinguished representative of the USSR knows this—the government of the United States has established a special office within the Department of Justice, an office that is assiduously investigating these cases, and, when it has enough evidence, it goes to court and tries to persuade a jury that these Nazis should be deported because they had entered the United States under false pretenses. The government does not always win; but it sometimes wins. And a Nazi is sometimes deported. Another Nazi, knowing that the government had very good evidence against him, voluntarily left the country. But, Mr. Chairman, no one familiar with a legal system that guarantees a fair trial before a jury chosen from among the people should be surprised when a jury votes against the government. These things happen in the United States, Mr. Chairman—I mean, these verdicts in favor of a defendant. It may be regrettable, but that is the price we pay for due process of law.

Mr. Chairman, I want to acknowledge the assistance given my government by the Soviet Union in the collection of evidence against these former Nazis. The Soviet Union has been cooperative—fully cooperative, marvelously cooperative. I know this because a former student of mine, now working in the special office of the Department of Justice, has at least twice been to the Soviet Union for the purpose of examining Soviet records of Nazi war crimes, and he assures me that the Soviet officials have gone out of their way to be cooperative.

We only wish the Soviet Union had been more cooperative with the French and British in 1939. That is to say, we wish that the Soviets had opposed Nazi Germany then as vigorously as they did when they themselves were invaded. Instead, in the summer of 1939 they signed a non-aggression treaty with Nazi Germany. I'm referring, of course, to the Molotov-Ribbentrop Pact. Perhaps I should explain this to the distinguished representative of Poland where, apparently, the school textbooks no longer refer to it. Molotov was the Soviet foreign secretary and Ribbentrop was the foreign secretary of Nazi Germany, and, as the result of that agreement, the Nazis invaded Poland from the West (thereby beginning World War II) and the Soviets invaded Poland from the East, and there was no Poland left for the Polish people. I also feel obliged to remind the distinguished representative of the German Democratic Republic of some historical facts. He complained that Hitler owed his success to the failure of anyone or any country to resist him. That is too simple an explanation. It fails to take account of the assistance given Hitler by the Soviet Union. By entering into the non-aggression pact, the Soviet Union assured Hitler that he would not have to fight on two fronts, east as well as west.

How different would be our world today if Stalin had followed the example of, say, Winston Churchill! How many lives would have been saved if, instead of cooperating with Hitler, instead of invading gallant Finland, the Soviet Union had cooperated with France, Britain, and Poland. Among other blessings, Poland might have been Poland today.

Mr. Chairman, the system that produced Hitler is dead. We can all be thankful for that. But the system and ideology that produced Stalin is not dead; it has its representatives in this very room. This Commission would be well-advised if it were to concern itself with this lively form of totalitarianism. Thank you, Mr. Chairman.

CHAPTER 6

TAKING THE UNITED NATIONS SERIOUSLY

Ambassador Jeane Kirkpatrick tells the story of being visited by a deputation of angry women demanding to know why the United States, alone, had voted against a General Assembly resolution having to do with women's rights. Patiently, she explained that the resolution contained an outright lie and that the United States could not, or, so long as she had anything to do with it, would not, support any such resolution. Challenged to point to the mendacious element, she replied that she had no doubt that Third World women were oppressed, but that it was not true that multinational corporations were responsible for this oppression. That, she said, was the outright lie.

This did not, however, end the exchange, not that anyone was willing to dispute that particular point with her. That is, no member of this deputation insisted that it was indeed Nippon Motors that introduced Indians to *suttee* as well as to Subarus, or that the women of Iran are forced to wear the chador as the result of a plot hatched in the boardroom of Burlington Mills, or, for one more example, that female circumcision was unknown in the Third World before the advent of Texas Instruments. The exchange continued because these veteran observers of the United Nations apparently believed that the truth or falseness of a resolution plays (and, as they saw it, ought to play) little or no part in the decision of whether it deserves to be supported. Unlike Kirkpatrick, they did not take the U.N. seriously.

Still, there is something to be said for their position. The U.N. is the only organization with which I have been associated where it is taken for granted that members do not necessarily speak the truth. Thus, at this year's session in Geneva, the thirty-ninth since its founding in 1948, there was no angry, or even incredulous, response from the Human Rights Commission when the chief Soviet delegate explained that the wall between East and West Germany—and the barbed wire fences, the mine fields, and the automatically triggered shotguns—was intended *not* to keep the East Germans *in*, but rather to keep the West Germans *out*. He knew he was not telling the truth (he was V.A. Zorin, the 1948 "Butcher of Prague"); everybody in the chamber knew he was not telling the truth; and he must have known that everybody knew he was not telling the truth. But he said it and (except for the Americans) the Commission listened to him calmly, or better, imperturbably. So it was when the representative of Afghanistan admitted that, yes, chemical weapons were being used in his country, but not by the government or its gallant Soviet ally; no, he said without blinking an eye, they were being used by the tribesmen who were being supplied by the Americans. So, too, it was when Yugoslavia asserted that the Israeli cabinet had "planned" the Sabra and Shatilla massacres (a resolution embodying this charge as well as a denunciation of the Camp David accords was adopted by a vote of twenty-six to seven with ten abstentions), and when "the distinguished representative of the Libyan Arab Jamahiriya"—that is, Colonel Qaddafi's man—assured the Commission that nothing characterizes his country better than its well-known toleration of the variety of religious beliefs—or, at least, of those religious beliefs that "come from Heaven," as opposed to those that come from the "Zionist entity."

Having to listen to this sort of speech day after day and, in the case of some of them, year after year, tends to make the U.N. delegates cynical. This tendency is surely exacerbated by some of the resolutions "debated" and adopted: the ritualistic and, in the Human Rights Commission, the week-long condemnations of South Africa, and especially the resolution condemning "all totalitarian or other ideologies and practices, particularly Nazi, fascist or neo-fascist." At Geneva this year, this hardy perennial—it pops up at every session of the Commission as well as at every session of the General Assembly—was introduced by the following co-sponsors (and I shall let the list speak for itself): Afghanistan, Bulgaria, Bylorussian SSR, Cuba, Czechoslovakia, German Democratic Republic, Hungary, Libyan Arab Jamahiriya, Mongolia, Mozambique, Nicaragua, Poland, Ukrainian SSR, and Vietnam. As usual, the Western countries moved an amendment replacing the words "particularly Nazi, fascist, and neo-fascist" with the words "including Nazi, fascist, and neo-fascist." This was intended to demonstrate their ability to recognize a Soviet trick when they see one. As usual, the co-sponsors accepted the amendment. This was intended to demonstrate their willingness to be accommodating in what they would have everybody believe is a common effort to advance the cause of human rights in the world. As usual, the resolution was then adopted by consensus, but with the United States refusing to participate in the vote. And this was intended to demonstrate that the United States, at least, takes such matters seriously.

The truth is, however, that it is easier to be cynical than to be serious about the U.N. In 1982, thanks largely to the Herculean efforts of American delegates Michael Novak and Richard Schifter, the Human Rights Commission, by a narrow margin, adopted a resolution calling upon the Secretary General of the United Nations to appoint a special representative to investigate the human rights situation in Poland. After a delay of suspicious duration, which was ended only by Ambassador Kirkpatrick's personal intervention, the special representative was in fact appointed. Unfortunately, but not surprisingly, the Polish government did not permit him to set foot in the country. In 1983, thanks largely to Schifter's efforts, the Commission renewed his mandate, whereupon and immediately the Polish representative announced that, of course, he would again be excluded from that country. And there, one might be inclined to conclude, the matter will rest. The passage of the resolution—duly reported by Radio Free Europe—represented a message of support if not of hope to the people of Poland, and it would surely be foolish to minimize the importance of this. The Soviet delegation certainly did everything in its power to prevent it. But, however assiduous their efforts to influence world opinion, Communist tyrants are themselves not moved by it, even when it is embodied in U.N. resolutions. There is no public opinion in the Soviet Union, and it is the Soviet Union that calls the shots in Poland.

To take human rights seriously is to join the authors of the Declaration of Independence in holding it to be self-evidently true that all men are created equal insofar as they are endowed by nature with certain unalienable rights. These are rights owed to no accident of birth, color, faith, or ethnic affiliation; nor do they derive from government. Indeed, it is precisely in order "to secure these rights" that governments are instituted in the first place, and governments are properly judged by the extent or degree to which they do so.

The basic weakness of the U.N. is that few of the countries and, perhaps, even fewer of the representatives, subscribe to this understanding of human rights. This is to be expected from the self-styled Marxist countries, of which there are many (the Soviet Union alone can be said to have six of the forty-three seats on the Human Rights Commission: one in its own name and the others under the names of Bulgaria, Cuba, Mozambique, Nicaragua, and Ukrainian SSR). It is to be expected because, although the Soviets on the Commission do not like to be publicly reminded of it, Karl Marx himself had nothing but contempt for the very idea of human rights; he repeatedly referred to them as "the so-called rights of man." The essence of his position on rights is contained in the following statement, which is quoted from the official Soviet edition of his works: "Above all, we note the fact that the so-called rights of man, the *droits de l'homme* as distinct from the *droits du citoyen*, are nothing but the rights of egoistic men, of man separated from other men and from the community." Or, as he wrote in the same pages ("Essay on the Jewish Question"), they are the so-called rights of unemancipated men, men not yet set free by the historical process. Thus, the only rights "enjoyed" by the citizens of the Soviet Union are those the party or government (the agent of history) is willing to grant, such as the "right" to work—in Siberia, if the party so decides.

Among the non-Marxist countries in the U.N. there seems to be an understanding—implicit more than explicit, but an understanding nevertheless—that a human right is whatever the U.N. declares to be one. This is why they work so hard to have resolutions adopted, and why they so sharply criticize the United States for sometimes voting against them or, worse, for refusing to ratify one of the covenants.

But it is precisely because the United States takes human rights seriously that it refuses to ratify the Covenant on Economic, Social and Cultural Rights, for example. Such documents do nothing to advance the cause of human rights properly so called. On the contrary, by formally declaring such things as paid vacations to be human rights, they debase, or depreciate, or bring into contempt the very idea of such rights. One does not have to be an historian to imagine the response of mankind (to whose opinions they were paying a "decent respect"), if Jefferson and his colleagues of 1776 had written: that all men are created equal, that they are endowed by their creator with certain unalienable rights, that among these are life, liberty, and a paid vacation.

And it is precisely because it takes human rights seriously that the United States, alone, refuses to support resolutions referring to the so-called "right to development." Like health, wealth, and wisdom, economic development may be desirable; and if human beings are to be fed, clothed, and housed in a manner compatible with human dignity, it may also be a necessity. But it is not a right—whose is the corresponding duty?—and, no matter what U.N. majorities have declared, it is emphatically not a right belonging to states. Such a "right" would inevitably be exercised by governments, and exercised too often at the expense of individual human beings whose rights will be ignored or denied.

Third World countries come to the U.N. with demands that, taking advantage of the terms in which the Western liberal democracies originally defined the U.N., they state as their rights. Some of these are demands—for example, those embodied in the so-called New International Economic Order—that can be satisfied only by the Western countries or at their expense; this ensures them the support of the Soviet bloc. The majority thus created controls the agenda— most of the resolutions and reports have a Third World provenance—and does most of the talking, and the Western countries offer only a token resistance. Most of them can be depended upon to find reasons to go along with this majority—to join consensus, as the saying goes—whether to avoid displeasing a former colony (with which they want to trade), or to avoid being harassed by their own left-wing press, or with the assumption that nothing the U.N. does really matters, or, finally, because in a parliamentary situation it is customary to be accommodating. But what is at stake here are "fundamental human rights," and fundamental principles are not debatable; they are not defined in a parliamentary debate.

Accommodation and compromise are appropriate in a national parliament where it can (and must) be assumed that members are united in their loyalties, principles, and purposes or ends, and where compromise affects only the means by which ends are to be reached. Among the so-called United Nations (where even the meaning of peace is disputed), there is no common understanding of these "fundamental human rights," and any attempt to define them is almost certain to depreciate or deform them.

A nation that takes human rights seriously must refuse to join in this process, even if it must stand alone, and even if it makes people angry.

CHAPTER 7

WHO'S AFRAID OF AGEE-WOLF

The Soviet Union may have its equivalents of Philip Agee and Louis Wolf, but it surely does not have its equivalent of what might be called the Agee-Wolf problem. Nothing, not political consideration and certainly not legal principle, would prevent the Soviets from dealing unhesitatingly and summarily with any former KGB agent who published "Dirty Work: The KGB in Western Europe," as Mr. Agee, a former CIA agent, sought to expose U.S. intelligence activities abroad, or any dissident editor who took it upon himself to name Soviet names in a covert action information bulletin, as Mr. Wolf, a self-described journalist, does with CIA names.

What characterizes a political problem is the absence of a solution, in the strict sense of that term, and what characterizes the Soviet Union is its proclivity for solutions, including simple if not yet final solutions. It is not an accident, as the Marxists would say, that we do things differently.

So far we have done nothing definitive. Congress is considering two bills making it a crime for the Agees and the Wolfs of the world to disclose the names of our covert intelligence agents, but as one might expect there is opposition. The civil libertarians and various representatives of press and bar insist that to the extent these bills are constitutional they will be ineffective and to the extent they will be effective they are unconstitutional.

Faced with this apparent dilemma the House voted for effectiveness, which it did by substituting the broader language of the original Senate bill, and the Senate Judiciary Committee voted for constitutionality, which it did by substituting the narrower language of the original House bill, language designed to make it more certain that the law will not be used to punish or inhibit legitimate reporting. And there, for the time being, the matter stands. (Being a bicameral body, the Congress—up to a point—can take dilemmas in its stride.)

The constitutionality problem has little or nothing to do with the Agees of the world. Almost everyone, even the American Civil Liberties Union, agrees that Congress may properly forbid someone, "having or having had authorized access to classified information that identifies a covert agent," intentionally to disclose any information "identifying such covert agent to any individual not authorized to receive classified information." Which is to say, almost everyone agrees that the Constitution does not forbid Congress, by law, to attempt to put the Agees out of business. The problem has to do with the Wolfs, who unlike the Agees, are not and have never been intelligence agents.

Not much is likely to be gained by calling them before grand juries and asking them to disclose their sources. Should they refuse to answer, they could, of course, be cited for contempt, and it would not be unconstitutional to put them in jail if convicted. In his testimony before the Senate Select Committee on Intelligence, Ford Rowan, an attorney but also a former NBC correspondent, said he would "go to jail to protect the identity of a source who gives [him] information."

Unfortunately, unlike Mr. Rowan, others might be likely to protect their sources not by refusing to respond to questioning but by responding falsely. Asked to name their

Agees (having already named our agents), they would be likely to insist that all their information came from public sources accessible to anyone willing to do a little digging. (It is said that for years it was possible to identify the CIA agents on our embassy staffs simply by checking State Department registers where their names did not appear.) In such cases it would not be a simple matter, in an American court, to prove they were lying. This is one reason that Congress is proposing to deal with them directly by making it a crime for them to publish.

Even as publishers and editors of covert action information bulletins, however, they represent the press and claim all the constitutional rights to which the press is entitled. If Floyd Abrams is correct (he was counsel for the *New York Times* in the Pentagon Papers case), the press has the right to publish anything of this sort that comes to its attention, whether classified (the name of covert agents) or unclassified (the sailing dates of troop ships, or, more likely, the imminent departure of an airborne division to the Persian Gulf). In his testimony, he said it was his view "that if Agee sits up on a rostrum or hands out leaflets or writes a book, that anyone who hears what he has to say is constitutionally free to repeat it." Thus, whereas the press is not constitutionally free to publish pornographic and libelous material, the Wolfs of the press (if Mr. Abrams is correct) are free to publish the names of covert agents.

Congress, for its part, is not contending that the Constitution permits it to enact an American version of the British Official Secrets Act. On the contrary, both House and Senate bills are aimed not at the press in general but precisely at those who, so to speak, make it their particular or explicit business to disclose the names of our covert agents. ("Whoever, in the course of a pattern of activities intended to identify and expose covert agents....")

The House bill would require the government, when prosecuting a name-dropping publisher, to prove that he intended to expose these agents "with reason to believe that [by so doing he] would impair or impede the foreign intelligence activities of the United States." The Senate Judiciary Committee's bill would impose the stricter requirement that the government prove "intent to impair or impede" these activities. Considering the clear and present danger of the world in which it is our misfortune to be living—let's call it, the world according to Brezhnev and Qaddafi—one might think that both bills, and especially the latter, would survive constitutional challenge. This is not, however, the view of the ACLU. In its testimony, it insisted that "a citizen has the right to impair and impede the functions of a Government agency, whether it is the Federal Trade Commission or the CIA."

With all sorts of qualifications, amendments or emendations, a citizen might in fact be able to agree with that statement, just as he might have been able to agree with E.M. Forster when he said that, if faced with the choice between betraying a friend or betraying his country, he hoped he would have the courage to stand by the friend; or John Le Carre's statement in his introduction to *The Philby Conspiracy:* "We shall never create a society that is proof against his kind. . . . Philby is the price we pay for being moderately free."

Such sentiments have a pleasing resonance in our liberal ears, especially after Watergate and Vietnam. As the Chesterfield cigaret ads used to proclaim, they satisfy. Still, *any* country and *any* friend? And *whatever* the cost of betrayal of country?

And when making an appointment to, say, the British secret service, especially to its counter-espionage branch, would it not have been proper—would it have been illiberal—to demand greater assurances than that a Philby or a Burgess, or a Maclean was a member in good standing in the Atheneum and had been schooled at Westminster and Trinity College, Cambridge? And, when setting out to impair or impede the work of a government agency, is it really a matter of indifference whether the agency is the CIA or the FTC? Or do we say such things because we believe that the Philbys, Agees and Wolfs can't really hurt us, not fatally; that whatever they try to do and even succeed in doing, the liberal democracies, and especially the United States, will prevail?

The source of this unfounded confidence is, admittedly, the Constitution itself, or more precisely the principles it embodies. What, after all, is liberal democracy if not the regime that emphasizes the importance of the private life, the regime whose institutions are intended to protect the private realm—voluntary associations, families, friends—and its loyalties?

E.M. Forster had it exactly backwards: In the liberal democratic world, courage is required to choose not friend over country but rather country over friend. Anyone can test this by asking himself what his inclinations would be when confronted with treachery on the part of son or daughter, wife, mother, father, or friend. (And what better friendships than those formed at Cambridge or any other university where, in the company of great teachers and books, youthful tastes are educated and minds purged of their prejudices?) We are not Spartans. On the other hand, as the late Justice Robert H. Jackson once said, the Constitution was not supposed to be a "suicide pact."

The libertarian notwithstanding, before this legislative session comes to an end we shall almost certainly have an Intelligence Identities Protection Act; Congress may or may not be afraid but it cannot afford to ignore Agee-Wolf. Judging from the narrow margin (one vote) by which the Senate committee adopted the more liberal amendment, we shall probably have the version that passed the House.* And then, like almost all our political issues, Agee-Wolf will go to the courts.

---

*This, essentially, is what happened on June 23, 1982. See 96 stat. 122; 50 USCA 421(c).

PART III

DOMESTIC POLITICS

CHAPTER 8

BEYOND THE (GARBAGE) PALE OR DEMOCRACY, CENSORSHIP AND THE ARTS

I

The case against censorship is very old and very familiar. Almost anyone can formulate it without difficulty. One has merely to set the venerable Milton's *Areopagitica* in modern prose, using modern spelling, punctuation, and examples. This is essentially what the civil libertarians did in their successful struggle with the censors. The unenlightened holder of the bishop's imprimatur, Milton's "unleasur'd licencer" who has never known "the labour of book-writing," became the ignorant policeman or the bigoted school board member who is offended by *Mrs. Warren's Profession*, or the benighted librarian who refuses to shelf *The Scarlet Letter*, or the insensitive customs official who seizes *Ulysses* in the name of an outrageous law, or the Comstockian vigilante who glues together the pages of every copy of *A Farewell to Arms* she can find in the bookstore. The industrious learned Milton, insulted by being asked to "appear in Print like a punie with his guardian and his censors hand on the back of his title to be his bayle and

Reprinted, with the permission of The Public Affairs Conference Center, Kenyon College, from Harry M. Clor (ed.), *Censorship and Freedom of Expression: Essays on Obscenity and the Law* (Chicago: Rand McNally & Co., 1971).

119

surety," was replaced by Shaw, Hawthorne, Joyce, or Hemingway, and those who followed in their wake, all victims of the mean-spirited and narrow-minded officials who were appointed, or in some cases took it upon themselves, to judge what others should read, or at least not read. The victory of truth when it grapples with falsehood became the victory of "enduring ideas" in the free competition of the market. With these updated versions of old and familiar arguments the civil libertarians have prevailed.

They prevailed partly because of the absurdity of some of their opposition, and also because of a difficulty inherent in the task their opponents set for themselves. The censors would proscribe the obscene, and even assuming, as our law did, that obscene speech is no part of the speech protected by the First Amendment to the Constitution and may therefore be proscribed without violation of the Constitution, it is not easy to formulate a rule of law that distinguishes the nonobscene from the obscene. Is it the presence of four-letter words? But many a literary masterpiece contains four-letter words. Detailed descriptions of sexual acts? James Joyce provides these. Words tending to corrupt those into whose hands they are likely to fall? But who is to say what corrupts or, for that matter, whether anything corrupts or, again, what is meant by corruption? Is it an appeal to a "prurient interest" or a work that is "patently offensive"? If that is what is meant by the obscene, many a "socially important work," many a book, play or film with "redeeming social value" would be lost to us. The college professors said so, and if college professors do not know the socially important, who does? Be that as it may, they succeeded in convincing the Supreme Court, and the result was the complete rout of the "forces of reaction." To the college professors, therefore, as well as to the "courageous" publishers and the "public-spirited" attorneys who had selflessly fought the cases through the courts, a debt of gratitude is owed by the lovers of Shaw, Hawthorne, Joyce, and Hemingway—and others too numerous to detail here. In the same spirit one might say that never has there been such a flourishing of the arts in this country.

Astonishingly, the editors of the *New York Times* disagree, and in an editorial printed on April 1, 1969, under the heading "Beyond the (Garbage) Pale," they expressed their disagreement in language that we have been accustomed to read only in the journals of the "reactionary right."

The explicit portrayal on the stage of sexual intercourse is the final step in the erosion of taste and subtlety in the theater. It reduces actors to mere exhibitionists, turns audiences into voyeurs and debases sexual relationships almost to the level of prostitution.

It is difficult to see any great principle of civil liberties involved when persons indulging themselves on-stage in this kind of peep-show activity are arrested for "public lewdness and obscenity"—as were the actors and staff of a recently opened New York production that, in displaying sodomy and other sexual aberrations, reached the *reductio ad obscenum* of the theatrical art. While there may be no difference in principle between pornography on the stage, on the screen and on the printed page, there is a difference in immediacy and in direct visual impact when it is carried out by live actors before a (presumably) live audience.

The fact that the legally enforceable standards of public decency have been interpreted away by the courts almost to the point of no return does not absolve artists, producers or publishers from all responsibility or restraint in pandering to the lowest possible public taste in quest of the largest possible monetary reward. Nor does the fact that a play, film, article or book attacks the so-called "establishment," revels in gutter language or drools over every known or unknown form of erotica justify the suspension of sophisticated critical judgment.

Yet this does seem to be just what has been suspended in the case of many recent works, viz. one current bestseller hailed as a "masterpiece," which, wallowing in a self-indulgent public psychoanalysis, drowns its literary merits in revolting excesses of masturbation and copulation.

The utter degradation of taste in pursuit of the dollar is perhaps best observed in films, both domestic and foreign such as one of the more notorious Swedish imports, refreshingly described by one reviewer unafraid of being called a "square" as "pseudo-pornography at its ugliest and least titillating and pseudo-sociology at its lowest point of technical ineptitude."

Far from providing a measure of cultural emancipation, such descents into degeneracy represent caricatures of art, deserving no exemption from the laws of common decency merely because they masquerade as drama or literature. It is preposterous to banish topless waitresses when there is no bottom to voyeurism on the stage or in the movie houses.

In the end, however, there may be an even more effective answer. The insensate pursuit of the urge to shock, carried from one excess to a more abysmal one, is bound to achieve its own antidote in total boredom. When there is no lower depth to descend to, ennui will erase the problem.[1]

This must be reckoned an astonishing statement because in the liberal world for which the *Times* speaks it has not been customary—on the contrary, it has been quite unfashionable—to cast any doubt on the wisdom of the anticensorship policy so long pursued by the leaders of this world. Now suddenly the *Times*, contrary to what its readers expect of it and even to the general tenor of its own drama and literary pages, registers its misgivings. This is not what they wanted to heppen. In their struggle against the censor they did not mean to defend "the explicit portrayal of sexual intercourse" on the stage or in films; they did not have in mind "sodomy and other sexual aberrations." They intended to protect the freedom of the arts from bigoted censors; they were defending *Ulysses* when the customs laws would have excluded it from the country, and sensitive foreign films, such as *Les Amants*, from Ohio's laws; but they certainly did not intend to establish a place for "revolting excesses of masturbation and copulation."

Nine months later one of the country's principal foes of censorship checked in with the same disclaimer. *Ulysses*, yes, said Morris Ernst, but "sodomy on the stage or masturbation in the public arena," no! Although it never appeared to figure with any prominence, or figure at all for that matter, in the arguments that had made him one of the foremost civil liberties lawyers in the country, Ernst now insists that he had always made it clear that he "would hate to live in a world with utter freedom." He deeply resents "the idea that the lowest common denominator, the most tawdry magazine, pandering for profit... should be able to compete in the marketplace with no restraints." The free marketplace has become the dirty marketplace, and Ernst wants no part in it and no responsibility for it.[2]

But surely this was inevitable? Pornography and the taste for it are not new phenomena. What is new is the fact that it can display itself openly in the marketplace, so to speak, whereas in the past it had been confined by the laws to the back alleys, or to the underworld, where its sales were limited not by a weakness of the potential demand but rather by the comparative inaccessibility of the market. Prodded by the civil libertarians, the Supreme Court made pornography a growth industry by giving it a license to operate in the accessible and legitimate market, thereby bringing buyer and seller together. True, the Court did not directly license *Oh! Calcutta!* or *Che!* but so long as the Court is consistent these works are certain to benefit from the licenses given *Les Amants* and *Fanny Hill* and the others. Consider the state of the law developed on their behalf. So long as a work is not "*utterly* without redeeming social value" (and the emphasis is the Supreme Court's), it cannot be proscribed even if it is "patently offensive" and is found by a jury to appeal to a "prurient interest." All that is needed to save any work from the censor, or the police, is some college professor willing to testify as to its "social value" or "social importance," and there is no shortage of such professors with such testimony. Indeed, the work has not been written, staged or filmed that cannot find its champions among the professors.[3]

It was not supposed to turn out this way. Some invisible and benign hand was supposed to operate in this market too, and guarantee the triumph of the true and the beautiful. "People," said Justice William O. Douglas in one of the obscenity cases only a couple of years ago, "are mature enough to pick and choose, to recognize trash when they see it, to be attracted to the literature that satisfies their deepest need, and...to move from plateau to plateau and finally reach the world of enduring ideas." This is the liberal faith and the *Times* shared it, and it is worth noting that even in its distress it refuses to forsake it altogether. The editors express their disgust with what has happened, but they must know that this will be unavailing with those who are themselves disgusting. Certainly the "artists, producers [and] publishers...pandering to the lowest public taste in quest of the largest possible monetary reward" are not going to forgo this reward simply because some fainthearted libertarians, even on the *Times*, look upon their work as disgusting. "I paid to see filth and I want filth," said the woman from Connecticut by way of protesting a showing of an expurgated *I Am Curious (Yellow)*. She paid to see filth and, no matter what the *Times* says, there will always be "artists, producers [and] publishers" to see to it that she gets her money's worth. That is why there used to be laws against filth, because the legislators who wrote these laws knew full well the fruitlessness of relying on admonition or expressions of disgust. The *Times* does not call for the refurbishment of these laws, but appeals instead to the "laws of common decency," as if these so-called laws had not passed into desuetude with the demise of the statute laws that constituted their foundation. So it is that, in the end, they return to the old liberal faith in an invisible hand that will provide our salvation: "When there is no lower depth to descend to, ennui will erase the problem."

Such a conclusion is pitifully inadequate, but it is an accurate reflection of the thinking that has been done on this issue during our time. Neither the *Times* nor Morris Ernst has a grasp of the principle with which—or even a suitable vocabulary in which—to challenge the powerful orthodoxy that has long governed the public discussion of censorship and the arts. To be a liberal is to be against censorship or it is to be nothing—or so it has been thought—and after a career spent arguing against it, it is not easy to formulate an argument in its favor. They deserve our gratitude nevertheless, for, although they leave it undefined, their disclaimers do have the merit of acknowledging that there is something wrong with things as they are, that there *is* a problem. The respectability attached to their names makes it easier to reexamine this problem.

II

Just as it is no simple task to formulate a rule of law that distinguishes the nonobscene from the obscene, it is still more difficult to distinguish the obscene from the work of genuine literary merit. In fact, it is impossible, and our failure to understand this may be said to be a condition, if not a cause, of our present situation. Our laws proscribe obscenity as such and by name, and we are unwilling to admit that great literary and dramatic works can be, and frequently are, obscene. In combination these two facts explain how it came about that we now have, with the sanction of the law, what is probably the most vulgar theatre and literature in history. The paradox is readily explained. The various statutes making up the law have made obscenity a criminal thing, and our judges assume that if a work of art is really a work of art, and not vulgar rubbish, it cannot be obscene. Thus, Judge John M. Woolsey, in his celebrated opinion in the *Ulysses* case, recounts how he had asked two literary friends whether the book was obscene within the legal definition, which he had explained to them, and how they had both agreed with him that it was not. But of course *Ulysses* is obscene. Not so obscene as an undoubted masterpiece, Aristophanes' *Assembly of Women*, for example, which would not be a masterpiece—which would not be anything—were its obscenity removed, but obscene nevertheless. The trouble stems from the fact that the Tariff Act of 1930 would exclude "obscene" books from the country, and Judge Woolsey, being a sensible man, did not want this to happen to *Ulysses*. So he fashioned a rule to protect it. But the same rule of law protects *The Tropic of Cancer*, because according to the rule's necessarily clumsy categories, the latter is no more obscene than the former, however it compares on another scale and whatever the distances separating its author, Henry Miller, and James Joyce as poets. Eventually, and for the same reason, the protection of the law was extended to *Trim, MANual,* and *Grecian Guild Pictorial,* the homosexual magazines involved in a case before the Supreme Court in 1962, and then to *Fanny Hill.* At this point, if one ignores the *Ginzburg* aberration and the recent children's cases,[4] the censors seem to have given up, and we have—well, anything that anyone will pay to see or read. Thus, having begun by exempting the work of art from the censorship laws, we have effectively arrived at the civil libertarian's destination: the case where the Supreme Court throws in its hand and concludes that there is no such thing as obscenity. If *Oh! Calcutta!* is not obscene, what is?

Underlying this unfortunate development is the familiar liberal idea of progress. Rather than attempt to inhibit artists and scientists, the good polity will grant them complete freedom of expression and of inquiry, and will benefit collectively by so doing. What is good for the arts and sciences is good for the polity: this proposition has gone largely unquestioned among us for 200 years now. The case for censorship rests on its denial, and can be made only by separately examining its parts. What is good for the arts and sciences and what is good for the polity? The case for censorship arises initially out of a consideration of the second question.

The case for censorship is at least as old as the case against it, and, contrary to what is usually thought today, has been made under decent and democratic auspices and by intelligent men. To the extent to which it is known today, however, it is thought to be pernicious or, at best, irrelevant to the enlightened conditions of the twentieth century. It begins from the premise that the laws cannot remain indifferent to the manner in which men amuse themselves, or to the kinds of amusement offered them. "The object of art," as Lessing put the case, "is pleasure, and pleasure is not indispensable. What kind and what degree of pleasure shall be permitted may justly depend on the law-giver."[5] Such a view, especially in this uncompromising form, appears excessively Spartan and illiberal to us; yet Lessing was one of the greatest lovers of art who ever lived and wrote.

We turn to the arts—to literature, films, and the theatre, as well as to the graphic arts which were the special concern of Lessing—for the pleasure to be derived from them, and pleasure has the capacity to form our tastes and thereby to affect our lives, and the kind of people we become, and the lives of those with whom and among whom we live. Is it politically uninteresting whether men and women derive pleasure from performing their duties as citizens, parents, and spouses or, on the other hand, from watching their laws and customs and institutions ridiculed on the stage? Whether the passions are excited by, and the affections drawn to, what is noble or what is base? Whether the relations between men and women are depicted in terms of an eroticism wholly divorced from love and calculated to destroy the capacity for love and the institutions, such as the family, that depend on love? Whether a dramatist uses pleasure to attach man to what is beautiful or to what is ugly? We may not be accustomed to thinking of these things in this manner, but it is not strange that so much of the obscenity from which so many of us derive our pleasure today has an avowed political purpose.[6] It would seem that these pornographers know intuitively what liberals—for example, Morris Ernst—have forgotten, namely, that there is indeed a "causal relationship...between word or pictures and human behavior." At least they are not waiting for behavioral science to discover this fact.

The purpose is sometimes directly political and sometimes political in the sense that it will have political consequences intended or not. This latter purpose is to make us shameless, and it seems to be succeeding with astonishing speed. Activities that were once confined to the private scene—to the "ob-scene," to make an etymological assumption—are now presented for our delectation and emulation in center state. Nothing that is appropriate to one place is inappropriate to any other place. No act, we are to infer, no human possibility, no possible physical combination or connection, is shameful. Even our lawmakers now so declare. "However plebian my tastes may be," Justice Douglas asked somewhat disingenuously in the *Ginzburg* case, "who am I to say that others' tastes must be so limited and that others' tastes have no 'social importance'?" Nothing prevents a dog from enjoying sexual intercourse in the marketplace, and it is unnatural to deprive man of the same pleasure, either actively or as voyeurs in the theatre. Shame itself is unnatural, a convention devised by hypocrites to inhibit the pleasures of the body. We must get rid of our "hangups."

But what if, contrary to Freud and to what is generally assumed, shame is natural to man in the sense of being an original feature of human existence, and shamelessness unnatural in the sense of having to be acquired? What if the beauty that we are capable of knowing and achieving in our lives with each other derives from the fact that man is naturally a "blushing creature," the only creature capable of blushing? Consider the case of voyeurism, a case that, under the circumstances, comes quickly to mind. Some of us—I have even known students to confess to it—experience discomfort watching others on the stage or screen performing sexual acts, or even the acts preparatory to sexual acts, such as the disrobing of a woman by a man. This discomfort is caused by shame or is akin to shame. True, it could derive from the fear of being discovered enjoying what society still sees as a forbidden game. The voyeur who experiences shame in this sense is judging himself by the conventions of his society and, according to the usual modern account, the greater the distance separating him from his society in space or time, the less he will experience this kind of shame. This shame, which may be denoted as concealing shame, is a function of the fear of discovery by one's own group. The group may have its reasons for forbidding a particular act, and thereby leading those who engage in it to conceal it—to be ashamed of it—but these reasons have nothing to do with the nature of man.

Voyeurism, according to this account, is a perversion only because society says it is, and a man guided only by nature would not be ashamed of it.

According to another view, however, not to be ashamed—to be a shameless voyeur—is more likely to require explanation, for voyeurism is by nature a perversion.

> Anyone who draws his sexual gratification from looking at another lives continuously at a distance. If it is normal to approach and unite with the partner, then it is precisely characteristic of the voyeur that he remains alone, without a partner, an outsider who acts in a stealthy and furtive manner. To keep his distance when it is essential to draw near is one of the paradoxes of his perversion. The looking of the voyeur is of course also a looking at and, as such, is as different from the looks exchanged by lovers as medical palpation from the gentle caress of the hand.[7]

From this point of view, voyeurism is perversion not merely because it is contrary to convention, but because it is contrary to nature. Convention here follows nature. Whereas sexual attraction brings man and woman together seeking a unity that culminates in the living being they together create, the voyeur maintains a distance; and because he maintains a distance he looks at, he does not communicate; and because he looks at he objectifies, he makes an object of that with which is is natural to join. Objectifying, he is incapable of uniting and therefore of love. The need to conceal voyeurism—the concealing shame—is a corollary of the protective shame, the shame that impels lovers to search for privacy and for an experience protected from the profane and the eyes of the stranger. The stranger is "at odds with the shared unity of the [erotic couple], and his mere presence tends to introduce some objectification into every immediate relationship."[8] Shame, both concealing and protective, protects lovers and therefore love. And a polity without love—without the tenderness and the charming sentiments and the poetry and the beauty and the uniquely human things that depend on it and derive from it—a polity without love would be an unnatural monstrosity.[9]

To speak in a manner that is more obviously political, such a polity may even be impossible, except in a form unacceptable to free men. There is a connection between self-restraint and shame, and therefore a connection between shame and self-government or democracy. There is therefore a danger in promoting shamelessness and the fullest self-expression or indulgence. To live together requires rules and a governing of the passions, and those who are without shame will be unruly and unrulable; having lost the ability to restrain themselves by observing the rules they collectively give themselves, they will have to be ruled by others. Tyranny is the mode of government for the shameless and self-indulgent who have carried liberty beyond any restraint, natural and conventional.

Such was the argument made prior to the twentieth century, when it was generally understood that democracy, more than any other form of government, required self-restraint, which it would inculcate through moral education and impose on itself through laws, including laws governing the manner of public amusements. It was the tyrant who could usually allow the people to indulge themselves. Indulgence of the sort we are now witnessing did not threaten his rule, because his rule did not depend on a citizenry of good character. Anyone can be ruled by a tyrant, and the more debased his subjects the safer his rule. A case can be made for complete freedom of the arts among such people, whose pleasures are derived from activities divorced from their labors and any duties associated with citizenship. Among them a theatre, for example, can serve to divert the search for pleasure from what the tyrant regards as more dangerous or pernicious pursuits.[10]

Such an argument was not unknown among thoughtful men at the time modern democracies were being constituted. It is to be found in Jean-Jacques Rousseau's *Letter to M. d'Alembert on the Theatre*. Its principles were known by Washington and Jefferson, to say nothing of the Antifederalists, and later on by Lincoln, all of whom insisted that democracy would not work without citizens of good character; and until recently no justice of the Supreme Court and no man in public life doubted the necessity for the law to make at least a modest effort to promote that good character, if only by protecting the effort of other institutions, such as the church and the family, to promote and maintain it. The case for censorship, at first glance, was made wholly with a view to the political good, and it had as its premise that what was good for the arts and sciences was not necessarily good for the polity.

There was no illusion that censorship laws would be easy to administer, and there was a recognition of the danger they represented. One obvious danger was that the lawmakers will demand too much, that the Anthony Comstocks who are always present will become the agents of the law and demand not merely decency but sanctity. Macaulay stated the problem in his essay on Restoration Comedy (mild fare compared to that regularly exhibited in our day):

> It must, indeed, be acknowledged, in justice to the writers of whom we have spoken thus severely, that they were to a great extent the creatures of their age. And if it be asked why that age encouraged immorality which no other age would have tolerated, we have no hesitation in answering that this great depravation of the national taste was the effect of the prevalence of Puritanism under the Commonwealth.
>
> To punish public outrages on morals and religion is unquestionably within the competence of rulers. But when a government, not content with requiring decency, requires sanctity, it oversteps the bounds which mark its proper functions. And it may be laid down as a universal rule that a government which attempts more than it ought will perform less.... And so a government which, not content with repressing scandalous excesses, demands from its subjects fervent and austere piety, will soon discover that, while attempting to render an impossible service to the cause of virtue, it has in truth only promoted vice.

The truth of this was amply demonstrated in the United States in the Prohibition era, when the attempt was made to enforce abstemiousness and not, labels to the contrary, temperance. In a word, the principle should be not to attempt to eradicate vice—the means by which that might conceivably be accomplished are incompatible with free government—but to make it difficult, knowing that while it will continue to flourish covertly, it will not be openly exhibited. And that was thought to be important.

It ought to be clear that this old and largely forgotten case for censorship was made by men who were not insensitive to the beauty of the arts and the noble role they can play in the lives of men. Rousseau admitted that he never willingly missed a performance of any of Molière's plays, and did so in the very context of arguing that all theatrical productions should be banned in the decent and self-governing polity. Like Plato he would banish the poets, yet he was himself a poet—a musician, opera composer, and novelist—and demonstrated his love for and knowledge of poetry, or as we would say, the arts, in his works and in his life. But he was above all a thinker of the highest rank, and as such he knew that the basic premise of the later liberalism is false. A century later John Stuart Mill could no longer conceive of a conflict between the intrinsic and therefore legitimate demands of the sciences and the intrinsic and therefore legitimate demands of the polity; whereas Rousseau had argued that the "restoration" of the arts and sciences did not tend to purify morals, but that, on the contrary, their restoration and popularization would be destructive of the possibility of a good civil society. His contemporaries were shocked and angered by this teaching and excluded Rousseau from their society; if we were taught by them and more directly by Mill and his followers—Justice Douglas, for example—we might tend to dismiss it as the teaching of a madman or fool. Are we, however, still prepared to stand with Mill and his predecessors against Rousseau to argue that what is good for science is necessarily good for civil society? Or have certain terrible events and conditions prepared us to reconsider that issue? If so, and especially in the light of certain literary and theatrical events, we might be prepared to reconsider the issue of whether what is good for the arts is necessarily good for civil society.

III

In practice censors have acted out of an unsophisticated concern for public morality, with no concern for the arts and with no appreciation of what would be sacrificed if their policy were to be adopted. Their opponents have resisted them out of a sophisticated concern for the freedom of expression, but with no concern for the effect of this on public morality. It would appear that concern for public morality requires censorship and that concern for the arts requires the abolition of censorship. The law developed by our courts is an attempt to avoid this dilemma by denying that it exists. But with what results? Rousseau predicted there would be not only a corruption of public morality but a degradation of the arts. His case for censorship appears only at first glance to be made wholly with a view to protecting the simple and decent political order from corruption at the hands of literature and the theatre; it was in fact also a case made with a view to preventing the corruption of the arts themselves. Their popularization would be their degradation. To deny the tension between politics and the arts is to assume that the subject requires no governing, that what is produced by writers and dramatists may be ignored by the law in the same manner that the production of economic goods and services was once said to be of no legitimate concern of the law. The free market will be permitted to operate, with the result that what appears in print and on the stage will be determined by the tastes operating in that market, which in a democracy will be a mass market. The law will no longer attempt to influence this market; having denied the distinction between the nonobscene and the obscene, it will in fact come to deny the distinction between art and trash. This is what has happened. Justice Douglas, who told us that the "ideal of the Free Society written into our Constitution ... is that people are mature enough ... to recognize trash when they see it," also denies that anyone, mature or immature, can define the difference between art and trash. "Some like Chopin, others like 'rock and roll.' Some are 'normal,' some are masochistic, some deviant in other respects.... But why is freedom of the press and expression denied them? When the Court today speaks of 'social value' does it mean a 'value' to the majority?... If a publication caters to the idiosyncracies of a minority, why does it not have 'social importance'?"[11] To him, whether a publication has "social value" is answered by whether anyone wants to read it, which is to say that any publication may have "social value." It is all a question of idiosyncratic taste: some like Chopin, some like rock and roll; some are normal—or as he writes it, "normal"—and some masochistic or deviant—or, as he ought to have written it, "deviant." These statements of course make nonsense of his business of ascending "from plateau to plateau and finally reach[ing] the world of enduring ideas"; because if everything has value, and if there is no standard by which to judge among them, then there is no upward or downward, no "plateau" higher than another "plateau," no art or trash, and, of course, no problem. Art is now defined as the "socially important," and this, in turn, is defined by Douglas as anything anyone has a taste for.

It is true that Douglas is uniquely vulgar for a Supreme Court justice, but his colleagues have not been far behind him on the substantive issue. In principle they acknowledge the category of socially "important" publications and productions, but they do not depend on an educated critical judgment to define it. They simply accept the judgment of any literary hack willing to testify, which amounts to transferring the mass market to the courtroom. It was solemnly said in testimony that *Fanny Hill* is a work of social importance, which was then elaborated as "literary merit" and "historical value," just the sort of thing to be taught in the classroom (and, as Douglas argued, in sermons from the pulpit). Another "expert witness" described it as a work of art that "asks for and receives a literary response." Its style was said to be "literary" and its central character, in addition to being a whore, an "intellectual," which is probably understood to be the highest praise within the power of these experts to bestow. An intellectual, the court was then told, is one who is "extremely curious about life and who seeks . . . to record with accuracy the details of the external world"—in Fanny's case, such "external details" as her "physical sensations."

Censorship, undertaken in the name of the public necessity to maintain the distinction between the nonobscene and the obscene, has the secondary effect of lending some support to the distinction between art and trash. At a minimum it requires a judgment of what is proper and what is improper, which is to say a judgment of what is worthy of being enjoyed and what is unworthy, and this has the effect of at least supporting the idea that there is a distinction to be made and that the distinction is important. Our law as announced by the judges of our highest court now denies this, explicitly in the case of Douglas and implicitly in the case of his colleagues making up the rest of the Court's majority. The law has resigned in favor of the free mass market, and it has done so not because the free market is seen as a mechanism best calculated to bring about a particular result (for example, the material wealth desired by the *laissez-faire* economists) but because it attaches no significance to the decisions the market will make. The popularization of the arts will not lead to their degradation because there is no such thing as degradation.

The *New York Times* does not agree with this when it calls for "sophisticated critical judgment" to save us from the pile of muck that now passes for art. But the "sophisticated critical judgment" of its own drama and book pages praised the very works condemned in the editorial; besides, much of this market is impervious to "sophisticated critical judgment." This is confirmed in the *Times* itself in a piece printed a few months later on the first page of the Sunday drama section: "Nobody yet knows how to control the effect of nudity for a production's purposes, but producers encourage it anyhow. Why? The explanation, I should think, is obvious: sex, as always, is good box office."[12] Exactly. It was the law, not the critics, that kept the strip tease and the "skin-flick" confined to the illegitimate theatre, and it is foolish to think, or to have thought, that the critics alone will be able to keep them there, or, in fact, from flourishing in the legitimate theatre. That game is caught, as Lincoln would have put it. What remains at large, unanswered, is whether "sophisticated critical judgment" can preserve artistic tastes in another part of the same theatre, or whether there will be any "sophisticated critical judgment." To ask this is to wonder whether the public taste—or at least a part of the public taste—can be educated, and educated with no assistance from the law. This is an old question; to ask it is to return to Rousseau's quarrel with Voltaire and the Enlightenment, and to Tocqueville and John Stuart Mill—in short, to the beginnings of modern democracy where, in political philosophy, the question received thematic treatment.

The principle of modern democracy is the natural equality of all men, and the problem was to find some way of preventing this principle from becoming all-pervasive, and especially from invading the arts and sciences themselves. Stated otherwise, the problem was to find a substitute for the aristocratic class which had formerly sustained the arts and sciences, some basis on which, or some citadel from which, the arts and sciences could resist public opinion. The constitutional principle of freedom of speech and press would, perhaps, protect them from hostile political passions, but this institutional device would not protect them from the much more subtle danger, corruption by public opinion, of coming to share the public's taste and of doing the public's work according to the public's standards. One solution, it was hoped by some, would be the modern university, which, as Allan Bloom has recently written, was to be "a center for reflection and education independent of the regime and the pervasive influence of its principles, free of the over-whelming effect of public opinion in its crude and subtle forms, devoted to the dispassionate quest for the important and comprehensive truths."[13] Tenure and academic freedom would protect the professors of the arts and sciences, and thereby protect the arts and sciences themselves, and the students would be educated in the principles of the arts and sciences and their tastes formed accordingly. The education of the public's taste in the arts, which will prevent the popularization of the arts from becoming the cause of their degradation, must take place in the universities if it is to take place at all.

But the so-called expert witnesses who testified in the obscenity cases came from the universities. *Fanny Hill*'s champions were university professors, and not, by any means, in minor institutions. To rely on the professors to provide the "sophisticated critical judgment" or to educate the tastes of the mass market, or of any part of it, is to ignore what is going on in the universities. Several years ago Cornell paid $800 to a man to conduct (lead? orchestrate? create?) a "happening" on campus as part of a Festival of Contemporary Art. This happening consisted of the following: a group of students was led to the city dump where they selected the charred remains of an old automobile, spread it with several hundred pounds of strawberry jam, removed their shirts and blouses, and then danced around it, stopping occasionally to lick the jam. By 1970 standards this is not especially offensive; it is silly, as so many "college boy" antics have been silly. What distinguishes it from goldfish swallowing and panty raids is that it was conducted under official university auspices and with the support and participation of professors.

The call for a "sophisticated critical judgment" is merely a variety of the general call for education, which libertarians have customarily offered as an alternative to the policy of forbidding or punishing speech. It is an attractive alternative, attractive for its consistency with liberal principles as well as for its avoidance of the difficulties accompanying a policy of censorship; unfortunately, in the present intellectual climate, education in this area is almost impossible. Consider the case of the parent who wants to convince his children of the impropriety of the use of the four-letter verb meaning to copulate. At the present time the task confronting him is only slightly less formidable than that faced by the parent who would teach his children that the world is flat. Just as the latter will have to overcome a body of scientific evidence to the contrary, the former will have to overcome the power of common usage and the idea of propriety it implies. Until recently propriety required the use of the verb "to make love,"[14] and this delicacy was not without purpose. It was meant to remind us—to *teach* us, or at least to allow us to be taught—that, whereas human copulation can be indistinguishable from animal copulation generally, it ought to be marked by the presence of a passion of which other animals are incapable. Now, to a quickly increasing extent, the four-letter verb—more "honest" in the opinion of its devotees—is being used openly and therefore without impropriety. The parent will fail in his effort to educate because he will be on his own, trying to teach a lesson his society no longer wants taught—by the law, by the language, or by the schools. Especially by the schools. When in 1964 the University of California at Berkeley could not find a reason to censure the students for whom "free speech" meant the brandishing of the four-letter verb on placards, it not only made legitimate what had been illegitimate, but announced that from that time forward it would not attempt to teach its students anything contrary to their passions—sexual, political, or, with reference to drug use, physiological. What became true then at Berkeley is now true generally. The professors have nothing to teach their students. The younger ones have joined the students and have come to share their tastes and their political passions; the older ones are silent, and together they are in the process of abdicating to the students their authority to govern the universities, to enforce parietals, to prescribe the curriculum, and even their right to teach them. Critical judgment is being replaced by "doing your own thing," which is what Justice Douglas was talking about, and this being so, it is doubtful, to say the least, whether the universities will be able to educate the taste of anyone. And if this is not done in the universities, where can it be done?[15] Where in the midst of all the vulgarity and this incessant clamor for doing one's own thing can be found a refuge for the arts? There can be no "sophisticated critical judgment" without it.

IV

One who undertakes to defend censorship in the name of the arts is obliged to acknowledge that he has not exhausted his subject when he has completed that defense. What is missing is a defense of obscenity. What is missing is a defense of the obscenity employed by the greatest of our poets—Aristophanes and Chaucer, Shakespeare and Swift—because it is impossible to believe, it is unreasonable to believe, that what they did is indefensible; and what they did, among other things, was to write a good deal of obscenity. Unfortunately, it would require a talent I do not possess to give a sufficient account of it.

They seemed to employ it mainly in comedy, but their purpose was not simply to make us laugh. Comedy, according to Aristotle,[16] makes us laugh at what is ludicrous in ugliness, and its purpose is to teach, just as tragedy teaches by making us cry before what is destructive in nobility. The latter imitates what is higher, the former what is lower, but they are equally serious; Aristotle discussed both, and Shakespeare, for example, was a comic as well as a tragic poet.

Those aspects of his soul that make man truly human and distinguish him from all other beings—higher or lower in the natural order of things—require political life. And no great poet ever denied this. Man's very virtues, as well as their counterparts, his vices, require him to be governed and to govern; they initiate demands that can be met only in political life, but the poet knows with Rousseau that the demands of human virtue cannot be fully met in political life because they transcend political life. The poet knows the beauty of that order beyond the polity; he reminds us that there is an order outside the conventional and that we are part of that natural order, as well as of the conventional. Shakespeare knows with Rousseau that there is a tension between this natural order and the conventional or legal order, and his purpose is to resolve it, at least for some men, at the highest possible level. They must first be shown that the conventional world is not the only world—that beyond Venice there is Belmont[17]—and here is where obscenity may play a part. It can be used to ridicule the conventional. But it is used in the name of the natural, that order outside the conventional according to which the conventional may be criticized and perhaps, if only to an extent, reformed. Obscenity in the hands of such a poet can serve to *elevate* men, elevate them, the few of them, above the conventional order in which all of us are forced to live our mundane lives. Its purpose is to teach what is truly beautiful—not what convention holds to be beautiful—and to do so by means of pleasure, for obscenity can be pleasurable.

Shakespeare expresses this conflict between nature and law in Edmund's soliloquy at the beginning of Act I, Scene 2, of *King Lear:*

> Thou, Nature, art my goddess; to thy law
> My services are bound. Wherefore should I
> Stand in the plague of custom, and permit
> The curiosity of nations to deprive me,
> For that I am some twelve or fourteen moonshines
> Lag of a brother? Why bastard? wherefore base?
> When my dimensions are as well compact,
> My mind as generous, and my shape as true,
> As honest madam's issue? Why brand they us
> With base? with baseness? bastardy? base, base?
> Who, in the lusty stealth of nature, take
> More composition and fierce quality
> Than doth, within a dull, stale, tired bed,
> Go to th' creating a whole tribe of fops,
> Got 'tween asleep and wake?—Well, then,
> Legitimate Edgar, I must have your land:
> Our father's love is to the bastard Edmund
> As to th' legitimate: fine word,—*legitimate*!
> Well, my legitimate, if this letter speed,
> And my invention thrive, Edmund the base
> Shall top th' legitimate. I grow; I prosper:—
> Now, gods, stand up for bastards!

This serves to illustrate a theme to which great poets address themselves—what is right by law and what is right by nature—and in the development of which the obscenity in comedy has a legitimate and perhaps even noble role to play. When it is so used it is fully justified, especially because great poetry even when it is obscene is of interest only to a few— those who read it primarily for what is beyond its obscenity, that towards which obscenity points. But when obscenity is employed as it is today, merely in an effort to capture an audience or to shock without elevating, or in the effort to set loose idiosyncratic "selfs" doing their own things, or to bring down the constitutional order, it is not justified, for it lacks the ground on which to claim exemption from the law. The modern advocates of obscenity do not seem to be aware of this consequence of their advocacy. They have obliterated the distinction between art and trash, and in so doing they have deprived themselves of the ground on which they might protest the law. What possible argument could have been used against the police had they decided to arrest the participants in the Cornell "happening" for indecent exposure, or against a law forbidding these festivals of contemporary "art"? In this generous world the police must be accorded a right to do their "own thing" too, and they would probably be able to do it with the support of the majority and therefore of the law. In a world of everyone doing his own thing, the majority not only rules but can do no wrong, because there is no standard of right and wrong. Justice Douglas sees his job as protecting the right of these contemporary "artists" to do their own thing, but a thoughtful judge is likely to ask how an artistic judgment that is wholly idiosyncratic can be capable of supporting an objection to the law. The objection, "*I* like it," is sufficiently rebutted by the response, "*we* don't."

How to express in a rule of law this distinction between the justified and the unjustified employment of obscenity is no simple task. That I have argued and that I willingly concede. I have also argued that it cannot be done at all on the premise from which our law has proceeded. I have, finally, tried to indicate the consequences of a failure to maintain the distinction in the law: not only will we no longer be able to teach the distinction between the proper and the improper, but we will no longer be able to teach—and will therefore come to forget—the distinction between art and trash. Stated otherwise, censorship, because it inhibits self-indulgence and supports the idea of propriety and impropriety, protects political democracy; paradoxically, when it faces the problem of the justified and unjustified use of obscenity, censorship also serves to maintain the distinction between art and trash and, therefore, to protect art and, thereby, to enhance the quality of this democracy. We forgot this. We began with a proper distrust of the capacities of juries and judges to make sound judgments in an area that lies outside their professional competence; but led by the Supreme Court we went on improperly to conclude that the judgments should not be made because they cannot be made, that there is nothing for anyone to judge. No doubt the law used to err on occasion; but democracy can live without *Mrs. Warren's Profession*, if it must, as well as without *Fanny Hill*— or to speak more precisely, it can live with the error that consigns *Mrs. Warren's Profession* to under-the-counter custom along with *Fanny Hill*. It remains to be seen whether the true friend of democracy will want to live in the world without under-the-counter custom, the world that does not know the difference between *Mrs. Warren's Profession* and *Fanny Hill*.

CHAPTER 9

FOR CAPITAL PUNISHMENT

Until recently, my business did not require me to think about the punishment of criminals in general or the legitimacy and efficacy of capital punishment in particular. In a vague way, I was aware of the disagreement among professionals concerning the purpose of punishment—whether it was intended to deter others, to rehabilitate the criminal, or to pay him back—but like most laymen I had no particular reason to decide which purpose was right or to what extent they may all have been right. I did know that retribution was held in ill repute among criminologists and jurists—to them, retribution was a fancy name for revenge, and revenge was barbaric—and, of course, I knew that capital punishment had the support only of policemen, prison guards, and some local politicians, the sort of people Arthur Koestler calls "hang-hards" (Philadelphia's Mayor Rizzo comes to mind). The intellectual community denounced it as both unnecessary and immoral. It was the phenomenon of Simon Wiesenthal that allowed me to understand why the intellectuals were wrong and why the police, the politicians, and the majority of the voters were right: we punish criminals principally in order to pay them back, and we execute the worst of them out of moral necessity. Anyone who respects Wiesenthal's mission will be driven to the same conclusion.

Of course, not everyone will respect that mission. It will

strike the busy man—I mean the sort of man who sees things only in the light cast by a concern for his own interests—as somewhat bizarre. Why should anyone devote his life— more than thirty years of it—exclusively to the task of hunting down the Nazi war criminals who survived World War II and escaped punishment? Wiesenthal says his conscience forces him "to bring the guilty ones to trial." But why punish them? What do we hope to accomplish now by punishing SS Obersturmbannführer Adolf Eichmann or SS Obersturmführer Franz Stangl or someday—who knows?— Reichsleiter Martin Bormann? We surely don't expect to rehabilitate them, and it would be foolish to think that by punishing them we might thereby deter others. The answer, I think, is clear: We want to punish them in order *to pay them back*. We think they must be made to pay for their crimes with their lives, and we think that we, the survivors of the world they violated, may legitimately exact that payment because we, too, are their victims. By punishing them, we demonstrate that there are laws that bind men across generations as well as across (and within) nations, that we are not simply isolated individuals, each pursuing his selfish interests and connected with others by a mere contract to live and let live. To state it simply, Wiesenthal allows us to see that it is right, morally right, to be angry with criminals and to express that anger publicly, officially, and in an appropriate manner, which may require the worst of them to be executed.

Modern civil-libertarian opponents of capital punishment do not understand this. They say that to execute a criminal is to deny his human dignity; they also say that the death penalty is not useful, that nothing useful is accomplished by executing anyone. Being utilitarians, they are essentially selfish men, distrustful of passion, who do not understand the connection between anger and justice, and between anger and human dignity.

Anger is expressed or manifested on those occasions when someone has acted in a manner that is thought to be unjust, and one of its origins is the opinion that men are responsible, and should be held responsible, for what they do. Thus, as Aristotle teaches us, anger is accompanied not only by the pain caused by the one who is the object of anger, but by the pleasure arising from the expectation of inflicting revenge on someone who is thought to deserve it. We can become angry with an inanimate object (the door we run into and then kick in return) only by foolishly attributing responsibility to it, and we cannot do that for long, which is why we do not think of returning later to revenge ourselves on the door. For the same reason, we cannot be more than momentarily angry with any one creature other than man; only a fool or worse would dream of taking revenge on a dog. And, finally, we tend to pity rather than to be angry with men who—because they are insane, for example—are not responsible for their acts. Anger, then, is a very human passion not only because only a human being can be angry, but also because anger acknowledges the humanity of its objects: it holds them accountable for what they do. And in holding particular men responsible, it pays them the respect that is due them as men. Anger recognizes that only men have the capacity to be moral beings and, in so doing, acknowledges the dignity of human beings. Anger is somehow connected with justice, and it is this that modern penology has not understood; it tends, on the whole, to regard anger as a selfish indulgence.

Anger can, of course, be that; and if someone does not become angry with an insult or an injury suffered unjustly, we tend to think he does not think much of himself. But it need not be selfish, not in the sense of being provoked only by an injury suffered by oneself. There were many angry men in America when President Kennedy was killed; one of them—Jack Ruby—took it upon himself to exact the punishment that, if indeed deserved, ought to have been exacted by the law. There were perhaps even angrier men when Martin Luther King, Jr., was killed, for King, more than anyone else at the time, embodied a people's quest for justice; the anger—more, the "black rage"—expressed on that occasion was simply a manifestation of the great change that had occurred among black men in America, a change wrought in large part by King and his associates in the civil-rights movement: the servility and fear of the past had been replaced by pride and anger, and the treatment that had formerly been accepted as a matter of course or as if it were deserved was now seen for what it was, unjust and unacceptable. King preached love, but the movement he led depended on anger as well as love, and that anger was not despicable, being neither selfish nor unjustified. On the contrary, it was a reflection of what was called solidarity and may more accurately be called a profound caring for others, black for other blacks, white for blacks, and, in the world King was trying to build, American for other Americans. If men are not saddened when someone else suffers, or angry when someone else suffers unjustly, the implication is that they do not care for anyone other than themselves or that they lack some quality that befits a man. When we criticize them for this, we acknowledge that they ought to care for others. If men are not angry when a neighbor suffers at the hands of a criminal, the implication is that their moral faculties have been corrupted, that they are not good citizens.

Criminals are properly the objects of anger, and the perpetrators of terrible crimes—for example, Lee Harvey Oswald and James Earl Ray—are properly the objects of great anger. They have done more than inflict an injury on an isolated individual; they have violated the foundations of trust and friendship, the necessary elements of a moral community, the only community worth living in. A moral community, unlike a hive of bees or a hill of ants, is one whose members are expected freely to obey the laws and, unlike those in a tyranny, are trusted to obey the laws. The criminal has violated that trust, and in so doing has injured not merely his immediate victim but the community as such. He has called into question the very possibility of that community by suggesting that men cannot be trusted to respect freely the property, the person, and the dignity of those with whom they are associated. If, then, men are not angry when someone else is robbed, raped, or murdered, the implication is that no moral community exists, because those men do not care for anyone other than themselves. Anger is an expression of that caring, and society needs men who care for one another, who share their pleasures and their pains, and do so for the sake of the others. It is the passion that can cause us to act for reasons having nothing to do with selfish or mean calculation; indeed, when educated, it can become a generous passion, the passion that protects the community or country by demanding punishment for its enemies. It is the stuff from which heroes are made.

A moral community is not possible without anger and the moral indignation that accompanies it. Thus the most powerful attack on capital punishment was written by a man, Albert Camus, who denied the legitimacy of anger and moral indignation by denying the very possibility of a moral community in our time. The anger expressed in our world, he said, is nothing but hypocrisy. His novel *L'Etranger* (variously translated as *The Stranger* or *The Outsider*) is a brilliant portrayal of what Camus insisted is our world, a world deprived of God, as he put it. It is a world we would not choose to live in and one that Camus, the hero of the French Resistance, disdained. Nevertheless, the novel is a modern masterpiece, and Meursault, its antihero (for a world without anger can have no heroes), is a murderer.

He is a murderer whose crime is excused, even as his lack of hypocrisy is praised, because the universe, we are told, is "benignly indifferent" to how we live or what we do. Of course, the law is not indifferent; the law punished Meursault and it threatens to punish us if we do as he did. But Camus the novelist teaches us that the law is simply a collection of arbitrary conceits. The people around Meursault apparently were not indifferent; they expressed dismay at his lack of attachment to his mother and disapprobation of his crime. But Camus the novelist teaches us that other people are hypocrites. They pretend not to know what Camus the opponent of capital punishment tells us: namely, that "our civilization has lost the only values that, in a certain way, can justify that penalty . . . [the existence of] a truth or a principle that is superior to man." There is no basis for friendship and no moral law; therefore, no one, not even a murderer, can violate the terms of friendship or break that law; and there is no basis for the anger that we express when someone breaks that law. The only thing we share as men, the only thing that connects us one to another, is a "solidarity against death," and a judgment of capital punishment "upsets" that solidarity. The purpose of human life is to stay alive.

Like Meursault, Macbeth was a murderer, and like *L'Etranger*, Shakespeare's *Macbeth* is the story of a murder; but there the similarity ends. As Lincoln said, "Nothing equals *Macbeth*." He was comparing it with the other Shakespearean plays he knew, the plays he had "gone over perhaps as frequently as any unprofessional reader ... *Lear, Richard Third, Henry Eighth, Hamlet*"; but I think he meant to say more than that none of these equals *Macbeth*. I think he meant that no other literary work equals it. "It is wonderful," he said. *Macbeth* is wonderful because, to say nothing more here, it teaches us the awesomeness of the commandment "Thou shalt not kill."

What can a dramatic poet tell us about murder? More, probably, than anyone else, if he is a poet worthy of consideration, and yet nothing that does not inhere in the act itself. In *Macbeth*, Shakespeare shows us murders committed in a political world by a man so driven by ambition to rule that world that he becomes a tyrant. He shows us also the consequences, which were terrible, worse even than Macbeth feared. The cosmos rebelled, turned into chaos by his deeds. He shows a world that was not "benignly indifferent" to what we call crimes and especially to murder, a world constituted by laws divine as well as human, and Macbeth violated the most awful of those laws. Because the world was so constituted, Macbeth suffered the torments of the great and the damned, torments far beyond the "practice" of any physician. He had known glory and had deserved the respect and affection of king, countrymen, army, friends, and wife; and he lost it all. At the end he was reduced to saying that life "is a tale told by an idiot, full of sound and fury, signifying nothing"; yet, in spite of the horrors provoked in us by his acts, he excites no anger in us. We pity him; even so, we understand the anger of his countrymen and the dramatic necessity of his death. Macbeth is a play about ambition, murder, tyranny; about horror, anger, vengeance, and, perhaps more than any other of Shakespeare's plays, justice. Because of justice, Macbeth has to die, not by his own hand—he will not "play the Roman fool, and die on [his] own sword"—but at the hand of the avenging Macduff. The dramatic necessity of his death would appear to rest on its *moral* necessity. Is that right? Does this play conform to our sense of what a murder means? Lincoln thought it was "wonderful."

Surely Shakespeare's is a truer account of murder than the one provided by Camus, and by truer I mean truer to our moral sense of what a murder is and what the consequences that attend it must be. Shakespeare shows us vengeful men because there is something in the souls of men—then and now—that requires such crimes to be revenged. Can we imagine a world that does not take its revenge on the man who kills Macduff's wife and children? (Can we imagine the play in which Macbeth does not die?) Can we imagine a people that does not hate murderers? (Can we imagine a world where Meursault is an outsider only because he does not *pretend* to be outraged by murder?) Shakespeare's poetry could not have been written out of the moral sense that the death penalty's opponents insist we ought to have. Indeed, the issue of capital punishment can be said to turn on whether Shakespeare's or Camus' is the more telling account of murder.

There is a sense in which punishment may be likened to dramatic poetry. Dramatic poetry depicts men's actions because men are revealed in, or make themselves known through, their actions; and the essence of a human action, according to Aristotle, consists in its being virtuous or vicious. Only a ruler or a contender for rule can act with the freedom and on a scale that allows the virtuousness or viciousness of human deeds to be fully displayed. Macbeth was such a man, and in his fall, brought about by his own acts, and in the consequent suffering he endured, is revealed the meaning of morality. In *Macbeth* the majesty of the moral law is demonstrated to us; as I said, it teaches us the awesomeness of the commandment Thou shalt not kill. In a similar fashion, the punishments imposed by the legal order remind us of the reign of the moral order; not only do they remind us of it, but by enforcing its prescriptions, they enhance the dignity of the legal order in the eyes of moral men, in the eyes of those decent citizens who cry out "for gods who will avenge injustice." That is especially important in a self-governing community, a community that gives laws to itself.

If the laws were understood to be divinely inspired or, in the extreme case, divinely given, they would enjoy all the dignity that the opinions of men can grant and all the dignity they require to ensure their being obeyed by most of the men living under them. Like Duncan in the opinion of Macduff, the laws would be "the Lord's anointed," and would be obeyed even as Macduff obeyed the laws of the Scottish kingdom. Only a Macbeth would challenge them, and only a Meursault would ignore them. But the laws of the United States are not of this description; in fact, among the proposed amendments that became the Bill of Rights was one declaring, not that all power comes from God, but rather "that all power is originally vested in, and consequently derives from the people"; and this proposal was dropped only because it was thought to be redundant: the Constitution's preamble said essentially the same thing, and what we know as the Tenth Amendment reiterated it. So Madison proposed to make the Constitution venerable in the minds of the people, and Lincoln, in an early speech, went so far as to say that a "political religion" should be made of it. They did not doubt that the Constitution and the laws made pursuant to it would be supported by "enlightened reason," but, fearing that enlightened reason would be in short supply, they sought to augment it. The laws of the United States would be obeyed by some men because they could hear and understand "the voice of enlightened reason," and by other men because they would regard the laws with that "veneration which time bestows on everything."

Supreme Court justices have occasionally complained of our habit of making "constitutionality synonymous with wisdom." But the extent to which the Constitution is venerated and its authority accepted depends on the compatibility of its rules with our moral sensibilities; despite its venerable character, the Constitution is not the only source of these moral sensibilities. There was even a period, before slavery was abolished by the Thirteenth Amendment, when the Constitution was regarded by some very moral men as an abomination: William Lloyd Garrison called it "a covenant with death and an agreement with Hell," and there were honorable men holding important political offices and judicial appointments who refused to enforce the Fugitive Slave Law even though its constitutionality had been affirmed. In time this opinion spread far beyond the ranks of the original abolitionists until those who held it composed a constitutional majority of the people, and slavery was abolished.

But Lincoln knew that more than amendments were required to make the Constitution once more worthy of the veneration of moral men. This is why, in the Gettysburg Address, he made the principle of the Constitution an inheritance from "our fathers." That it should be so esteemed is especially important in a self-governing nation that gives laws to itself, because it is only a short step from the principle that the laws are merely a product of one's own will to the opinion that the only consideration that informs the law is self-interest; and this opinion is only one remove from lawlessness. A nation of simply self-interested men will soon enough perish from the earth.

It was not an accident that Lincoln spoke as he did at Gettysburg or that he chose as the occasion for his words the dedication of a cemetary built on a portion of the most significant battlefield of the Civil War. Two-and-a-half years earlier, in his First Inaugural Address, he had said that Americans, north and south, were not and must not be enemies, but friends. Passion had strained but must not be allowed to break the bonds of affection that tied them one to another. He closed by saying this: "The mystic chords of memory, stretching from every battlefield, and patriot grave, to every living heart and hearthstone, all over this broad land, will yet swell the chorus of the Union, when again touched, as surely they will be, by the better angels of our nature." The chords of memory that would swell the chorus of the Union could be touched, even by a man of Lincoln's stature, only on the most solemn occasions, and in the life of a nation no occasion is more solemn than the burial of the patriots who have died defending it on the field of battle. War is surely an evil, but as Hegel said, it is not an "absolute evil." It exacts the supreme sacrifice, but precisely because of that it can call forth such sublime rhetoric as Lincoln's. His words at Gettysburg serve to remind Amerians in particular of what Hegel said people in general needed to know, and could be made to know by means of war and the sacrifices demanded of them in wars: namely, that their country is something more than a "civil society" the purpose of which is simply the protection of individual and selfish interests.

Capital punishment, like Shakespeare's dramatic and Lincoln's political poetry (and it is surely that, and was understood by him to be that), serves to remind us of the majesty of the moral order that is embodied in our law, and of the terrible consequences of its breach. The law must not be understood to be merely a statute that we enact or repeal at our will, and obey or disobey at our convenience— especially not the criminal law. Wherever law is regarded as merely statutory, men will soon enough disobey it, and will learn how to do so without any inconvenience to themselves. The criminal law must possess a dignity far beyond that possessed by mere statutory enactment or utilitarian and self-interested calculations. The most powerful means we have to give it that dignity is to authorize it to impose the ultimate penalty. The criminal law must be made awful, by which I mean awe-inspiring, or commanding "profound respect or reverential fear." It must remind us of the moral order by which alone we can live as *human* beings, and in America, now that the Supreme Court has outlawed banishment, the only punishment that can do this is capital punishment.

The founder of modern criminology, the eighteenth-century Italian Cesare Beccaria, opposed both banishment and capital punishment because he understood that both were inconsistent with the principle of self-interest, and self-interest was the basis of the political order he favored. If a man's first or only duty is to himself, of course he will prefer his money to his country; he will also prefer his money to his brother. In fact, he will prefer his brother's money to his brother, and a people of this description, or a country that understands itself in this Beccarian manner, can put the mark of Cain on no one. For the same reason, such a country can have no legitimate reason to execute its criminals, or, indeed, to punish them in any manner. What would be accomplished by punishment in such a place? Punishment arises out of the demand for justice, and justice is demanded by angry, morally indignant men; its purpose is to satisfy that moral indignation and thereby promote the law-abidingness that, it is assumed, accompanies it. But the principle of self-interest denies the moral basis of that indignation.

Not only will a country based solely on self-interest have no legitimate reason to punish; it may have no need to punish. It may be able to solve what we call the crime problem by substituting a law of contracts for a law of crimes. According to Beccaria's social contract, men agree to yield their natural freedom to the "sovereign" in exchange for his promise to keep the peace. As it becomes more difficult for the sovereign to fulfill his part of the contract, there is a demand that he be made to pay for his nonperformance. From this comes compensation or insurance schemes embodied in statutes whereby the sovereign (or state), being unable to keep the peace by punishing criminals, agrees to compensate its contractual partners for injuries suffered at the hands of criminals, injuries the police are unable to prevent. The insurance policy takes the place of law enforcement and the *posse comitatus*, and John Wayne and Gary Cooper, give way to Mutual of Omaha. There is no anger in this kind of law, and none (or no reason for any) in the society. The principle can be carried further still. If we ignore the victim (and nothing we do can restore his life anyway), there would appear to be no reason why—the worth of a man being his price, as Beccaria's teacher, Thomas Hobbes, put it—coverage should not be extended to the losses incurred in a murder. If we ignore the victim's sensibilities (and what are they but absurd vanities?), there would appear to be no reason why—the worth of a woman being *her* price—coverage should not be extended to the losses incurred in a rape. Other examples will no doubt suggest themselves.

This might appear to be an almost perfect solution to what we persist in calling the crime problem, achieved without risking the terrible things sometimes done by an angry people. A people that is not angry with criminals will not be able to deter crime, but a people fully covered by insurance has no need to deter crime: they will be insured against all the losses they can, in principle, suffer. What is now called crime can be expected to increase in volume, of course, and this will cause an increase in the premiums paid, directly or in the form of taxes. But it will no longer be necessary to apprehend, try, and punish criminals, which now costs Americans more than $1.5 billion a month (and is increasing at an annual rate of about 15 percent), and one can buy a lot of insurance of $1.5 billion. There is this difficulty, as Rousseau put it: To exclude anger from the human community is to concentrate all the passions in a "self-interest of the meanest sort," and such a place would not be fit for human habitation.

When, in 1976, the Supreme Court declared death to be a constitutional penalty, it decided that the United States was not that sort of country; most of us, I think, can appreciate that judgment. We want to live among people who do not value their possessions more than their citizenship, who do not think exclusively or even primarily of their own rights, people whom we can depend on even as they exercise their rights, and whom we can trust, which is to say, people who, even in the absence of a policeman, will not assault our bodies or steal our possessions, and might even come to our assistance when we need it, and who stand ready, when the occasion demands it, to risk their lives in defense of their country. If we are of the opinion that the United States may rightly ask of its citizens this awful sacrifice, then we are also of the opinion that it may rightly impose the most awful penalty; if it may rightly honor its heroes, it may rightly execute the worst of its criminals. By doing so, it will remind its citizens that it is a country worthy of heroes.

CHAPTER 10

THE STATE OF THE NATION'S MORALE

The celebration of the Bicentennial was a heartening experience for "Stars and Stripes Forever" Americans, among whom I unabashedly number myself, and especially for such an American who for seven years had been living and teaching outside the country. At the University of Toronto, in the course of lecturing on Tocqueville's *Democracy in America,* I once asked the class the question of where Canadians got their heroes. "Do you," I suggested, "get them from Canadian history?" To my great embarrassment, the class of more than a hundred students broke out in a roar of laughter. With the memory of that event still fresh in my mind, I watched Americans pay joyous homage to Jefferson, Adams, Washington, and the rest—the American heroes whom four score and seven years later Lincoln was to call "our fathers." In July 1979, however, only three years after the Bicentennial, President Carter said the country was experiencing a crisis of confidence that "strikes at the very heart and soul and spirit of our national will." America had apparently become like Canada, a nation uncertain of its purpose, "losing [its] confidence in the future [and] beginning to close the door on [its] past." So said Jimmy Carter.

So, too, said Daniel P. Moynihan, not yet a United States senator. Writing in the Bicentennial issue of *The Public Interest*, Moynihan said sadly that in "no one thing has the American civic culture declined more in recent decades than in the symbols of love of country, and in . . . pride in the nation." So, too, said Daniel Bell, one of our leading intellectuals. Writing in the same issue of *The Public Interest*, Bell asked: "Do most Americans today believe in 'Americanism'? Do people identify achievement and equality with pride in nation, or patriotism?" He said it was an "open question."

Were they, or are they, correct in their assessments of the condition of our morale? A good deal depends on the answer to that question because, quite clearly, in the immediate future the American people will have to be asked to make some painful decisions. For most of the years since World War II, the country has been able to combine a commitment to the welfare state at home with a strong anti-Soviet policy abroad, but the party that fostered this and best exemplified it, the Democratic party, began to die when President Lyndon Johnson refused to ask the people to pay for the Vietnam War, and it was buried on the floor of the 1972 convention in Miami. (What remains of *that* party calls itself the Coalition for a Democratic Majority, many of whom supported Ronald Reagan in 1980.) In the future, which has already arrived, politics in America will not follow Harold Lasswell's familiar formulation of who gets what, when, and how; in our future, politics will more likely be a question of who loses what, when, and how much. Can the people accept this or are they, as Mr. Carter said they were, morally sick? That, I think, depends to a great extent on the kind of leadership they get.

One of the striking things about Mr. Carter's "malaise" speech was that it contained no evidence of the condition it deplored. There was surely nothing new, or even necessarily improper, about a Congress being "twisted and pulled in every direction by hundreds of well-financed special interests"; and none of the comments he elicited from the people justified his statement that "after listening to the American people I have been reminded again that all the legislatures in the world can't fix what's wrong with America." What Carter viewed as extraordinary, James Madison had recognized as everpresent. He wrote in *Federalist* 10:

> The regulation of these various and interfering interests forms the principal task of modern legislation and involves the spirit of party and faction in the necessary and ordinary operations of government.

Indeed, it was not even clear that Mr. Carter intended to be taken seriously, or, if he did, that he knew what he was talking about; in the very paragraph where he spoke of a severe crisis of confidence, he assured us that "our political and civil liberties . . . will endure." If we could have been sure of that—and we had his reiterated word for it—what was the problem? Some of us would have been happy to settle for secure political and civil liberties, especially when, as he went right on to say, our economic and military might were "unmatched." Free, rich, strong, what in the world ailed us?

The opinions reported in this issue of *Public Opinion* do not *prove* Carter, Moynihan, and Bell wrong in their assessments of the moral state of the nation, but they are worth reporting because they suggest that the people are in a healthier condition than up to now their leaders have been willing to assume. (In one of their 1976 television debates Mr. Ford and Mr. Carter were asked whether they foresaw the necessity to ask the people to make sacrifices and, if so, of what sort. Both began by saying they would demand sacrifices, of course, and both ended by promising goodies.) These polls show that for the overwhelming majority of the people, America is still "the very best place in the world to live," and not simply because of its material prosperity. Indeed, and the point deserves to be emphasized, material prosperity seems to have very little to do with it. Asked to explain why they are proud to be American (and almost everyone indicated such pride), only 4 percent of the respondents mentioned the country's prosperity, whereas 69 percent, a number that must have included many who were not necessarily prosperous, pointed to its freedom. For them, apparently, the country continues to be "the land of the free," and some 80 percent of Americans "think the United States has a special role to play in the world." That, too, deserves to be emphasized, because the survival of rights in the world does indeed depend upon a strong United States; but, on the other hand, no opinion survey is capable of demonstrating what the people would be willing to do in order to keep it that way. When it comes to assessing or ascertaining the morale of the country, a law demanding military service, for example, is likely to provide a more reliable answer than is a public opinion poll.

I use this example of compulsory military service not merely because all the evidence suggests that the all-volunteer policy is an utter failure and that the armed forces can be resuscitated only by a reinstitution of the draft, but because the armed forces are an instrument of foreign policy and it is principally in its dealings with foreign powers that a nation learns whether its morale is good. It is here that the American people are now going to be tested, and their leaders, beginning with the leaders of the Republican party, are going to be tested.

I use this example for still another reason: the nation is celebrating its first Fourth of July under the new Republican administration, and Republican administrations especially do not readily issue calls to arms or, for that matter, calls for sacrifices of any sort. (It has never been easy for democracies to demand sacrifices.) Not since McKinley has the country gone to war under a Republican president, and not since Theodore Roosevelt has it had a Republican president who, in his appeals to the people, found it natural or easy to employ the language of the citizen rather than that of the bourgeois. (By doing so, Roosevelt succeeded mainly in splitting the party, with his faction, in the course of time, finding a more comfortable home among the Democrats.)

It was Rousseau who, looking at the new world wrought

by the political philosophers Hobbes and Locke, first used the term "bourgeois" in contradistinction to the older term "citizen." For him, the bourgeois was the man whose primary concern is self-preservation, or in Locke's formulation, comfortable self-preservation, which means that in his dealings with others he is inclined to think only of himself. He finds himself at home in a civil society founded on Lockean principles and, being so founded, such a society gives the appearance of being dedicated to the pursuit of individual goods rather than to a common good. By nature free and equal and owing allegiance to no man and no cause beyond his own preservation, such a person enters civil society chiefly, as Locke says, to preserve his right to acquire property, property being the chief means of his preservation. The civil society he builds is much more likely to defend itself with an all-volunteer force, allowing market forces to determine the levels of pay, rather than demand military service of its members. It will take the form of a freely competitive commercial republic, and of our two major political parties the Republicans have always (or, at least, since Lincoln's time) been more at home in the commercial republic. It was not a Republican who said, for example, ask not what your country can do for you but rather what you can do for your country. Republicans ask the government to get off the people's backs so as to allow them to compete in the free market (their extreme right wing—the so-called libertarians—calls upon the government to wither away); the words "duty" and "free market" belong to different political lexicons.

Republicans since Theodore Roosevelt's time have not taken readily to foreign policy. From their perspective, foreign policy is unnatural and, well, foreign. A sound foreign policy at this juncture might require us to cease all trade with the Soviet Union (except in the area of cultural exchange whereby they send us ballet dancers and classical musicians, a fair number of whom defect, and we send them rock music, which has the salutary effect of corrupting their youth), but Republicans take naturally to trade and give it up with the greatest reluctance. One can readily imagine President Reagan himself standing at the Berlin Wall and saying, *"Ich bin ein Berliner,"* or even better, *"Ich bin auch ein Berliner,"* but he heads a party that would prefer to hear him say, "Ich bin ein Kansas wheat farmer." (And from a certain perspective, why not?)

On the other hand, Republicans are also much less likely than Democrats to speak of compassion and the necessity to be governed by it in all their official actions. This, I think, is good, because the politician who pretends to great compassion also tends to democratic sycophancy—and sycophancy is the greatest failure of leadership—he flatters the people in a servile manner. Mr. Carter's "malaise" speech provides us with a good example of this. If it were true that the American people had lost confidence in their institutions, Mr. Carter's pious exhortations—"have faith," "join hands," "say something good about the country"— were not calculated to restore that confidence. A truly demoralized country—Germany in the latter days of the Weimar Republic, for example, or France on the eve of World War II and again in 1958 during the last days of the Fourth Republic—would greet these *niaiseries* with the contempt they would deserve in such circumstances. If what was wrong with America in 1979 could not have been fixed by "all the legislatures in the world," then surely it could not have been cured by a physician who, having told the patient that he was seriously ill, proposed to allow him to prescribe his own treatment. Yet this is what Carter did; not from him came a prescription of bitter medicine, even though his diagnosis would have called for it. "I will," he said, "continue to travel this country [in order] to hear the people of America." He would hear them, talk with them, jog among them, mingle with them, learn from them, and be restored by them. This was Carter the populist talking, and like all populists he proposed to go to the people and drink from the cup of their wisdom. Demcratic sycophancy, as Plato was the first to point out, is always a great temptation, and Jimmy Carter in his cardigan was obviously not the man to resist it.

Instead, he promised to make the government "as good, as compassionate," as the American people.

As Clifford Orwin has shown in an unusually brilliant essay in *The American Scholar* (Summer 1980), compassion as a political principle arose, almost of necessity, out of representative government. "Its function," Orwin points out, "has been to vouch for representativeness when other tokens have not sufficed to do so." According to our political theory, it was consent that was supposed to vouch for representativeness; or, stated otherwise, representation was supposed to rest on and be made legitimate by consent: "You elected me, therefore I represent you." All of this is implied in the Declaration of Independence: "[Representative] governments are instituted among men, deriving their just powers from the consent of the governed." Even as these Lockean principles were being adopted and enshrined in America, however, Rousseau over in France was denying that representative government could be vouched for, or made legitimate, by consent. To state the problem in its simplest terms, the elected representatives—those to whom the people have given their consent—will not be representative of the people because they will inevitably have interests different from those of the great body of the electorate; as Orwin says in a reference to the French Revolution, "seigneur and serf were no more [but] the comfortable and the wretched remained," and it would be the comfortable who would be elected (or would become comfortable on being elected). Thus, the elected representatives (Robespierre, for example) came to realize that they could not adequately represent their nominal constituents—*unless* they could demonstrate their compassionate concern for them. "Compassion alone could transmute the comfortable into true representatives of the wretched." And if, on the whole, it has been the Republicans who have identified themselves with competition, it has been the Democrats, and especially the Democrats from Franklin Roosevelt's time to the present, who have emphasized their compassion. The richer they are—for example, Teddy

Kennedy at last summer's Democratic convention—the more strident becomes their insistence that they care about the poor, the sick, the old. It is not sufficient to *sympathize* with them; the truly compassionate politician must *em*pathize with them. (O brave new verb, that has such usage in't!) Only in this way can he establish his *bona fides.*

The venerable sage of the *New York Times,* James Reston, remarked all this for us when, ruminating on the occasion of Lyndon Johnson's death, he said the great choice confronting the nation was that between a competitive society and a compassionate one (and he counseled compassion). If only the choice were so simple.

The trouble is, compassion too readily becomes softness; indeed, the worst charge that can be leveled against its votaries is, as Orwin points out, not that of being "bleeding-heart liberals" (they shrug that off) but of being insensitive. (They take umbrage at that charge.) Hence, they heap on us welfare program upon welfare program and broaden the definition of those in need, for they know of no way to demonstrate their continuing concern for the poor other than by continually attempting to relieve their lot. Better that the poor be kept poor; in this way compassion will never lack objects.

When the time comes that a choice has to be made between guns and butter, they will choose butter by denying the need for guns. Their compassion not only dictates this choice but facilitates it, because where others see enemies, the compassionate politician will tend to see humanity (for, above all, he is a humanitarian), and humanity knows no national boundaries. For this reason, a compassionate foreign policy is a soft foreign policy, and instead of hardware it relies on software: "diplomacy," aid programs, and, ultimately, world government. Compassion's perfect secretary of state is the one who believes that the world's leaders "share similar dreams and aspirations" (presumably, the dream of being able to relieve the lot of the poor) and who resigns when the leader of his own country sends a military force on a rescue mission.

Still, so long as compassion does not take this extreme form, it is much easier to ascend to a concern for one's country from a concern for one's countrymen (compassion) than it is from a concern for oneself alone. Which is to say, the distance between compassion and patriotism is shorter than that between self-interest and patriotism. So, historically, it has been easier for the Democrats to take the country into war and for the Republicans to make peace; for the Democrats to take the country into a league of nominally united nations (for, as I indicated, compassion tends eventually to leap over national boundaries) and for the Republicans to urge a retreat into isolationism; for a Democratic president to impose an embargo on shipments of grain to our enemies and for a Republican president to lift it; for a Democratic president to require registration of draft-age men and for a Republican president to refuse to use it.

By dwelling on the single quality (competition or compassion) that seems best to characterize each of our two major parties, I have exaggerated the distance between them. In the event, of course, Americans are not divided into two clashing armies; to vary Jefferson's formulation only slightly, Americans are all Republicans, all Democrats, and it is by no means impossible to create a single patriotic public out of these elements. In this project, Mr. Reagan enjoys a few distinct advantages over his predecessor. It is not necessary for him to assure the people, and continually reassure them, that he will not lie to them. While he may once have been an actor, there is obviously nothing artificial about him as a man; he is, and is seen to be, the genuine article. His manner is immediately engaging, and he possesses an abundance of those qualities, none of them contrived or even practiced, that permit him to charm everyone in his presence—even Speaker Thomas P. O'Neill, as the speaker grudgingly admitted—and, with the aid of television, he can readily bring the entire nation into his presence. Without being bathetic, he succeeds in evoking a patriotic response from his audiences, and he is not likely to vitiate it by admonishing them to lose their "inordinate" fear of communism or by planting a kiss on Mr. Brezhnev's cheek. He is popular.

He is especially popular among Republicans, and I cannot believe that he could not have overcome the pressure put on him to lift the grain embargo or to exchange the AWACS for Saudi oil. Electorally speaking, the Republicans have no place else to go; if the President leads, they will follow.

It is otherwise with the Democrats, or with the Democratic element within most of us, by which I mean to emphasize that they (or we) present a special problem for any president who knows that we must face up to the hardness of our times. Someone once said that in these times of voter alienation, whoever would command our suffrage must contrive to remain one of us—understanding this, Mr. Carter chose to run against the "them" of Washington—and Mr. Reagan, despite his preference for horseback riding over softball and jogging, has managed to do that. But to accomplish what his office now requires, he must persuade us to sacrifice for the country we say we love. He must build a public. Yet, the building of a public, or to say the same thing, the molding of a public opinion, is not one of his constitutionally prescribed powers.

A president of the United States may be *primus inter pares* (and that only temporarily) but he heads an "administration" not a government; he administers or "presides" over the public administration of the affairs of the people, whose servant he is. The trouble is, the times require him to be a servant as Jeeves was a servant to Bertie Wooster: he must somehow contrive to govern his masters. President Washington was able to escape this necessity because, although he may have been the unanimous choice of the people, he was not popularly elected. In our compassionate times, if a president is going to succeed in getting the people to accept the burdens he would lay upon them, he must show that there are burdens that lie heavily on him; if the people must suffer, so must the president, and at least as much. There is something profoundly appropriate in the fact that our greatest president was also our greatest sufferer; in addition to that, and perhaps not by chance, he had the most profound understanding of public opinion in a democracy.

"In this and like communities," Lincoln said in the first of his formal debates with Douglas, "public sentiment is everything. With public sentiment, nothing can fail; without it nothing can succeed. Consequently he who moulds public sentiment, goes deeper than he who enact statutes or pronounces [judicial] decisions. He make statutes and decisions possible or impossible to be executed."

Lincoln faced a nation much more sharply divided than we are today, or for that matter, than we have been at any other time in our history. His task was to unite the nation on the principles on which it had been founded, but this required not simply a restoration of what had been at the beginning; it required, as he was to say at Gettysburg, a *new* birth of freedom. It required the creation of a public dedicated to that newly born freedom. It required him to persuade the people that popular sovereignty understood simply as majority rule was pernicious because it would permit a majority to deny the natural rights of a minority. Which is to say, for the sake of minorities and what is more remarkable, for the sake of what was then a widely despised minority, he had to persuade the majority to accept limits on its power. To do this, he had to defeat in free and open debate the greatest and most eloquent populist this country has ever produced, Stephen A. Douglas. The contest between Lincoln and Douglas was not, however, merely one of oratory; it was one of intellect. Lincoln may have lost the senatorship they were contesting, but he won the debate; the north proved willing to fight for the principle that all men are created equal insofar as they are all endowed with natural rights to life, liberty, and the pursuit of happiness.

Preventing southern secession, however, was only a necessary condition of a new birth of freedom; it was not, and Lincoln never had any doubt about this, a sufficient condition. A nation held together by force of arms alone could not be a free nation; this is the principal point in the Gettysburg Address. Men died at Gettysburg to save the nation, but the work they did on that battlefield was "unfinished," and so Lincoln called upon the living to dedicate themselves to the great task remaining before them: "It is rather for us to be here dedicated to the great task remaining before us—that from these honored dead we take increased devotion—that we here highly resolve that these dead shall not have died in vain—that this nation, under God, shall have a new birth of freedom—and that government of the people, by the people, for the people, shall not perish from the earth."

To make the point I want to make here, I must make it clear that the Gettysburg Address was, and was intended by Lincoln to be, the major event of his presidency and the major article of his statecraft. In it he said the world would little note nor long remember what he and the other orators on that field and on that day said, but he had good reason to know that the country would remember what he said, and he was right. Some of us—thanks to television perhaps many of us—have seen the film *Ruggles of Red Gap*, in which Charles Laughton plays the role of a gentleman's personal gentleman (a Jeeves of sorts) who is lost by his English aristocrat employer to an American in a poker game in Paris, and taken by his new employer to Red Gap, Wyoming. The film is about the Americanization of Ruggles, and one poignant scene in a typical western saloon of the time is used to illustrate the completion of the process. The occasion calls for Ruggles to recite an American speech, and, of course, he recites the Gettysburg Address, beautifully. (How else?) Of all our speeches and documents, the screen writer (or book author, I don't know which) selected this one. It is the most famous of our speeches, the best statement of what it means to be an American, and the second most famous of our public documents. The most famous is the Declaration of Independence, written four score and seven years earlier, and it is so in our day largely because of Lincoln's words at Gettysburg.

He knew what he was doing at Gettysburg; he had that speech and that occasion in his mind at least as early as 1861 when he delivered his First Inaugural. On that occasion, he pleaded with the southern states not to secede, but he knew they would—some already had—and he knew there would be a war and, with the war, battlefields and the occasions for his kind of public speech. That, I think, is sufficiently clear from his peroration: "I am loth to close," he said. "We are not enemies, but friends. We must not be enemies. Though passion may have strained, it must not break our bonds of affection. The mystic chords of memory, stretching from every battlefield, and patriot grave, to every living heart and hearth-stone, all over this broad land, will yet swell the chorus of the Union, when again touched, as surely they will be, by the better angels of our nature." At Gettysburg, surrounded by the graves of patriots—for where else can one speak as Lincoln spoke?—he created new "mystic chords" stretching from a new battlefield and new graves to every living heart and hearth-stone, and he touched them in such a way that we can still hear the chorus they sounded. To make certain that we could still hear that chorus, he managed—I am tempted to see the hand of God in it—to have himself assassinated as soon as the war was over. He was, as I said, our greatest sufferer, but he was more than that. He was the democratic leader par excellence.

The example of Lincoln allows us to understand the distinction Robert Nisbet has drawn for us between popular and public opinion. Public opinion has much deeper causes and the making of it requires virtues in addition to those that are popular. During his years in office, Lincoln was not the most popular of presidents; indeed, in the election of 1864, his margin of victory over George McClellan, a general who, it is almost true to say, never won a battle, was by no means overwhelming. He did not always say to the people what they wanted to hear. But as Lord Charnwood says in his superb memoir of Lincoln, "When it was all over it seemed to the people that he had all along been thinking their real thoughts for them; but they knew that this was because he had fearlessly thought for himself."

CHAPTER 11

LET'S HEAR IT FOR THE ELECTORAL COLLEGE

Where the Electoral College is concerned, nothing fails to succeed like success. Once again it produced in 1980 a clear and immediately known winner; once again it gave us a constitutionally legitimate President. Once again it served to discourage third-party candidates, thus strengthening the two-party system which has served this country so well. And once again, in succeeding rather than failing, it failed to silence its critics.

The *Washington Post* didn't even wait for the votes to be counted before remounting its familiar assault on our method of choosing a President. In its November 5, "Morning-After" lead editorial, the *Post* again complained of an "absurdly dangerous" method of presidential selection, of the possibility that "runaway electors exercising their constitutionally given free choice [might] plunge the nation into political chaos," of a "relic" that will sooner or later "self-destruct," and of a "bomb waiting for the right circumstances to go off." (And all this when the only sound some of us heard was the popping of Republican champagne corks!)

As usual, these written complaints were accompanied by variations of that humorous Herblock cartoon, two since the election—the umpteenth one in the series—showing the Electoral College as the white-haired old man with the ear trumpet saying, as he strains to hear the results, "Don't expect me to get this right, bub," or words to that effect.

As in the past, the old man did get it right in 1980, but by doing so may only have added to the complaints that we can expect to hear in the future: The Electoral College is, so the critics will say, biased in favor of one of the two major parties. Worse (but this *sotto voce*), it now has a built-in bias in favor of candidates of the Republican Party.

Tom Wicker sounded this alarm in his *New York Times* column of November 28, and repeated it on December 19. "Earlier this year," he wrote on the 28th, "the Electoral College came under its quadrennial scrutiny because John Anderson's independent campaign threatened to deny any candidate an electoral majority and throw the decision into the House of Representatives. That didn't happen, but the election produced other reasons—particularly for the Democrats—to take a hard look at this political anachronism."

Whereas it used to be said that the system favored the Democrats, who could be expected to win the populous Eastern states with their large blocs of electoral votes, a "hard look" at the new political geography shows 17 Western states, typically underpopulated, typically Republican, and each casting, among its electoral votes, two votes that represent nothing more than the fact that it is a state. These two "extra" votes may be constitutional, but, say the critics, it is not democratic; Presidents, like the legislators in the Supreme Court's reapportionment decisions, should "represent people, not trees or acres." To represent people, Presidents must be elected directly by the people.

Why has the Constitution not been amended to permit direct popular election, or, as the *Post* asked the question, why does the nation continue to tolerate the Electoral College? Because, in fact, "there is no national consensus on what should replace it." True enough; but there is also no consensus that it should be replaced. As some of us have made a career of telling what used to be Birch Bayh's Subcommittee on the Constitution, there are good reasons why Presidents should not be chosen by direct popular vote.

The framers of the Constitution knew this and we ought to know it. They knew that we were—and we still are—a nation of minorities; they knew that we were—and we still are—a union of states with diverse interests (with different kinds of trees and acres, if you will). And they knew—and we have reason to know—that a President chosen by a simple numerical majority of the people might neglect the legitimate interests of those minorities and states.

"If the majority be united by a common interest," said Madison in *Federalist* 51, "the rights of the minority will be insecure." The American idea of democracy cannot be expressed in the simple but insidious formula, the greatest good for the greatest number. What the greatest number regards as its greatest good might very well prove to be a curse to those who are excluded from it. The American idea, which is expressed in the Declaration of Independence and embodied in various provisions of the Constitution, is that government is instituted to secure the rights of all. It was the considered judgment of the framers that a system of indirect rather than direct popular elections would be likely to produce Presidents politically free to do their constitutional duty, which was and is to secure the rights of all.

Admittedly, the Electoral College does not work exactly as the framers intended, but, in combination with our party system and the winner-take-all practice instituted by the laws of every state except Maine, it has worked in a manner approximating the intention. In practice, the electors are not independent, but neither are they simply dependent on the people at large.

Since the days of Martin Van Buren, the inventor of the modern party system, electors have been instructed by the political parties which, despite the proliferation of presidential primaries, continue to screen the candidates and, to that extent, to narrow the range of choice available to the voters. What is significant here is that, unlike the typical voter, who must depend on impressions gained from the press, party leaders are likely to have first-hand knowledge of the strengths and weaknesses of the candidates; furthermore, they will be more likely to take account of the variety of interest within the country.

In fact, they will be required to do so: Because of the Electoral College, popular votes are counted (or aggregated) not at the national level (where a minority interest is likely to be less visible) but at the state level, where the vote of any particular minority looms larger. So long as a minority is not distributed evenly throughout the country, but is concentrated in particular states, it is in its interest to oppose direct popular elections; most civil rights leaders have understood this. Is there, then, not something to be said for an electoral system that threatens to penalize a party and its candidate for failing to respect the rights of respectable minorities?

Of course, it is possible that some minority might be over-represented, just as it is possible that (because each state, regardless of its population, has at least three electoral votes) some states might be over-represented. But the critics have not been able to demonstrate that this has happened. What is demonstrable is that the presidential candidates have had to pay attention to the rights of minorities and the interests of states (with their peculiar trees and acres): Only twice in the 20th Century (the elections of 1960 and 1976) has the candidate with an electoral majority failed to win a majority of the states. Is there not something to be said for a system that threatens to penalize sectional candidates?

These arguments are not likely to convince the critics who think that political legitimacy can be conferred only by simple popular majorities and would design their electoral systems accordingly. To the extent that they live in the Northeast, however, which is suffering a relative loss of population and a real loss of representation in the House of Representatives, they might be moved by an appeal to their political interests narrowly defined.

Mr. Wicker, for example, acknowledges that the electoral power of the "Republican" Sun Belt will increase as its population increases. The time might come when "Democratic" Rhode Island, Connecticut, and—who knows?—even New York with its peculiar trees and acres might need those two "extra" electoral votes. At that time he might be more inclined to appreciate that a President has the constitutional duty to represent everyone: those who vote for him, those who vote against him, and even those who do not bother to vote.

CHAPTER 12

THE MINISTRY OF LOVE

> He did not know where he was. Presumably he was in the
> Ministry of Love; but there was no way of making certain.
> George Orwell, *Nineteen Eighty-Four.*

So far there have been only a handful of sexual harassment
cases decided in the federal courts, and none has reached the
Supreme Court. The typical case involves a young woman
who is hired as an office worker and, after a few months
during which time she has become eligible for promotion to a
secretarial position, is invited to lunch by her supervisor. He
says he wants to discuss her fitness report and future
prospects with the firm, and that this can best be done in a
quiet setting; after a cocktail or two, he makes a sexual
advance, indicating that her prospects would be materially
enhances were she to consent. Replying that she will "ne'er
consent," and unlike Byron's Julia meaning it, she proceeds
to file a complaint with higher management. After a cursory
investigation, an embarrassed higher management decides to
take no action, or arranges a transfer, or, in the extreme case,
discharges her as a troublemaker. Rarely, if ever, is the
supervisor transferred or discharged. She goes to court.

Sometimes the sexual advances are more direct. A
physical assault in the stockroom serves to demonstrate (and

is intended to demonstrate) what the job will require of the female applicant; it is a job description of sorts. Promises of promotion and salary increases are made behind a file cabinet by bosses with busy hands. Sometimes, quite apart from the man making it, the proposition is tempting, promising a position with "greater responsibilities" combined with an airline ticket to romantic places—on company (but not unaccompanied) business. And there is even a case—and surely not a unique case—where a frustrated middle manager discharges his assistant because, though spurning his persistent advances, she readily submits to a co-worker's. (The co-worker happens to be the son of a vice-president of the firm.)

These various facts tell a familiar story, one known to many men, most working women (or so we are told), and to all movie-goers, who have seen it told sometimes as "An American Tragedy" but usually as a comedy in which (to go back in time a bit) a Franchot Tone or George Brent makes a sophisticated pass at a Rosalind Russell or Claudette Colbert and, in return, gets a resounding slap on the kisser, as we were wont to say in those days. But while most cases of sexual harassment do not end in what can fairly be described as tragedy, they are surely not suitable material for comedy and ought not to be treated as such. One well-known law professor maintains that sexual harassment of working women "has been one of the most pervasive but carefully ignored features of our national life." For our failure to recognize this, and do something about it, we are about to pay a price: the sexual harassment of working women has now been declared a discriminatory and therefore unlawful employment practice under federal law, and the enforcement of that law has been made the business of one of Washington's most zealous administrative agencies, the Equal Employment Opportunity Commission. In April of this year, the EEOC issued its Interim Guidelines on Sexual Harassment, and presumably, these will serve to put an end to the inconsistency and indecision that have characterized the courts' handling of this issue.

II

Someone not familiar with recent developments in what we naively persist in calling our federal system might well wonder how local lechery is properly the business of the national government. What clause of the Constitution authorizes this sort of regulation? The answer is, if the company is one employing a minimum of fifteen persons, it is an "industry affecting commerce," and, as such, is subject to federal regulation. After all, the Constitution expressly authorizes Congress to regulate commerce among the states, and only a slight rearrangement of the terms is required to show that Congress' power to regulate commerce implies the use of the commerce power to regulate acts of congress, at least those that would be consummated in a commercial setting.

Furthermore, as these things are seen from Washington, almost every "setting" is commercial and subject to federal regulation, including private educational institutions. As I was told by one EEOC official (who found it amusing that I should raise the question), Yale is an industry affecting interstate commerce because it buys a lot of equipment outside Connecticut. It also gathers "raw material" from around the country and the world, then works on that "material" for a term of years, and finally sends it (reprocessed one might say) out to a national and world market. Who is to say that this does not make it a commercial enterprise? (Certainly not the prestigious universities; they find it more convenient to appoint Vice Presidents for compliance than to take the government to court.)

Thus, some of the cases under investigation by the EEOC involve allegedly lecherous professors and their female students who, in exchange for sexual favors, are promised high grades and other marks of preferment. (Yale has already been hauled into federal court on sexual harassment charges.) This, we are told in the literature, is a widespread practice, although in my experience, which may, of course, be parochial or atypical, the literature has got it backwards.

(Professor Berns, isn't there *something* I can do to raise this grade? . . .)

The principal statutory basis of EEOC's jurisdiction over sexual harassment is Title VII of the Civil Rights Act of 1964. When the bill that became this law reached the floor of the House of Representatives, the relevant section read as follows: "It shall be an unlawful employment practice for an employer—(1) to fail or refuse to hire or to discharge any individual, or otherwise to discriminate against any individual with respect to his compensation, terms, conditions, or privileges of employment, because of such individual's race, color, religion, or national origin." Nothing was said about sex. It was courtly Howard Smith of Virginia—"Judge Smith" as he was known during his many years as chairman of the House Rules Committee—who introduced the amendment to insert the word "sex" after the word "religion." No champion of the rights of man, let alone women, Smith obviously thought that by adding this provision he would kill the legislation. Of course, he insisted he was serious in his professed concern for women's rights; he even read a constituent's letter asking Congress to do something—what, she did not say—about the fact that there were then some 2,661,000 more women than men living in the United States, thus making it difficult, if not impossible, for "every female to have a husband of her own." But his colleagues were not deceived by this bit of persiflage. Edith Green of Oregon, a staunch proponent of women's rights, opposed the amendment precisely because she feared it would "jeopardize our primary purpose," which, of course, was to do something about racial discrimination. Despite her efforts, however, the amendment was adopted; and despite its adoption, the bill became law and the EEOC was launched.

Still, one would have thought (and I have no doubt that, had they been asked, the members of the 88th Congress would have thought) that sexual discrimination is one thing and sexual harassment quite another. When a firm pays a man more than it pays a women doing comparable work, that is discrimination on the basis of sex. And when a hospital pays a class of workers, mostly men (say, doctors), more than it pays another class of workers, mostly women (say, nurses) doing "comparable" work, that is, or might in time prove to be, discrimination on the basis of sex. (The EEOC is vigorously pursuing this business of "comparable" work.) But are women as a class being treated unequally when some but not all of them are being propositioned with a promise of a pay raise? As Dorothy Parker reminded us when she pointed out that "men seldom make passes at girls who wear glasses"—she said that some time ago—it is, of course, true that not all women are treated equally; but the EEOC has not yet indicated any intention of attempting to do something about that familiar form of unequal treatment. In what sense, then, is the sexual harassment of *a* woman a form of discrimination against women? To refuse to hire a black person simply because he is black is surely discrimination against a class of persons and, as such, is surely forbidden by the statute. To refuse to hire (or to pay lower wages to) a woman simply because she is a woman is discrimination against a class of persons and, just as clearly as in the first case, is surely forbidden by the statue. But, to repeat, how can it be said that the sexual harassment of some—but surely not of all?—women is a form of discrimination against women as women? Or, once more, would it not astonish the man who demands sexual favors of a woman to be told that he is biased against women?

EEOC's answer to this simple-minded objection was best expressed by a federal court in a 1977 case. What is a violation of Title VII, said the court, is not that the supervisor demanded sex but that he made it a condition that "he would not have fastened on a male employee."

But surely that depends on the sexual proclivities of the supervisor? Some may prefer women, but others may prefer men. Are they all guilty of discrimination? Two years earlier, a different federal court made this point when it said that it would be "ludicrous to hold that the sort of activity involved here was contemplated by the [Civil Rights] Act because to do so would mean that if the conduct complained of was directed equally to males there would be no basis for suit." And it is no answer to this to say that, while possible, it is highly unlikely that an office manager, for example, will one day demand sexual favors of a female stenographer and the next day of a male mailroom clerk. Are there no female office managers?

Besides, it is not the office manager who commits this form of sexual harassment, not the office manager as individual male (or female); it is the company in whose name he (or she) offers the job, promotion, or salary increase. He (or she) might be sued as individuals in a state court—in some jurisdictions sexual harassment is treated as assault or battery, for example—but only Bausch and Lomb, or the Bank of America, or the Public Service Electric and Gas Company may be sued for sexual harassment in a federal court; and it is not easy to understand how the Bank of America can be said to be discriminating on the basis of sex if some of its branch managers fondle female tellers and others fondle male tellers. In terms of discrimination, one would have thought such a company could claim to have an exemplary record. Be that as it may—indeed, be the statute as it may—"it is much too late in the day to contend that Title VII does not outlaw terms of employment for women which differ appreciably from those set for men"; so said a federal judge in 1977. What he seems to have meant is that, typically, it is the man who supervises, the man who makes the sexual advance, and the woman, not the man, who is asked to do more than ought to be required of an employee. Under *current* social conditions, as Catherine A. MacKinnon argues in *Sexual Harassment of Working Women*, "no man would be in the same position as a woman, even if he were in identical circumstances." Which is to say, no man would be in the same position as a woman, even if he were in the same position as a woman. Logically and biologically, says MacKinnon, it might be reasonable to equate the sexual harassment of men and the sexual harassment of women— and indeed it might—but in this society, in this sexist society, in this society where laws have to be enacted in order to ensure women their rights, it is not reasonable. This seems to be the theory on which the EEOC is proceeding.

From all that appears in the Interim Guidelines, women as well as men can harass and men as well as women can be the victims of harassment. This regulatory neutrality conforms to the Constitution as well as to the various provisions of the Civil Rights Act, which are both gender-blind and color-blind. But so long as American society remains sexist, as well as racist, or so long as women, as well as blacks, are victims of past discrimination, the Commission's efforts will be extended mainly if not exclusively on their behalf. Thus, it is the female worker who is being invited—indeed, encouraged—to file complaints of harassment with the Commission, and it is on her behalf that the Commission, after investigating the complaints, will either file suit in the federal courts or issue, to the complainant, a Notice of Right to Sue.

Somewhat surprisingly, the Guidelines do not contain a definition or description of sexual harassment. We are told that it may be "either physical or verbal in nature," but there is not a clue as to what sort of act or what sort of language will be held to constitute the offense. This, said the EEOC, will be done "on a case by case basis," and the employers of American will have to wait on these events.

One thing, however, is made very clear: whatever the offense proves to be, the employer will be held responsible for it—"regardless of whether the specific acts complained of were authorized or even forbidden by the employer and regardless of whether the employer knew or should have known of their occurence"; so say the Guidelines. Nothing will be gained by the employer showing that the supervisor lacked authority to make the offer of preferment or was, in fact, violating company policy when he made it; or even that the sexual advance was made away from company premises and outside company time. In short—to state this in terms familiar to lawyers who remember their tort law on vicarious liability—there is no recognition of the practice of employees, or servants, or agents, to go off on a "frolic and detour" of their own. ("It is not contested that the defendant was possessed of a cart and horse, or that plaintiff was proceeding on foot across a certain public and common highway, to wit, Bishopsgate Street, or that he was struck by said horse and cart which was coming from the direction of Shoreditch and was being driven in a careless manner by the defendant's servant, or, as a consequence, that plaintiff suffered a fracture of the leg, causing him pain and great expense, and additional expense in having to retain diverse persons to superintend his business for six calendar months; but, nevertheless, if the servant, instead of being on his master's business at the time and acting against his master's implied commands, was going on a frolic of his own, then the master is not liable.") By deciding to impose strict liability on the employer, the EEOC hopes to influence the federal courts which have been divided on the issue.

It is easier to see where the employer's responsibility begins than where it will end. In the cases now being collected and processed by the Commission, the supervisor's advances were spurned and his conditions rejected. But it does not always work this way. What is the Commission going to do when the proposition is accepted—and the supervisor being a man of his word—the compliant woman is hired, promoted, or given a salary increase denied to others? Will "honest madam"—that's Shakespeare's term—be entitled to bring an action against the employer? Could it not be said that, by being virtuous, she is denied (or, at least, is denying herself) an equal employment opportunity? And what sort of an investigation would be required to determine whether she has a justified complaint? (In the case coming closest to this situation, the woman did her part by yielding, but the supervisor reneged, and not only reneged but promoted another woman, and—since hell hath no fury like a woman scorned—the first woman sued. Can she recover damages from the company? Can she recover if it can be proved that the second woman also yielded?)

And what about the compliant woman's male co-worker? Since the typical supervisor is male and, for the time being at least, not homosexual, can it not be said that this male co-worker is being denied an equal employment opportunity? Catherine McKinnon thinks he might have a case. Whatever his other qualifications, he obviously has less to offer of what it really takes (but ought not to take), and simple justice would suggest that he be entitled to maintain an action under Title VII. Of course, he will have to show that the woman was promoted *because* she yielded to the sexual advance, and he will have to prove that she did in fact yield; but in a large company and over a period of time he might be able to offer statistical proof that women were being promoted more than men, and that some of them at least must have yielded, because any other explanation of their disproportionate advancement would be statistically improbable. Collecting these statistics will be burdensome, difficult, and expensive, but, in the case of large companies, not impossible. For the others, the EEOC will have to rely on traditional investigative techniques, here applied to what at least some of the persons involved regard as their private lives.

More disquieting still are suggestions in the Guidelines (which EEOC officials do not hesitate to confirm) that employers now have "an affirmative duty to maintain a workplace free of sexual harassment and intimidation." To squeeze these juices out of the already crumpled pulp of Title VII, the Commission has to argue that it is an unlawful employment practice to fail to prevent such things as sexual banter in the work place. That is to say, there is here no question of a supervisor imposing an unequal and therefore discriminatory condition on women, a condition he would not normally impose on his male employees; what is here declared to be an unlawful employment practice is the failure to provide a working environment "uncontaminated" by sexual harassment. Thus, a statute forbidding discrimination with respect to the "conditions" of employment—which would seem to mean that, just as an employer may not discriminate with respect to "compensation" (by paying women less than men), or with respect to "terms" of employment (by requiring women to work longer hours), or with respect to "privileges" of employment (by denying them holidays or rest periods given to men), so it may not discriminate with respect to "conditions" of employment (by demanding more of women by way of qualifications or output than it demands of men)—this statute is now being interpreted to require employers to provide working "conditions" that meet the Commission's idea of an environment free of what it calls intimidation. On this reading of the statute, an employer discriminates when he intimidates, and he intimidates when he fails to cleanse the environment of polluting talk, or pictures, or whatever. (This, too, will be worked out "on a case by case basis.")

Enforcement of this provision will not be an easy task. The *Playboy* centerfolds that decorate walls in the warehouse or the "girlie" calendars hanging above the desk of the Parts Department foreman will, admittedly, present no evidentiary problem. They are readily visible and, upon complaint, can be ordered removed, and inspection can readily determine whether the order has been obeyed. (Whether such an order can survive constitutional challenge—on freedom of expression grounds—is something else again.) But what about oral harassment, that is, talk, whistling, or vulgar noises? And obscene gestures? Here the Commission will be dealing not with what was said by a supervisor to a subordinate—which, because it was said in private, is difficult enough to ascertain—but with what was said or done by one worker to another worker. Lewd whistling might pollute the atmosphere, but, depending on how it is received, it might not; and the two cases will be difficult to distinguish. Suppose a male worker is in the habit of whistling at two stenographers, one of whom, appreciating this form of attention and the flattery it implies, smiles or glows with secret pleasure, and the other of whom, feeling insulted by what she regards as a vulgar display of bad manners, files a complaint with the EEOC? An offense under the statute? And suppose one woman files a complaint because she is offended by the sight of a romantic couple displaying their affection for each other during office hours? Again, we shall have to wait on the cases.

Fortunately, in these sexually polluted atmosphere cases, the Commission will not hold employers strictly liable for the (unappreciated) acts, words, sounds, or gestures of their male employees; they will be liable only if they fail to take "immediate and appropriate corrective action." Employers will, of course, be grateful for this uncharacteristic display of generosity on the Commission's part, and we can expect them to cooperate eagerly with the teams of inspectors dispatched by its regional offices to determine whether the atmosphere has, in fact, been cleaned up.

Nevertheless, employers will make a serious mistake if they think they need only be concerned with how their male employees behave. While I should hesitate to say that, by their deportment or, more immediately, by their dress, women can themselves pollute a working environment, I do think they can be accessories before the fact of its pollution. As the Commission has acknowledged, however, grudgingly, women can be provocative; and it would be unfair to admonish or, in the grave case, to discharge the whistling office boy while ignoring the nubile stenographer whose "daring decolletage" may have provoked his whistle. Rather than having to devote what will surely be thousands of personhours investigating such cases, it might be preferable to impose dress codes on female employees.

The most serious objection to this may be constitutional: if it's a constitutional right to express one's hostility to the country by affixing its flag to the seat of one's pants, or if, contrary to board of education regulations, school children have a constitutional right to express themselves by wearing armbands, then stenographers may have a constitutional right to express themselves in a slit skirt. Then, too, some women, and especially those who like men and look upon the workplace as a good place to meet and attract them, will resent being told what to wear at work and what not to wear; and like those women of Iran, they are not likely to be mollified by the reassurance that it is all in a good cause. But their resentment will have to be weighed in the balance with the fact that men can be aroused by what women wear and, being aroused, can be provoked to do or say things they may later regret. As I was informed by officials in EEOC's Office of Policy Implementation, it was the Commission's recognition of this provocation problem that partly explains the absence in the Guidelines of a precise description of what constitutes sexual harassment. Perhaps, then, the final Guidelines will take into account not only what he said or did but what she said or did (including what she wore). They will be grossly unjust if they do not because, contrary to the assumption in sexual harassment literature, it is women, not men, who are ultimately responsible for what might be called the moral tone of any place where men and women are assembled, even, I think, the workplace. (Tocqueville observed this of American women 150 years or so ago, and I think it is still true.) Men may tell the bawdy jokes, but they will do so in the company of women only with their consent, or with the consent of at least one woman present. In general, men will be what women want them to be. ("Do you want to know men?" asked Rousseau, "study women.") Even young boys know this—or, at least, come to recognize it when, later on in their lives, they recall the first time they cavorted before girls or, in the familiar ways, endeavored to please them. If they are at all reflective, they might also come to recognize the peculiar power wielded by women (even young women) over men (and especially young men): they can make them ashamed of what in themselves displeases women. An employer's "affirmative duty to maintain a workplace free of sexual harassment" will require that he take account of this power women have over men.

This is certain to cause employers all sorts of trouble, especially if they try to impose dress codes; but here the EEOC can be of assistance. It can issue national guidelines, and the typical employer, rather than engaging in a running battle with his female employees (who will constantly remind him of the greater freedom allowed by other companies), will eagerly adopt and enforce them. Here, for the Commission's own guidance, is one modest proposal: Rule 2 (Rule 1 will have to deal with slit skirts): "The nipples of the female breast (see 45 *Code of Federal Regulations* 11.3 [a]) shall not be allowed to protrude so far as to be visible in outline through the dress, blouse, or sweater." In a few years—say, by 1984—we can expect the *Federal Register* to have many pages of such rules.

III

On March 24, 1978, President Carter issued Executive Order 12044, "Improving Governmental Regulation." Its purpose was to ensure, to the extent possible, that regulations be simple and clear, that legislative goals be achieved effectively and efficiently, and that unnecessary burdens, on the economy as well as on individuals, be avoided. If regulations are judged likely to have a major impact on the economy, or any part of it, their issuance must be accompanied by what is called a "regulatory analysis," explaining the problems, the alternative approaches to dealing with it, and justifying the approach being taken. If, on the other hand, the agency determines that its regulations will not have a major impact on the economy, it is required officially to say so. This the EEOC did when, in the *Federal Register*, it published its Interim Guidelines on Sexual Harassment.

I have no disposition to quarrel with this assessment; adherence to the Guidelines may impose some economic costs on industry, but these costs will probably be insignificant and, anyway, unlike the costs of putting "scrubbers" on the nation's coal-burning furnaces, are probably incalculable. If enforced in the same zealous spirit that has sometimes characterized the Commission's work in the area of racial discrimination, however, the Guidelines will certainly have an impact on the commercial environment and on the men and women who work in it—I mean, an impact other than, or in addition to, the one nominally sought by the Commission. Their enforcement will take the national government into an area where it does not belong and require it to do things that may not properly be done by a government founded on liberal principles.

In our time, the government may fix our prices, limit our emissions, forbid our effluents, bus our children, set our quotas, prescribe our diets, and proscribe our medicines, and some sort of case can be made for each of these regulatory policies. (Rather the COWPS, EPA, OSHA, FDA, EEOC, FTC, and the rest, than—to take the extreme cases—runaway inflation, unbreathable air, undrinkable water, explosive grain elevators, poisoned mothers and deformed babies, or morally corrupting television programs.) But now this national government is threatening the essentially and necessarily private realm of the erotic.

Of course this will be denied by the Commission. It will protest that its concern is the workplace, not the bedroom; but many lovers who end up in the bedroom meet in the workplace. That its purpose is the prevention of sexual harassment, not the inhibiting of romance; but in its efforts to identify the one, it will intrude upon the other. That it will not interfere with the easy and sometimes playful familiarity that characterizes the relations of men and women. That its simple goal is a workplace where men look upon women as equals and not as sex objects; but even the man at work is aware that women are different, and the difference is sexual, and that to deny the difference is to destroy the relationship. That it will provide no congenial forum for the malicious and false accusation; but men will accept that assurance only at their peril. That it will never use its power vindictively against firms or organizations that have the courage or temerity to oppose it; but there are organizations—a couple of little private and wholly privately funded colleges come to mind—that can demonstrate the worthlessness of such assurances. That it is aware that women can provoke men, and that Rousseau was right when he said that women give the law in love because, "according to the order of nature, resistance belongs to them."

In the sexual harassment literature there is no such thing

as romance; there is only commercial or power relationships—marriage, prostitution, or harassment—in which
women are required to exchange "sexual services for material
survival." And there are no significant natural differences
between men and women. That, the feminists say, is the
trouble with the law: it reinforces the pernicious and
unscientific view that there is an essential difference between
men and women, and it is this view that is responsible for
sexual harassment. It allows men, indeed, it encourages men,
to define women on the basis of their sexuality, whereas,
according to nature, the differences between man and
women are insignificant. One's sexual identity is determined
by social factors—as MacKinnon puts it, the most salient
determinents of sexuality "are organized in society, not fixed
in 'nature' "—and these social factors must be eliminated by
changing the laws.

Feminists have many quarrels with the law. For example,
they complain about what they refer to as the sexist
Constitution, yet one of the striking things about that
venerable document is that, even without amendment,
nothing in *it* prevented women from voting, and not a word
of it had to be changed before they were eligible to become
senators or members of the House of Representatives (or
even heads of federal agencies, such as the EEOC); and
nothing in it will have to be changed before a woman may be
elected President or appointed a Supreme Court justice.

They complain, too, about certain aspects of the criminal
law, and, specifically, about the fact that while sexual
harassment is technically a crime in most jurisdictions, the
rules of procedure and evidence make it difficult to gain
convictions. Juries are cautioned to be especially careful in
their evaluation of testimony, to take account of the
emotional involvement of witnesses and the fact that the
alleged offenses take place in private, thus making it difficult
to determine the truth respecting them. As MacKinnon says,
in the nasty fashion typical of her school, the law gives men a
"right to be let alone" and makes of this a "shield behind
which isolated women can be sexually abused one at a time."

(What she might have said is that, by respecting the privacy of the erotic relationship, the law gives men and women together the right to be let alone, and does this not in order to allow men to beat their wives or harass their secretaries with impunity—although that may be one of the consequences—but to allow them to desire each other, enjoy each other, give pleasure to each other, and consummate the love they bear for each other. Traditionally, love has been seen to be none of the government's business.)

Then they complain of tort law because it treats sexual harassment as a moral offense. "Every woman," said one judge quoted by MacKinnon, "has a right to assume that a passenger car is not a brothel and that when she travels in it, she will meet nothing, see nothing , hear nothing, to wound her delicacy or insult her womanhood." MacKinnon finds this insulting, a "disabling (and cloying) moralism." Sexual harassment is not, as the law of torts sees it, an offense against a woman but against women as a class; it is, she says, "less an issue of right and wrong than as issue of power."

With the assistance of the EEOC, the power of men will be balanced by the power of women, and, as my wife added, what we shall end up with is a balance of terror.

CHAPTER 13

THE TROUBLE WITH THE ERA*

I must say at the outset that I agree with the effort to abolish all statutes, ordinances, and regulations that discriminate against women. As someone who has taught constitutional law for thirty years, it has always seemed to me that the Supreme Court's decision in *Bradwell* v. *State of Illinois* (16 Wall. 130 [1873]), upholding the right of Illinois to exclude women from the practice of law, had to be ranked, if not, like *Dred Scott* v. *Sandford*, among the most pernicious decisions ever to come down from that Court, then, surely, among the least enlightened. It is astonishing now to notice that only one member of the Court (Chief Justice Salmon P. Chase) saw fit to dissent in that case and that even he was too timid to write an opinion. But, as the cigarette ads say, we've come a long way since then.

In fact, we've come a long way since 1972 when the Congress first proposed this amendment in this form. At least sixteen states now have constitutional provisions similar to the proposed ERA; Title VII of the Civil Rights Act of 1964 has been used effectively to extend the right of women to equal employment opportunity; and, in a handful of Fourteenth Amendment-equal protection cases, the Supreme Court has invalidated state-based discriminatory

---

*This statement on the proposed Equal Rights Amendment was presented to the Senate Judiciary Subcommittee on the Constitution on May 26, 1983.

provisions. In this connection, it is of interest to note that none of the subjects debated here in 1970 had to do with the right of young women to be accepted as students in the service academies at Annapolis and West Point. A policy that then seemed ill-advised to many has since been implemented to the satisfaction of almost everybody.

My opposition to this proposed Equal Rights Amendment is limited to its ambiguous wording: I don't know what it means—or, to state my objection more precisely, there is no agreement as to what it means. In fact, I would wager that a survey of congressional opinion would disclose that there is no agreement here as to what it means, not even among the resolution's co-sponsors. It speaks of equality of rights without identifying those rights. In this respect it should be compared with Article I, section 8, where Congress is authorized to secure for limited times the "exclusive right" of authors and inventors to their respective writings and discoveries, and with the Nineteenth and Twenty-sixth Amendments which specifically protect the right to vote. Such specificity is lacking in S.J. Res. 10. If adopted, it would be the only provision in the Constitution bestowing or protecting a right without identifying the right.

It might, of course, be said that identification is unnecessary; that the language, being absolute in its terms, permits no exceptions or qualifications; that it means that the rights enjoyed by men cannot be denied to women or, conversely, that the rights enjoyed by women cannot be denied to men. That is to say, as drafted, this constitutional language forbids all laws, federal as well as state, that classify by sex. But I know of no one who in fact favors this interpretation, not even the authors of that landmark article in the *Yale Law Journal*.[1] They say the "constitutional mandate must be absolute," but they don't really mean to say that all gender classifications must be forbidden. Their constitutional amendment would permit laws taking account of physical characteristics unique to one sex or the other— for example, laws respecting wet nurses and sperm banks.[2] It would also permit laws resting on some other constitutional right, such as the right to privacy.[3] (This was intended to reassure those opponents of the ERA who feared that its adoption would outlaw the separation of the sexes in public restrooms.) Thus, while insisting that the mandate must be absolute, they would permit exceptions which they call qualifications. Is this what the co-sponsors of S.J. Res. 10 mean? I don't know and, I submit, neither does this committee.

Other supporters of the proposed amendment are even less absolutist in their reading of its terms. Generally speaking, their intention is to make sex, like race, a suspect classification, suspect—and therefore harder to justify—but not absolutely forbidden, or suspect and therefore subject to a stricter judicial scrutiny. What this implies is that it is not necessary to know what the language means because in due course the courts will tell us what it means, and that it is altogether proper to delegate this authority to the courts. If this is the intention of S.J. Res. 10, I would ask its co-sponsors whether they are willing to accept *any* meaning the courts give its language. If so, I would charge them with treating the Constitution with contempt; if not, I would ask them to point to the standard on the basis of which they could charge the courts with having misinterpreted the language.

If it is said, as it was when the ERA was last debated here, that the courts will be guided by "legislative history," I would reply that what is being debated here is not a piece of legislation. It is a constitutional provision, and the Constitution does not derive from or come out of the legislature. The Constitution derives from the people in their sovereign capacity; as Hamilton made clear in *Federalist* 78, it is an expression of the people's will, and it can be amended only by a "solemn and authoritative act" of the people. That it is the people (and not the courts or the Congress) that may so act was described by Hamilton as the "fundamental principle of republican government." By Article V, Congress is authorized to propose amendments to the Constitution, but it is the people, acting through their representatives in the state legislatures or in the state conventions, who adopt amendments. And they ought to know what it is they are adopting. Or, they ought to know, and to know precisely, what it is they are being asked to adopt. Are the co-sponsors of S.J. Res. 10 willing to say to the people of the United States that by adopting this constitutional amendment they would be making sex a suspect classification, that they cannot be sure as to what that means, but that, in due course, the courts will let them know what that means?

Let me be more precise. Are the co-sponsors willing to say to the American people, "We don't know whether this amendment will invalidate a male-only draft, but, not to worry, the courts will tell you"? That we haven't been able to agree as to whether the states would still be entitled to require separate dormitories in their colleges and universities, but that in time the courts will decide, and that if they can't come to a common decision, a majority of the Supreme Court will settle the matter? That, truth to tell, some of us are of the opinion that the ERA will outlaw separate junior high schools, one for boys and one for girls, and that others—that is to say, other co-sponsors—are of the opinion that it will not outlaw them, but you the sovereign people of the United States ought not to let that bother you? That we all agree that Congress is already entitled to withhold financial support from private schools that segregate on the basis of race, but we haven't been able to make up our minds as to whether the ERA will require Congress to withhold it from private schools that segregate on the basis of sex? That most of us are persuaded that the courts are already authorized to grant affirmative relief in order to remedy the effects of past racial discrimination—for example, most of us believe that benign racial quotas are acceptable—but we are not sure about benign sex quotas, but, again, we are content to allow the courts answer that question, and answer it one way or the other? That we confess that we never thought about the issue of sex entitlements similar to racial entitlements—that is to say, whether the right of women to vote which, as we all know, now includes the right to be represented by a member of that racial group? (Or, to be more accurate, we haven't thought about whether a gender group's right to vote can, like a racial group's be "diluted" when the group is not sufficiently represented.) That—and this will be my last example—we have not wondered as to the effect of the ERA on what might be called the second-generation abortion cases, but we are delighted to leave that issue to the courts?[4]

I said at the outset that I am opposed to laws that discriminate against women, and I meant what I said. I also said that, even without an Equal Rights Amendment, we have made considerable progress toward the complete elimination of such laws; but I did not mean to suggest that we had succeeded in eliminating all of them. There is still work to be done. But to do that work does not require a constitutional amendment. All vestiges of discrimination can be eliminated by simple legislative enactment, many of them by acts of Congress. If, for the most obvious example, it is the will of Congress to draft women as well as men into the armed forces, thereby putting an end to a practice that discriminates against men, Congress need only say so. (And if the President vetoes the measure, it is clear from the number of co-sponsors of S.J. Res. 10 that the veto will be overridden.) And if the legislatures of the 35 states that, during the 1970s, ratified the ERA are truly determined to abolish single-sex public schools, equalize the laws respecting prostitution (by providing for the punishment of the men who purchase the services of women), abolish maximum hour laws for women, and so on, they need only say so. And it is difficult for me to believe that the remaining fifteen states could long sustain their isolation from what would then appear to be a national public opinion in favor of equality of treatment. I urge you to leave the Constitution alone.

Contrary to what is sometimes said, it is not a "sexist" document. It is in fact remarkable free of references to gender. Not one of its provisions had to be changed before a woman could serve in House or Senate or on the Supreme Court, or would have to be changed to allow a woman to be elected President. Not one of its provisions had to be changed before women could vote. The Constitution may not be perfect, but it is a better document now than it would be with this ERA.

That amendment should be labeled a judiciary act, an act extending the jurisdiction of the federal courts, an act inviting the courts (and ultimately the Supreme Court) to decide the particular issues that members of Congress would appear eager to avoid. It would of necessity foster still more judicial activism, and I am no friend of judicial activism. Unlike the friends of judicial activism, I do not believe that the good judge is one who asks himself what is good for the country and then seeks "to translate his answers to that question into constitutional law."[5] Officials with the power to decide "what is good for the country" are officials that I want to be able to vote out of office when, in my judgment, they decide wrong. This, I close by saying, was also the desire of the Framers of the Constitution.

PART IV

RACIAL POLITICS

CHAPTER 14

THE CONSTITUTION AND THE MIGRATION OF SLAVES

Shortly after the adoption of the Constitution, the South came to see the power granted to Congress to regulate commerce as a major threat to its domestic tranquility, for this power extended, or might reasonably be seen to extend, to the regulation of the slave trade, domestic as well as foreign. The question of the extent of federal power over commerce was, in the minds of Southerners, simply coincident with the question of the extent of federal power over slavery.[1] As Charles Warren puts it,

> the long-continued controversy as to whether Congress had exclusive or concurrent jurisdiction over commerce was not a conflict between theories of government, or between Nationalism and State-Rights, or between differing legal construction of the Constitution, but was simply the naked issue of State or Federal control of slavery.[2]

The friends of slavery had every reason to feel threatened by the commerce power. They had exacted a compromise at Philadelphia in 1787, according to which Congress was forbidden to abolish the slave trade for twenty years. But twenty years is not a long time in the affairs of nations—or institutions—and the day would inevitably come when Congress might exercise its power, with incalculable effect

Reprinted by permission of The Yale Law Journal Company and Fred B. Rothman & Company from the *Yale Law Journal* 78, pp. 198-228.

on the institution of slavery itself. Hence the very men who insisted on the right to buy and sell other men as articles of commerce denied that these other men were articles of commerce for purposes of the Constitution's commerce clause. In addition, to make doubly certain that Congress's power to regulate commerce would not threaten the existence of their "peculiar institution," Madison and others fostered what has become the traditional interpretation of the first clause of Article I, Section 9, denying all congressional power to regulate the internal slave trade, and leaving only importation from Africa to be prohibited after 1808.[3]

The clause in question reads as follows:

> The Migration or Importation of Such Persons as any of the States now existing shall think proper to admit, shall not be prohibited by the Congress prior to the Year one thousand eight hundred and eight, but a tax or duty may be imposed on such Importation, not exceeding ten dollars for each Person.

The controversy over the scope of this proscription centered about a dispute over the meaning of the phrase "such persons." If "such persons" referred exclusively to slaves, then Congress was limited in two respects by the clause: it could not before 1808 forbid the importation of slaves from abroad into the states originally existing and, secondly, could not until 1808 legislate so as to prevent the migration of slaves—that is, the movement of slaves—between or among the states originally existing, despite its expressly granted power over commerce among the states.

Such an interpretation could not be accepted by the South. If the clause were read as including a limitation on an underlying congressional power to regulate the movement of slaves between states, the removal of that limitation in 1808 would leave Congress free to stop not only the importation of slaves from abroad but all interstate traffic in them as well. The Southern response to this danger was to insist that the phrase "such persons" referred *not* to slaves alone, but to both slaves, who are "imported," and to white aliens, who "migrate," into the United States. Such a reading, by leaving no internal operation to the term "migration," restricted the limitation of the clause—and hence, by implication, the scope of the congressional power being limited—to entries into the United States from abroad. The question, and a great deal turned on the answer, is whether this Southern interpretation is a fair construction of the clause.[4]

I

The clause made its first appearance in the Constitutional Convention on August 6, in the Report of the Committee of Detail. At that time it read as follows: "No tax or duty shall be laid by the Legislature on articles exported from any State; nor on the migration or importation of such persons as the several states shall think proper to admit; nor shall such migration or importation be prohibited."[5] In this form the clause provoked an acrimonious debate concerning the whole subject of slavery. The South Carolinians and Georgians insisted that their states would never join the Union if the importation of slaves were forbidden; the others denounced "this infernal traffic" and the "pernicious effect on manners" caused by slavery. The debate was closed only when Gouverneur Morris proposed that "the whole subject" along with "the clause relating to taxes on exports & to a navigation act" be turned over to a committee. "These things," he said, "may form a bargain among the Northern & Southern States."[6]

This was precisely what happened. The Committee of Eleven, composed of one member from each state present, reported on August 24, recommending the elimination of the clause requiring a two-thirds majority for all "navigation acts" and the replacement of the absolute prohibition of laws forbidding the migration and importation of "such persons" by a provision forbidding such laws only until 1800.[7] The Southern states would not be able to protect themselves from laws favoring Northern shippers and discriminating against foreign shippers by rallying one-third plus one of the members of each house of Congress; nor, since navigation acts were acknowledged by everyone to be regulations of commerce, would they be able to protect the slave trade by this provision.[8] This was a concession to the Northern states. But the latter would not, even with a majority in each house, be able to ban "this infernal traffic" prior to 1800. This was the concession to the Southern states, specifically to South Carolina and Georgia who, alone at the time, insisted on importing further slaves. On the motion of Charles Cotesworth Pinckney, and over the objection of James Madison, who protested that "twenty years will produce all the mischief that can be apprehended from the liberty to import slaves," the prohibition was extended to 1808, and the compromise adopted by a vote of 7–4.[9]

Thus everyone, Southerner and Northerner, pro-slavery and anti-slavery, seems to have assumed from the beginning that the traffic in slaves was commerce and subject to Congress's power to regulate commerce. But the commerce power is not limited to foreign trade; on the contrary, Congress is expressly granted the power to regulate commerce "among the several states." Why, then, should it not follow that Congress had the power to regulate the domestic slave trade?

Quite apart from the logical extent of the commerce power, those who foresaw congressional abolition of slavery after 1808 must have assumed that control over internal commerce in slaves would be the instrument of that abolition.[10] Simple prohibition of importation could hardly have been expected to bring an end to the "peculiar institution." From the fragment preserved from the New Hampshire ratifying debate, for example, we learn that an "honorable member from Portsmouth boasted . . . '*that an end is then to be put to slavery.*'" This led Joshua Atherton to reply *not* that no such power was granted to Congress but rather that in 1808 "Congress may be as much, or more, puzzled to put a stop to it then, than we are now." Thus although the clause by itself "has not secured its abolition," it empowers Congress, if it so desires, to legislate toward that end.[11]

Madison, as we shall see, took essentially the same

position at the time of ratification. During the Missouri controversy some years later, however, he joined his colleagues from the South in insisting that Congress had no authority over the internal slave trade. The language of the clause, he wrote in 1819 in a letter to Robert Walsh, provided that "[C]ongress should not interfere until the year 1808; with an implication, that after that date, they might prohibit the importation of slaves into the States then existing, & previous thereto, into the States not then existing...."[12]

> But whatever may have been intended by the term "migration" or the term "persons," it is most certain, that they referred exclusively to a migration or importation from other countries into the U. States; and not to a removal, voluntary or involuntary, of slaves or freemen, from one to another part of the United States.[13]

Despite Madison's confidence, it is quite certain that the issue of Congress's power over the internal slave trade necessarily turned on the meaning accorded to the phrase "such persons." As pointed out above, if the phrase referred exclusively to slaves, Article I, Section 9 implied a congressional power to regulate the interstate slave trade.

It should be remembered that in its original version Article I, Section 9 provoked only a slave trade debate. Nor is there any doubt that in its amended version the clause was intended as a compromise between those who, in Madison's own words, wanted "an immediate and absolute stop to the [slave] trade" and those who "were not only averse to any interference on the subject," but went further to solemnly declare "that their constituents would never accede to a constitution containing such an article." Out of this conflict, Madison concludes, "grew the middle measure providing that Congress should not interfere until the year 1808...."[14] It would be odd indeed if in such circumstances the phrase "such persons" had been understood or intended to include white aliens as well as slaves.

Everyone knew why the term "such persons" was used instead of "slaves." Luther Martin, in his lengthy address to the Maryland legislature on the proposed Constitution, was not speaking for himself alone when he said that the delegates to the convention "anxiously sought to avoid the admission of expressions which might be odious in the ears of Americans...."[15] Madison, in the letter to Walsh quoted above, agreed: the convention, he said, "had scruples against admitting the term 'Slaves' into the Instrument."[16] Indeed, there is very little evidence contemporary with the writing and ratification of the Constitution to suggest that "such persons" was understood as anything more than a euphemism for "slaves." During the North Carolina debate, for example, Richard Spaight, who had been a delegate to the convention, was asked to explain the clause in question. He responded, with no reference to free aliens, that "the Southern States, whose principal support depended on the labor of slaves, would not consent to the desire of the Northern States to exclude the importation of slaves absolutely...."[17] Similarly, Luther Martin, who had been a member of the Committee of Eleven that had effected the compromise, described the deliberations over the clause without reference to anything except the slave trade:

> I found the *eastern* states, notwithstanding their *aversion to slavery*, were very willing to indulge the southern states at least with a temporary liberty to prosecute the *slave-trade*, provided the southern states would, in their turn, gratify them, by laying *no restriction on navigation acts*....[18]

The only references to free aliens during the ratification debates were made by Wilson of Pennsylvania and Iredell and Galloway of North Carolina. Wilson, in response to an objection that the tax provision would inhibit the "introduction of white people from Europe," pointed out that the tax might be laid on importation but not on migration, thus implying that migration referred to persons other than slaves.[19] Iredell made the same point during the North Carolina debates.[20] Against this must be put the testimony of Benjamin Rush, who assumed, and asserted that other anti-slavery men had also assumed, that after 1808 Congress would possess the authority to abolish slavery itself—presumably by prohibiting all commerce, both foreign and domestic, in slaves. Writing to Jeremy Belknap in 1788 he said:

> There was a respectable representation of [Quakers] in our [the Pennsylvania] Convention, all of whom voted in favor of the new Constitution. They consider very wisely that the abolition of slavery in our country must be gradual in order to be effectual, and that the section of the Constitution which will put it in the power of Congress twenty years hence to restrain it altogether was a great point obtained from the Southern States. The appeals, therefore, that have been made to the humane & laudable prejudices of our Quakers by our anti-federal writers upon the subject of negro slavery, have been treated by that prudent society with silence and contempt.[21]

This opinion respecting the temporarily dormant powers of Congress was not confined to Rush. In the Pennsylvania ratifying convention Thomas McKean also referred to a power in Congress to abolish slavery:

> In the first clause [of Article I, Section 9], there is a provision made for an event which must gratify the feelings of every friend to humanity. The abolition of slavery is put within the reach of the federal government.[22]

As early as October of 1787 Moses Brown of Rhode Island wrote to James Pendleton in Pennsylvania:

> It seems to Exhibit a poor Example of Confidence in Congress the Southern States being not willing to Leave the Commerce in Men under [Congress's] Controul and Regulation as well as other matters.... [H]ad the period of 21 years been fixed for Abolishing Slavery *as some writers your way seem to represent*, it would have been doing something....[23]

Nor were such opinions confined to private letters. Noah Webster wrote as follows in his tract written in defense of the proposed Constitution:

> The truth is, Congress cannot prohibit the importation of slaves, during that period; but the [state] laws against the importation into particular states, stand unrepealed. An immediate abolition of slavery would bring ruin upon the

whites, and misery upon the blacks, in the Southern states. The Constitution has therefore wisely left each state to pursue its own measures, with respect to this article of legislation, during the period of twenty-one years.[24]

Thus there is evidence that the anti-slavery men in the Northern states were assured by the Federalists that the bargain struck by them with the South was of limited duration, and that after 1808 Congress would possess the constitutional authority to act so as to abolish slavery. As Thomas Dawes said in the Massachusetts ratifying convention, in a few years slavery would be "abolished"; it would die not "of an apoplexy, but of a consumption," presumably at the hands of a Congress exercising control over the internal, as well as the external, commerce in slaves.[25]

The strongest argument in favor of the traditional interpretation of Article I, Section (reading "such persons" as including white aliens, limiting the term "migration" to them, and hence denying congressional authority to regulate the domestic slave trade under the commerce clause) is that had the alternative interpretation suggested here been taken seriously, the anti-Federalists in the South would have pointed to the threat to the institution of slavery represented by the interstate commerce power in order to rally pro-slavery sentiment against the proposed constitution. They did not do so. But their silence on the point is not conclusive. It could mean, as the traditional account would have it, that it was generally assumed that the clause referred to free whites immigrating into the country, and therefore that no power over interstate movement of slaves was implied. On the other hand, particularly since almost all vocal Southern opinion in the Constitutional Convention and the ratification debates was ultimately opposed to slavery, it could mean that the South was willing to concede what the North was in time going to insist upon: a power to limit slavery to its present boundaries. There seemed to be an assumption that, as Zachariah Johnson put it during the ratifying debates in Virginia, whether emancipation came late or soon, it was certain to come.[26] Congressional power over the interstate slave trade would pose no threat to men with such expectations.

Nevertheless, it is surprising how little was said in the South concerning this clause, surprising because the clause obviously affected commerce in slaves in *some* manner and because, just as obviously, Congress was being given authority to regulate domestic as well as foreign commerce. Even in Virginia, where the debates were particularly thorough and extensive, only a handful of references to the clause were made. And is it not astonishing that in the South Carolina ratifying convention the clause was not mentioned, even in passing?

In the Virginia debates George Mason deplored the fact that the proposed Constitution permitted the "nefarious" slave trade for another 20 years, as well as its failure to include a provision "securing to the Southern States [the slaves] they now possess"—which Lee of Westmoreland ridiculed as "two contradictory reasons" for opposing the Constitution.[27] Mason repeated these complaints four days later and was this time answered by Madison, who pointed out that however deplorable a temporary continuation of this "traffic" might be, the situation was at least an improvement because under the Articles of Confederation "it might be continued forever." He then went on to assure Mason that the "general government" would possess no power to "interpose with respect to the property in slaves now held by the states."[28] John Tyler, who like Mason later voted against ratification, followed by condemning the "impolicy, iniquity, and disgracefulness of this wicked traffic," and was answered by George Nicholas with much the same arguments that Madison had, a few minutes earlier, used against Mason.[29] In response to the fear that Congress would emancipate the slaves already held, Nicholas added that Congress "would only have a *general superintendency of trade*" after 1808. The Southern states, he said, had "insisted on this exception to that *general superintendency* for twenty years."[30] Shortly thereafter Governor Randolph, in an effort to meet the anti-Federalist argument concerning powers implied in the Constitution, used language suggesting, as had Nicholas, that Congress's powers after 1808 would extend to more than the mere importation of slaves:

> But the insertion of the negative *restrictions* [in Article I, Section 9] has given cause of triumph, it seems, to gentlemen. They suppose that it demonstrates that Congress are to have powers by implication.... I persuade myself that every exception here mentioned is an exception, not from general powers, but from the particular powers therein vested. To what power in the general government is the exception made respecting the importation of negroes?... This is an exception from the power given them of regulating commerce.[31]

Except for a later speech by Randolph repeating what he had already said and a passing reference by Mason, these were the only references to the clause during the Virginia debates.

In the South Carolina debates, if we are to believe the official journal of the convention as well as the local newspapers at the time, nothing at all was said respecting this clause. Yet South Carolina even then was the state most closely associated with the cause of slavery. The convention debated the proposed constitution clause by clause, finishing its discussion of Article I, Section 8, on Friday, May 16, 1788. The following day, discussion began with Article I, Section 10. Nor, as the convention proceeded through to the end of the Constitution, did it return to the missing clause. Is it possible to believe that this was the only part of the Constitution that was of no interest to the South Carolina convention, the only clause that provoked neither debate nor acknowledgement? Yet, while it received some mention earlier in the legislature,[32] all the sources agree that it was ignored officially in the ratifying convention, and none of them provides any clue as to what was said unofficially, for example, on that Friday night.[33]

Aside from the remarks of Wilson, Iredell, and Galloway in the Pennsylvania and North Carolina ratifying debates,[34] the only other suggestion at this time that "such persons" might include persons other than slaves is to be found in an exchange between Gouverneur Morris and George Mason in the Constitutional Convention itself. The second part of the migration or importation provision as reported by the Committee of Eleven read as follows: "... but a tax or duty may be imposed on such migration or importation at a rate not exceeding the average of duties laid on imports." Morris pointed out "that as the clause now stands [i.e., using the term "such persons" rather than "slaves"] it implies that the Legislature may tax freemen imported."[35] Mason then replied that the "provision as it stands was necessary for the case of Convicts in order to prevent the introduction of them."[36] The outcome of this exchange was an amendment, adopted unanimously, to allow a tax or duty to be imposed only on the importation—and not on the migration—of "such persons."[37]

This exchange between Morris and Mason and the remarks of Wilson, Iredell, and Galloway are, to repeat, the only evidence contemporary with the adoption of the Constitution that the term "such persons" was meant to be anything but a euphemism for "slaves." On the other hand, the record is equally barren of any statement that the word "migration" was intended to refer to the domestic slave trade.[38] That is to say, no one expressly stated that after 1808 Congress would be empowered to forbid the migration of slaves even among the states originally existing.[39] As we have seen, however, a number of men *did* say, in one way or another, that after 1808 Congress would be able to act to abolish slavery or to bring about its abolition.[40]

Nor can the inconclusive nature of available evidence contemporaneous with the adoption of the Constitution be made up for by looking to later interpretations of the clause, however clear they may seem. Opinions expressed on the question of congressional power over commerce in slaves in the years following the establishment of the Government are inevitably colored by the writer's views on the increasingly sensitive slavery question, and are therefore suspect. This became clear as early as 1790 during the debate in the House of Representatives on the anti-slavery petitions presented by the Pennsylvania Quakers and by Benjamin Franklin's Society for Promoting the Abolition of Slavery. The petitions were referred to a special committee which reported in part as follows:

> That, from the nature of the matters contained in these memorials, they were induced to examine the powers vested in Congress, under the present Constitution, relating to the Abolition of Slavery, and are clearly of opinion:
>
> First, That the general government is expressly restrained from prohibiting the importation of such persons as any of the States now existing shall think proper to admit until the year 1808.
>
> Secondly, That Congress, by a fair construction of the Constitution, are equally restrained from interfering in the emancipation of slaves, who already are, or who may, within the period mentioned [i.e., prior to 1808], be imported into, or born within, any of the said States.[41]

Smith of South Carolina greeted this report, and not without reason, with the statement that it "appeared to hold out the idea that Congress might exercise the power of emancipating after the year 1808." Elias Boudinot of New Jersey admitted as much, saying that "Congress could not interfere in prohibiting the importation, or promoting the emancipation of them prior to that period."[42] Smith and his Southern colleagues therefore moved that the Report of the Special Committee be referred to the Committee of the Whole House, which in its report replaced the offensive second paragraph with a new one stating flatly that "Congress have no authority to interfere in the emancipation of slaves, or in the treatment of them within *any* of the States. . . ."[43] The House, some of its members obviously being in a conciliatory mood, voted 29–25 to insert *both* reports in the Journal,[44] thereby acknowledging its indecision, or its inability to agree, on this matter of constitutional interpretation.

The same sort of disagreement occurred in 1798 during the debate on the alien part of the infamous Alien and Sedition Laws. Somewhat at a loss to explain where the

Constitution authorized Congress to enact a law expelling aliens, one of the supporters of the Alien Friends bill, Samuel Sewell of Massachusetts, hit upon the commerce clause. Robert Williams of North Carolina then replied that he thought it "a curious idea, that all emigrants coming to this country should be considered as articles of commerce." But even if it were granted, he continued, Congress's power is limited to "laying a tax of ten dollars upon their migration, as the migration cannot be prohibited till the year 1808." How, he asked, can "gentlemen . . . contend, from this clause of the Constitution, that Congress has a right to prevent the migration of foreigners, or remove them after they arrive"? If this could be done, then slaves "may also be sent out of the country," and the Southern states would never permit this.[45] The power to expel aliens conjured in the minds of the Southerners the prospect of a federal law expelling slaves. Abraham Baldwin of Georgia then took up the cause of the South, which led to an interesting exchange on the precise point of the meaning of the term "such persons." He thought Article I, Section 9, "forbidding Congress to prohibit the migration, etc., was directly opposed to the principle of this bill."

> He recollected very well that when the 9th section . . . was under consideration in the Convention, the delegates from some of the Southern States insisted that the prohibition of the introduction of slaves should be left to the State Governments; it was found expedient to make this provision in the Constitution; there was an objection to the use of the word slaves, as Congress by none of their acts had ever acknowledged the existence of such a condition. It was at length settled on the words as they now stand, "that the migration or importation of such persons as the several states shall think proper to admit, should not be prohibited till the year 1808." It was observed by some gentlemen present that this expression would extend to other persons besides slaves, which was not denied, but this did not produce any alteration of it.[46]

This statement was hotly contradicted by the Speaker of

the House, Jonathan Dayton of New Jersey, who happened to be the only other member of the House who had been a delegate to the Constitutional Convention. Baldwin's words could only be ascribed "either to absolute forgetfulness, or to willful misrepresentation," he said, made "to suit the particular purposes of the opponents of the Alien bill." He insisted that "in the discussion of [Article I, Section 9's] merits, no question arose, or was agitated respecting the admission of foreigners, but on the contrary, that it was confined simply to slaves...." Everyone knew the reasons for changing the term. And

> until the present debate arose, he had never heard that any one member supposed that the simple change of the term would enlarge the construction of this prohibitory provision, as it was now contended for. If it could have been conceived to be really liable to such interpretation, he was convinced that it would not have been adopted, for it would then carry with it a strong injunction upon Congress to prohibit the introduction of foreigners into the newly erected states immediately, and into the then existing states after the year 1808, as it undoubtedly does, that of slaves after that period.[47]

Since the records of the Convention are almost completely barren on this question, it is impossible to determine who, Baldwin or Dayton, is correct. As we saw above,[48] Gouverneur Morris had indeed raised a question concerning the meaning of the clause, but whether this gave rise to an agitation "respecting the admission of foreigners," we cannot know.

What we do know, however, is that Baldwin's version became the Southerners' version, the version insisted on by the friends of or apologists for slavery. And we do know that the number of these apologists increased with the passage of time, and that opinions on the constitutional question, including those offered by Jefferson and Madison, changed accordingly. Dayton and his friends were to hear this Southern argument many times in the years that followed, especially during the Missouri controversy in 1819–20, though perhaps nowhere in a more specious version than that put forward by Charles Pinckney in the House of Representatives on February 14, 1820.

> The term, or word, migration, applies wholly to free whites.... The reasons of its being adopted and used in the Constitution ... were these; that the Constitution being a frame of government, consisting wholly of delegated powers, all power, not *expressly* delegated, being reserved to the people or the states, it was supposed, that, without some express grant to them of power on the subject, Congress would not be authorized ever to touch the question of migration hither, or emigration to this country, however pressing or urgent the necessity for such a measure might be; that they could derive no such power from the usages of nations, or even the laws of war; that the latter would only enable them to make prisoners of alien enemies, which would not be sufficient, as spies or other dangerous emigrants, who were not alien enemies, might enter the country for treasonable purposes, and do great injury.... [49]

In short, Article I, Section 9 had now become not a limitation on Congress's commerce powers, but a grant of power! Without the clause, its powers being limited to those "expressly delegated," Congress would not have been able to enact immigration laws! The article is a "negative pregnant, restraining for twenty years, and giving the power after." So pressing was the need to protect the country against these "spies or other dangerous emigrants" that the constitutional convention deliberately deprived Congress of all power to deal with them for twenty years! After this palpable nonsense, no one should be surprised to read Pinckney's conclusion that Congress's power to regulate commerce "between the States" was limited to "the commerce by water." Congress must be denied all power that touched the subject of slavery, and any argument, however specious, would be advanced in that cause.

To recapitulate briefly: the question of the extent of congressional power over slavery was intimately related to the meaning of the term "such persons" as it appears in the "migration or importation" clause in Article I, Section 9. We have seen that the term was a euphemism for slaves, adopted in order to avoid using "expressions which might be odious in the ears of Americans." A few men, with the exception of James Wilson all Southerners, used the term in a manner comprehending persons other than slaves—convicts, for example, or free whites. As to the clause as a whole, originally everyone saw it as a temporary restriction on Congress's power to regulate commerce—a power that extends to commerce among the states (and not merely by water) as well as to foreign commerce. It was also clear to everyone that slaves were capable of being articles of commerce. Thus, a number of men,[50] mostly Northerners but including James Madison, assumed that Congress, after 1808, would possess the authority, presumably derived from the power to regulate commerce, to abolish slavery, or to abolish slavery in some places, or to act in a manner calculated to have the effect of abolishing slavery. It is suggested, for example, that the antislavery Quakers of Pennsylvania would not have voted to ratify the Constitution without assurance that Congress would possess such a power; while, on the other hand, there were doubtless Southerners who would not have voted to ratify the Constitution unless they had believed that Congress would *not* possess such a power. The testimony of the men immediately concerned is thus not conclusive on the proper interpretation of Article I, Section 9. While the historical record demonstrates that the traditional reading of the clause can no longer be accepted without question, it is necessary to turn to a different mode of analysis to establish that the interpretation suggested here is more probably the originally intended meaning.

II

The clause in question reads: "The Migration or Importation of Such Persons as any of the States now existing shall think proper to admit, shall not be prohibited by the Congress prior to the Year one thousand eight hundred and eight...." At the very least this wording leaves Congress free, even before 1808, to prohibit the importation of slaves from abroad into a territory or a new state. Indeed, Congress exercised this power when organizing the Mississippi Territory, formed out of Georgia's western lands, and earlier when it re-enacted the law governing the Northwest Territory.[51] *Why*, it is natural to ask, *was this temporary restriction on the power of Congress itself restricted to the states originally existing?* It seems obvious that the purpose of the clause's particular wording was to enable Congress to prevent the spread of slavery beyond the boundaries of the existing slave states, without, at least for a time, encroaching on the established slave trade within them.[52] If the term "migration" were read as referring only to the immigration of free aliens from abroad and not to the interstate movement of slaves, however, as the South later insisted, this purpose could be defeated with ridiculous ease. Of what use is a power to prohibit the importation of slaves from abroad into newly created states or territories, if South Carolina or Georgia could import slaves and transport them with impunity into the same states or territories? If any force at all is to be accorded the limited congressional power to prohibit importation before 1808, the term "migration" must be read as referring to the internal movement of slaves. Only such an interpretation is consistent with the power Congress was given to prevent the spread of slavery. And only when, under increasing economic pressure from the North, the South became concerned with the territorial expansion of slavery, did it become necessary to reinterpret "migration" so as to deny the existence of any congressional power over interstate traffic in slaves.

Madison, who was so emphatic on the lack of national power over the internal slave trade in his 1819 letter to Robert Walsh,[53] seems to have been of a different opinion at the time he, along with Hamilton and Jay, was urging the adoption of the new Constitution:

> It were doubtless to be wished that the power of prohibiting the importation of slaves had not been postponed until the year 1808, or rather that it had been suffered to have immediate operation. But it is not difficult to account either

for this restriction on the general government, or for the manner in which the whole clause is expressed. It ought to be considered as a great point gained in favor of humanity that a period of twenty years may terminate forever, *within these States*, a traffic which has so long and so loudly upbraided the barbarism of modern policy....

Attempts have been made to pervert this clause into an objection against the Constitution by representing it on one side as a criminal toleration of an illicit practice, and on another as calculated to prevent *voluntary and beneficial emigration from Europe to America. I mention these misconstructions not with a view to give them an answer, for they deserve none, but as specimens of the manner and spirit in which some have thought fit to conduct their opposition to the proposed government.*[54]

Taking the phrase "within these states" at its face value, this 1788 opinion seems incompatible with what Madison wrote to Robert Walsh in 1819 during the Missouri dispute. It is difficult to see how Congress could have abolished the barbarous traffic (this "illicit practice") "within these States" unless it possessed a power over the movement of slaves from place to place "within these States," a power over the internal slave trade, and a power that was only temporarily and partially denied it by the clause in question. Until 1808 Congress was forbidden to prohibit the importation of slaves from abroad into the states then existing (but not into or within new states or territories). Migration, Madison is saying in 1788, is not to be understood as referring to "voluntary and beneficial emigrations from Europe to America"; the opponents of the new Constitution who have introduced this "misconstruction" into the debates do not even deserve an answer—in 1788. But by 1819, and in fact long before then, Madison had himself adopted this "perverted" view. Walsh taxed him with being inconsistent. He replied to Madison's letter of November 27, 1819, pointing out that it was inconsistent with the views Madison had expressed in *Federalist* 42. Madison replied as follows:

It is far from my purpose to resume a subject on which I

have, perhaps, already exceeded the proper limits. But, having spoken with so confident a recollection of the meaning attached by the convention to the term "migration," which seems to be an important hinge to the argument, I may be permitted merely to remark...that a consistency of the passage cited from the Federalist, with my recollections, is preserved by the discriminating term "beneficial," added to voluntary emigrations from Europe *to* America.[55]

It is difficult to understand how Madison thought this one word would save him. Why was it a misconstruction to say that Article I, Section 9 was "calculated to prevent voluntary and beneficial emigrations from Europe to America," and why would it *not* have been a misconstruction to say the clause was "calculated to prevent voluntary... emigrations from Europe to America"? What difference is made by the adjective "beneficial"? For twenty years the clause will not prevent any kind of immigration into the original states; after twenty years—to assume with the 1820 Madison that "such persons" also refers to persons other than slaves—Congress would have the power to prevent the "migration" of every variety of European immigrant, beneficial as well as baneful.

Of course Madison may have meant that although after 1808 Congress would certainly have the power to forbid voluntary emigration into the states originally existing, it could be assumed that Congress would not exercise its power so as to exclude *beneficial* voluntary emigration. In other words, Madison could be saying that Congress can be trusted to use its authority to prohibit the "migration" only of those white persons we do not want and not to exclude those white persons, those beneficial immigrants, we are eager to admit. He did not say this, but such an interpretation allows us to make some sense of what he did say.

Some sense, yes, but not very much. For the fact is that whereas under this interpretation Madison is saying that the clause reflects a trust in Congress wisely to exercise the power over immigration, the necessary implication of the fact that Congress was forbidden before 1808 to prohibit the migration of "such persons" is that the Founders were not willing to trust Congress with a power over migration into the original states! Not, that is, until 1808. Madison cannot have it both ways. Once committed to the position that "migration" refers to free aliens, he cannot escape self-contradiction.

Nor is this all. The original question still remains unanswered: why was Article I, Section 9's temporary restriction on the power of Congress itself restricted to the states originally existing? According to the latter-day Madisonian interpretation, although Congress would be forbidden until 1808 to prohibit the migration of free whites into the original states, it would not be forbidden during this period to prohibit their migration into the new states to be formed out of the Western Territories. Can this distinction be explained by any policy favored by the Southern, or even Northern, states in 1787? The difference with respect to the power over the importation of slaves is readily explained: South Carolina and Georgia wanted more slaves and hoped to import a sufficient number during the 20-year period of grace, while the Founders, conceding this to South Carolina and Georgia, limited the concession to them and the other original states in order to keep slaves out of the new states. That a similar distinction should have been made with respect to the migration of free whites is difficult to understand. Can it be argued that the original states also wanted to make certain that they would not be forbidden to admit beneficial white immigrants and, at the same time, that they were unconcerned about the migration of whites into the western lands? On the contrary, the record shows an intense concern with such migration. In the Virginia ratifying convention, for example, considerable time was spent discussing the question of the navigation of the Mississippi River. There was some fear that under the proposed constitution the new government might give up the right of free navigation which, the anti-Federalists argued, would jeopardize Virginia's policy of populating the western lands adjacent to the river. Under the Articles of Confederation, said William Grayson, people would continue to settle in these western lands, but deprive them of the hope and "privilege of navigating that river ... and the emigration will cease." It is interesting that during this discussion no reference was made by Grayson or Patrick Henry or any of the other anti-Federalists to Article I, Section 9; yet if the Southern interpretation of the clause is correct, Congress would have had the power to prohibit the migration of free whites into any part of the western lands lying outside the boundaries of the original states, both before and after 1808.[56] As General William Heath said in the Massachusetts convention, the "migration or importation, etc., is confined to the states now *existing only*; new states cannot claim it."[57]

In short, if the term "such persons" was intended to cover free white immigrants as well as slaves, it does not appear to make any sense to distinguish, as the clause does, between the states originally existing and any new states that would be formed.

Quite apart from the internal logic of Article I, Section 9, moreover, there is legislative evidence that Congress considered itself empowered to deal with the internal movement of slaves into the territories and new states formed from them. General Heath, in the passage just cited, goes on to point out that the Continental Congress, "by their ordinance for erecting new states, some time since, declared that the new states shall be republican, and that there shall be no slavery in them." He was referring to the famous Northwest Ordinance of 1787, enacted by the Continental Congress while the new Constitution was being written in Philadelphia, which provided in its sixth article that there "shall be neither slavery nor involuntary servitude in the said territory.... " It is important to note here, for reasons that will soon become clear, that in one of the first statues passed under the new Constitution, Congress re-enacted the Ordinance,[58] affirming its intention to follow the policy of the old Congress in keeping slavery out of the states to be formed from the western lands. Does this not indicate a belief that the national government possessed the authority to implement this policy? And is it not obvious that such a policy could have been defeated not only by the introduction of slaves from abroad, but also by the introduction of slaves from the states already existing? It was certainly obvious to the Congress that in 1804 enacted the law establishing the Territory of Orleans. In the tenth section of that statute Congress not only forbade the importation of slaves from abroad, but went on to add that it "shall not be lawful for any person or persons to import or bring into the said territory, *from any port or place within the limits of the United States* ... any slave or slaves, which shall have been imported since the first day of May [1798], into any port or place within the limits of the United States...."[59] This is a law regulating the movement of slaves *within* the United States. It does, at least as to slaves brought into the country after 1798, precisely what had to be done to enforce Congress's powers under the commerce clause and Article I, Section 9. As has been pointed out above, no purpose would be served by prohibiting the importation of slaves from abroad if they could, prior to 1808, be imported into South Carolina and then sent on to a new state or territory. In 1804 Congress understood this very well, and sought to prevent it by exercising either its power over the "migration" of "such persons" into a new territory—a power derived from its general authority over commerce among the states and, even before 1808, not limited by Article I, Section 9—or its authority to "make all needful Rules and Regulations respecting the Territory ... belonging to the United States...."[60]

In his 1819 letter to Walsh, Madison slides over this aspect of the 1804 Act. Indeed, it might even be said that he actively misrepresents it, although he concedes implicitly that the power being exercised was the power to regulate commerce. Congress, he says, "lost no time in applying the prohibitory power to Louisiana, which having maritime ports, might be an inlet for slaves from abroad. But they forebore to extend the prohibition to the introduction of slaves from other parts of the Union."[61] Not content with this flat misstatement of fact, Madison goes right on to deny that Congress, in any of the "Territorial governments created by them," had ever forbidden the existence of slavery. This statement apparently caused him some uneasiness, for two pages later he refers to the Northwest Ordinance, a piece of legislation of which Walsh could not be presumed to be ignorant. But he says of the Ordinance that it "proceeded from the old Congress, acting, with the best intentions, but under a charter which contains no shadow of the authority exercised." No mention whatever is made of the fact—and it must certainly have been known to him, for he was a member of the Congress that enacted the statute, and himself voted for it—that one of the first pieces of business in the new Congress, acting under the authority of the new Constitution, was to re-enact this famous anti-slavery ordinance.[62]

Nor was this the only example of Madison's willingness to use specious arguments to support his Southern views on the slavery question. In this same letter to Walsh he asserts that nothing was said in the Constitutional Convention indicating an intention to prevent the spread of slavery, a statement that cannot be believed. He then added the following:

> The case of the N. Western Territory was probably superseded by the provision against the importation of slaves by South Carolina and Georgia, which had not then passed laws prohibiting it. When the existence of slavery in that territory was precluded [by the Northwest Ordinance], the importation of slaves was rapidly going on, and the only mode of checking it was by narrowing the space open to them. It is not an unfair inference that the expedient would not have been undertaken, if the power afterward given to terminate the importation everywhere, had existed or been even anticipated.[63]

Consider first this last statement. Madison says that the provision prohibiting slavery in the Northwest Territory would not have been adopted had the Continental Congress anticipated the powers subsequently given to Congress in the new Constitution to forbid the importation of slaves. But when the new Congress re-enacted the Northwest Ordinance in 1789, they *did* know about this constitutional power and they did enact legislation designed to forbid slavery in the territories. Consider next the statement that the Northwest Ordinance prohibition was "probably superseded by the provision against importation by S. Carolina and Georgia...." What provision? Does he mean the act of Congress, effective January 1, 1808, forbidding all importation into the United States? But when it was enacted the only state permitting importation was South Carolina. So he must be referring to the Georgia statute of 1798 and the South Carolina statute of 1792 (repealed in 1803) forbidding importation from abroad, they being the only two states permitting importation at the time of the Northwest Ordinance.[64] Thus, these state laws superseded an act of Congress! This from the father of the Constitution whose supremacy clause states the opposite.

Walsh certainly was not deceived by the misinformation supplied him by Madison. In an "able and eloquent" monograph published shortly thereafter, and apparently long since forgotten,[65] he developed at some length the argument advanced here respecting Congress's power over the internal slave trade. To him

> the whole test [of Article I, Section 9] bespeaks a compromise in which, on the one hand, the privilege of multiplying the race of slaves within their limits, either by importations from abroad or domestic migration is reluctantly yielded for a term to those southern states who made this compliance a *sine qua non* of their accession to the union; while, on the other hand, the power is conceded, by implication, to the federal government, or preventing at once the extension of slavery beyond the limits of the old states—of keeping the territory of the union, and the new states, free from the pestilence; and ultimately of suppressing altogether the diabolical trade in human flesh, whether *internal* or external.[66]

To him the words "such persons" refer "exclusively to negro slaves," with the result that "migration" refers to the movement of slaves among the states and territories. Congress had to have this power, Walsh argues, because most of the territories and new states were, or would be,

> *inland,* and slaves could not be imported into them, but through the old states; which last circumstance—owing to the facility of concealing beyond detection, the foreign origin of slaves introduced,—would render futile any prohibitory regulations as to mere importation.[67]

As to the failure of Congress to forbid slavery in the new states of Kentucky, Tennessee, Alabama, and Mississippi, this did not bespeak a lack of constitutional authority; it derived rather from the fact that the states of Virginia, North Carolina, South Carolina, and Georgia, who owned the lands out of which these new states were formed, had insisted, in the acts ceding the lands to the United States, that slavery be permitted in them. But in the Northwest Territory and the Orleans Territory, part of the purchase from Napoleon's France, Congress acted free of such inhibitions and was able to exercise fully the powers bestowed on it by the Constitution.

III

At the time of the Constitutional Convention the South, although determined not to be stripped of the immediate benefits of slave-holding by the Northern states, was not inclined to defend the virtue or permanence of its "peculiar institution." In *Federalist* 42 the original Madison could look forward to the day when the barbarous slave trade would cease to exist *within* the United States, and men like Wilson openly proclaimed that the new Constitution laid the foundation "for banishing slavery . . . out of this country." But by the time of the Alien Act debates the Southerners, Madison among them, were denying congressional power over the internal slave trade; and in 1857 the Supreme Court of the United States, headed by a Southerner, found constitutional grounds for denying congressional power over slavery even in the territories, a power Congress had exercised from the very beginning.[68]

By 1857 most Southerners agreed with Lincoln that a house divided against itself on an issue as fundamental as slavery could not stand. Their solution, naturally enough, was to end the division by extending slavery throughout the nation. Lincoln warned of this in his debates with Douglas in 1858 when he showed how Taney's opinion in the *Dred Scott* case laid the foundation for a future decision prohibiting the states from excluding slavery from their limits.[69]

Jefferson and Madison, of course, never became advocates of slavery and did not espouse such a solution. Like most of their Southern colleagues during this early period, however, they were determined to keep the federal government from interfering with what to them was a purely local matter. To borrow a modern turn of phrase from another context, they were anti-antislavery men. Hence Jefferson's reaction to the Missouri controversy and specifically to the antislavery opposition to the admission of Missouri as a slave state. This was to him a Federalist plot, "a mere party trick," whereby the Federalists hoped to regain power by dividing the country along a geographical line that coincided with a division based on a moral principle. In proposing that Congress act to prevent slavery in Missouri, the antislavery people had sounded "a fire bell in the night" that awakened him, he said, and "filled [him] with terror." The regulation of "the condition of the different descriptions of men composing a State," and of their migration within the country was "the exclusive right of every State." For Congress to interfere would sound the "knell of the Union."[70] The antislavery people, and especially the new breed whose opposition to slavery was sparked by an evangelical fervor, must not be permitted to rule the country. To the same end, the powers of Congress must be confined within the narrowest of limits. Hence the assiduous effort of Southern judges, including Southern judges on the Supreme Court, to deny any power to Congress over persons as subjects of commerce.[71]

It is no doubt difficult to believe that men of the stature of Jefferson and Madison could have joined in a more or less deliberate campaign to distort the original meaning of the Constitution, and to do so on behalf of slavery. But consider Jefferson's words just quoted. In 1820 he was claiming that the regulation of "the condition of the different descriptions of men composing a state," and of their migration within the country, was "the exclusive right of every state." Yet as President he had approved the bill authorizing Ohio to adopt a state constitution and to enter the Union—*provided* "the same shall be republican, and not repugnant to the ordinance of the thirteenth of July [1787], between the original states, and the people and States of the territory northwest of the river Ohio."[72] Whatever the wishes of the people in the Ohio territory, they would not be permitted to enter the Union except as a free state: clearly Congress, in imposing such conditions upon Ohio's entry into the Union, had exercised a power over "the condition of the different descriptions of men composing a state." The antislavery provision of the 1787 Ordinance, moreover, had itself originated in a plan, drawn by Jefferson himself, to provide for the government of the new states to be formed out of the territories. This 1784 plan extended not merely to the territory north and west of the Ohio River, but "to all parts of the national domain," as Julian Boyd puts it, "those already acquired as well as those to be acquired in the future...."[73] This plan, which formed the basis of the 1784 ordinance for the temporary government of the Northwest Territory, provided that "after the year 1800 of the Christian era there shall be neither slavery nor involuntary servitude in any of the said states...." Although this antislavery provision was dropped from the 1784 Ordinance on final passage,[74] it reappeared in a slightly altered version in the famous 1787 Ordinance.

In 1819, as we have seen, Madison asserted that the Continental Congress had had no authority to adopt such a provision;[75] in 1820 Jefferson claimed that the states themselves, and only the states, had any control of the subject; and in our own time Julian Boyd has written that "there was nothing in the Articles of Confederation to warrant the abolition of slavery...."[76]

Yet the Continental Congress, working with a provision drawn by the earlier Jefferson, solemnly and officially forbade slavery not only in the territory but *in the states* to be formed out of the territory. Where did they think they got such authority? The final paragraph of Jefferson's 1784 plan reads as follows:

> [T]he preceding articles shall be formed into a Charter of Compact, shall be duly executed by the President of the U.S. in Congress Assembled [,] shall be promulgated, and shall stand as fundamental constitutions between the thirteen original states, and those now newly described, unalterable but by the joint consent of the U.S. in Congress Assembled and of the particular state within which such alteration is proposed to be made.[77]

Thus, according to Jefferson in 1784 and the entire Continental Congress in 1787 (with the sole exception of Robert Yates of New York, who also refused to vote for the new Constitution) the power to prohibit slavery did not derive from a power to regulate commerce among the states (the Articles of Confederation bestowed no such power on Congress) or even from a power to govern the territories (in Jefferson's plan the prohibition of slavery extended to the states as well as the territories), but from a power to make a compact, in this case a compact between the original states and the new states—states not yet existing but "newly described."

Whatever the status, or the legality, of such a compact and the powers derived from it,[78] the Continental Congress reasserted them in the 1787 Ordinance. The First Congress, acting under the new Constitution, implicitly asserted its power over slavery in the territories and in new states to be carved out of them when it re-enacted the 1787 Ordinance.[79] In 1802, when the Ohio bill was signed, Thomas Jefferson and Congress affirmed that power once again. Eighteen years later he claimed that such authority did not belong to the Government of the United States.

Such a denial of national authority is quite consistent with a principle long associated with Jefferson's name, but for Madison the theory of states' rights, which he espoused vigorously in the Virginia Resolutions of 1798 and implicitly throughout the later slavery debates, is directly and profoundly contrary to the principle of the large commercial republic on which his fame as a political thinker largely rests. In *Federalist* 10 he explained the necessity for size in a popularly governed republic:

> The smaller the society, the fewer probably will be the distinct parties and interests composing it; the fewer the distinct parties and interests, the more frequently will a majority be found of the same party; and the smaller the number of individuals composing a majority, and the smaller the compass within which they are placed, the more easily will they concert and execute their plans of oppression. Extend the sphere and you take in a greater variety of parties and interests; you make it less probable that a majority of the whole will have a common motive to invade the rights of other citizens. ... [80]

The *causes* of factions, those impassioned groups that pursue ends inimical to the common good, cannot be eliminated by any means consonant with republican principles. But their *effects* can be controlled. In size, both of population and territory, there is to be found a wholly republican remedy to the problem of republican, or popular government; for in a large republic there can be the variety of interests giving rise to the variety of factions needed to save the country from the oppressive rule of any one of them.

But size alone, Madison realized, will not necessarily produce the required diversity. It is "the possession of different degrees and kinds of property" that produces "a division of the society into different interests and parties."[81] What is called for is the promotion of these different kinds of property. And commerce and industry, Madison believed, breed this diversity of property and interests and help insure the necessary multiplicity of factions.[82] As Martin Diamond once said, "a large Saharan republic would be rent by the Marxist-like class struggle between date-pickers and oasis-landholders." Thus the rapid commercialization of the United States is one major premise on which Madison's famous argument rests. Yet within a very few years he took his stand with Virginia, whose economy rested on agriculture and the breeding of slaves to be used in agriculture elsewhere, against Hamilton, the great and consistent advocate of the large commercial republic.

The argument of *Federalist* 10 has another premise, this one more explicitly stated. To the extent that localities are marked by simple economies rather than by "variety and complexity" (and this will be the case if they do not combine and permit the growth of a large mass market), factions will be able to gain local political control. Thus if the decisive political decisions are made in the localities where "factious leaders" are in control, the size and diversity of the whole will be of no avail. Size and diversity will solve the problem of faction, which is *the* problem of popular government, only if the decisive political decisions are made in the arena where faction does not command—in the counsels of the national government. That is to say, the solution to the problem of popular government requires *one* country with a government empowered to govern in all matters affecting the country as a whole—"anything in the Constitution or Laws of any State to the contrary notwithstanding." Yet in connection with the Alien Act a decade later, when his Southern friends saw a threat to slavery,[83] Madison reacted by drafting the Virginia Resolutions, proclaiming the right of the "sovereign states" to exercise decisive political control. In short, he abandoned the large commercial republic solution and joined Jefferson, whose passion for the small agricultural republic is one of the commonplaces of American history.

It is possible, of course, that Madison had changed his mind; that he had become convinced that a commercial republic would lead to a vulgarization of humanity—that Rousseau was right in his criticism of Locke—and that the small, essentially rural, virtuous republic offered the only solution; that "moral and religious motives" could be relied on, or would have to be relied on because further reflection had convinced him of the inadequacy of the alternative. Or he may have been convinced by the policies of the Federalist administrations of Washington and Adams that, unless some radical changes were introduced into the constitutional system, there was a genuine danger of a centralized despotism, and that the most effective safeguard would be to shift the balance of power between the national government and that of the states. Such a shift, for such a reason, would only incidentally have the effect of leaving the states with complete authority to deal with the slavery problem. Whatever his reasons—and to account for them is a task for some future biographer—Madison turned his back on the republic that he, as much as any man, had brought into being. The later Madisonian republic, unlike the original, was no enemy to slavery, not even to its extension into the western lands.

Whether Congress, had it adhered to the original intent of Article I, Section 9, would have exercised its commerce powers to forbid the migration of slaves within the country after 1808 is, of course, a question we cannot answer. The early and almost unamimous embarrassment among Southerners concerning their "peculiar institution" soon gave way to praise of slavery as an institution beneficial alike to slaveholder and slave, a shift which was reflected in all national debates touching the issue and which produced, in time, such judicial decisions as *Dred Scott*. One cannot help wondering what the course of American history might have been if Madison and Jefferson had resolutely and publicly maintained their early hopes that Congress could do something about the evils of slavery and that it would "countenance the abolition" of the slave trade and adopt regulations forbidding the introduction of slaves "into the new States to be formed out of the Western Territory."[84] Instead they chose to act in the manner that inspired men such as John C. Calhoun. Similarly one cannot help wondering what the result might have been had all the states, Northern and Southern, been encouraged to approach one another in variety and complexity through the fostering of commerce in both regions. In *The Federalist* Madison had expressed the hope that with the passage of time and with an increase of commercial intercourse among the peoples of the various states, there would come a "general assimilation of their manners and laws."[85] But instead of fostering commercial policies which might have brought about a "general assimilation" characterized by antislavery "manners and laws," Madison and Jefferson denied the full scope of Congress's commercial powers, and Madison even vetoed the internal improvement bill designed to diversify the Southern economy.[86] In 1819, moreover, in his letter to Robert Walsh, Madison called for a "diffusion of the slaves" throughout the new states, arguing that this would facilitate their manumission and improve their "moral & physical condition." The more likely result, since the slave population was growing, would have been a "general assimilation of . . . manners and laws" quite the opposite of the sort he had originally hoped for. A civil war was required to prevent that.

CHAPTER 15

RACIAL DISCRIMINATION AND THE LIMITS OF JUDICIAL REMEDY

In the *Dred Scott* case of 1857, the Supreme Court held that Negroes were not and could never become citizens of the United States, because Negroes were not and could never be included among those men who were, by the Declaration of Independence, declared to be equally endowed by their Creator with certain unalienable rights. As if this were not enough, the Court held that Congress had no power to forbid slavery in the territories and, even worse, it provided the basis for a future declaration that no *state* had power to forbid slavery. Under these circumstances, it is not strange that this infamous decision, embodying this intention, was followed by Civil War, or that during that war the President proclaimed the emancipation of those Negroes held as slaves in the states whose people were in rebellion against the United States.

Though thus limited in its immediate application, the Emancipation Proclamation promised much more. Specifically, it promised Negroes legal membership in that body known, in the words of the Constitution's Preamble, as "the people of the United States," with the hope, if not in

Reprinted, with permission, from Robert A. Goldwin, ed., *100 Years of Emancipation* (Chicago: Rand McNally & Co., 1963)

every case the expectation, that legal membership would be followed by membership in the ultimate sense, that is, in the hearts and minds of their white fellow citizens. This has not yet happened. During the last quarter of the century since the Proclamation, the Negro, thanks mainly to a host of Supreme Court decisions striking down state discriminatory laws and practices, has managed to achieve a close approximation of legal equality, but membership in the ultimate sense has continued to be denied him. The Court has nullified verdicts handed down by juries from which Negroes have been systematically excluded; it has guaranteed them nonsegregated service in the dining cars of interstate trains and in the restaurants in interstate bus terminals; it has promoted Negro voting, even in primary and preprimary elections. It has, furthermore, invalidated racially-segregated schools, criminated the local police brute for his illegal treatment of Negroes, and nullified racially-restrictive real estate contracts. It has done these things and more. But it cannot force, or even goad, cajole, or drive (the terms are Roy Wilkins's) white parents to send their children to those schools; it cannot, in too many places, get a local jury to convict the brutal policeman; and it cannot prevent whites from moving out of the uncovenanted areas when Negroes move in.

Even as President Kennedy called for new legislation and an end to "the cruel disease of discrimination,"[1] the law was demonstrating its inability to overcome this discrimination which, together with the Negro's response to it, constitutes what is surely the most urgent national domestic political problem of our time. The problem derives from private conduct that springs from—from what? a fear of the Negro, a hatred stemming from guilt, a distrust, a dislike, a contempt, or simply a difference?—at any rate, an attitude that apparently cannot be legislated or "decisioned" out of existence. Perhaps we should have known this; perhaps we should have known that, generally speaking, the laws are dependent on the character of the people, not the reverse, and that laws in conflict with this character or with the sentiment that expresses it will not be obeyed. Perhaps we should have known that this anti-Negro sentiment would not yield to moral exhortation or federal troops or judicial decisions. And perhaps we should have known the price of a failure to recognize the limits of law.

This paper is not concerned with the failure of the exhortation—that, at least, is harmless—or with the use of troops; its concern is the unceasing effort to use the agencies of law against this anti-Negro sentiment, in the opinion or hope that the law will solve the problem. More precisely, it is concerned with the Supreme Court's failure to recognize the limits of the law and with the damage done to the law because of this failure. Not resting on principles "that satisfy the mind," as one friendly critic has said,[2] some of these decisions may not only fail to achieve their purpose (with what consequences to the morale of those who relied on them?), but they pose a serious threat to certain basic principles of American government, and they threaten to promote a contempt for the Court and for the law in general. In short, in its efforts, unsupported by public sentiment, to make Negroes a part of "the people of the United States" in every sense, the Court is threatening the true character and force of the Constitution ordained and established by "the people of the United States."

UNPRINCIPLED DECISIONS

It is outrageous for a state to take no action against the likes of Claude Screws, the Georgia sheriff who arrested a young Negro for the alleged theft of a tire, handcuffed him, then beat him to death with a "solid-bar blackjack about eight inches long and weighing two pounds."[3] Surely it is frustrating to see the state refuse to act and to see Screws acquitted of the only federal crime for which he could be indicted, that of willfully depriving Hall, the Negro, not of his life, but of his constitutional right not to be deprived of his life without due process of law, that is, without a fair trial. The *Screws* case involved a particularly heinous offense, but there are many injustices, and many of them hiding behind the barriers, or within the interstices, of the federal system. This explains, although it does not justify, the Court's impatience with the various limitations of the federal government's authority, and its willingness sometimes to sacrifice "principled adjudication," to "cut corners," to "take short cuts"—in brief, to be guided primarily, if not wholly, by a determination to redress the imbalance against Negroes, rather than by principles of constitutional law.

Most civil rights cases come to the Supreme Court under the Fourteenth and Fifteenth Amendments, but not all of them. Some have come under the commerce clause,[4] whose principles Thomas Reed Powell, one of the most distinguished of all authorities on the American Constitution, once said he could state in three sentences: "Congress may regulate interstate commerce. The states may also regulate interstate commerce, but not too much. How much is too much is beyond the scope of this statement."[5] The continuing problem in commerce clause cases arises when Congress has not regulated a subject of commerce; and since the first case in 1824, the Court has had the duty of deciding whether, in the absence of federal law, a particular state law, such as a licensing act or a tax, obstructs the free flow of commerce among the states, or constitutes a burden on it. Such cases will come to the Supreme Court so long as the federal system is maintained. One such case, which is also a civil rights case, is *Bob-Lo Excursion Co. v. Michigan*, decided in 1948.[6]

Bois Blanc Island (known in Detroit as Bob-Lo Island) lies just above the mouth of the Detroit River, fifteen miles upstream from the city. It is a part of the Province of Ontario, Canada, but almost all of it is owned by the Bob-Lo Excursion Company and is used as an amusement park for Detroiters, who are transported to it on two steamships owned by the company. In 1945, the company refused passage to a Negro girl, a member of a group of school girls on a holiday, on one of its steamships plying between Detroit and the island. For this it was convicted of violating a Michigan civil rights statute, and the Supreme Court of the

United States, on appeal, upheld the conviction. The company argued, citing a number of precedents in its favor, that the state law was unconstitutional as applied to its steamship because the steamship was engaged in foreign commerce, which only Congress may regulate. But the Court, not by any means unanimously, said, essentially, that though this was foreign commerce, it was not very foreign, and that therefore the state might regulate at least this aspect of it. One has only to change a couple of the presumably nonmaterial facts in the case to recognize that this case was not decided on the basis of any principle flowing from the commerce clause.

Suppose the action had arisen in Texas, for example, and the steamship carried passengers from Brownsville to some Mexican island, and that the excursion company refused passage to a Negro girl. There is no doubt whatever that if the company acted by virtue of a state segregation law, that law (in 1948) would have been invalidated as an unconstitutional regulation of foreign commerce; and if the company acted without authority from state law but simply on its own, it would have been held to have violated the Interstate Commerce Act. The decisive fact in the *Bob-Lo* case had nothing to do with whether the commerce involved was foreign or intrasate; the decisive fact was that the state law favored the Negro—just as in a case decided two years before, in which the Court had struck down a Virginia statute requiring segregation on buses,[7] including interstate buses, the decisive fact was the discrimination against the Negro. Yet both cases are indexed under commerce, and the opinions of the Court purport to be explications of the law of the commerce clause. True, not much had to be sacrificed in order to reach the decision upholding the right of a Negro girl to make the voyage to Bob-Lo Island with her classmates— the law of the commerce clause has survived decisions as unprincipled as that in the Bob-Lo case—but this one case is by no means unique.

Arkansas public school teachers are hired on a year-to-year basis. In 1958, the state enacted a statute compelling

every teacher, as a condition of employment, to submit an
affidavit listing all the organizations to which he belonged or
to which he had regularly contributed within the preceding
five years. B.T. Shelton, a teacher in the Little Rock schools
and a member of the National Association for the
Advancement of Colored People, suspecting, not without
reason, that members of the NAACP were not likely to have
their contracts renewed, refused to file the affidavit and
petitioned a federal district court to declare the statute
unconstitutional. This the district court refused to do, but
the Supreme Court reversed. With four justices dissenting,
the Court held the statute unconstitutional. On what
grounds? Not, quite evidently, on the ostensible grounds.

The Court did not hold that the states have no authority to
compel teachers to disclose the names of the associations to
which they belonged; indeed, it said "there can be no
question of the relevance of a State's inquiry into the fitness
and competence of its teachers," and it conceded implicitly
that to judge fitness and competence, the state may inquire
into a teacher's associations. "The question to be decided,"
the Court said, "is not whether the State of Arkansas can ask
certain of its teachers about all their organizational
relationships," but rather whether it may "ask every one of
its teachers to disclose every single organization with which
he has been associated over a five-year period."[8] Many
associational ties, it went on, "could have no possible bearing
upon the teacher's . . . competence or fitness." But if the state
may ask certain of its teachers about all their organizational
relationships," then it is not true that many of them "have no
possible bearing upon the teacher's . . . competence or
fitness"; all of them may have some bearing some time. At
any rate, the Court did not attempt to determine which
associational ties are related to competence or fitness and
which are not. All it said was that the statute was too broad—
while conceding that under some circumstances a statute
with the broadest possible scope, such as the one involved in
this case, would be perfectly valid. The four dissenters
expressed their view of all this with less acerbity than is

customary in such cases, perhaps because they agreed that it was a nasty thing Arkansas was (probably) trying to do to Negro teachers who belonged to the NAACP.

Nothing Mr. Justice Stewart said in his opinion for the majority can disguise what Alexander Bickel has called the decision's lack of "intellectual coherence."[9] This statute was invalidated, not because it was too broad, but because it was aimed at the NAACP; not because there was no rational connection between it and a state's legitimate interest in the competence or fitness of its teachers, but because five members of the Court, being determined to extend the protection of the Constitution to Negroes whenever they are threatened by a state law, were willing to forget the "restraints that attend constitutional adjudication," as Mr. Justice Harlan put it in dissent. Arkansas lost, not for any reason stated in the Court's opinion, but simply because it was engaged in a reprehensible course of action against its Negro citizens that the Court, with no more than a "thus saith the Lord," called unconstitutional.

To some undefinable extent, however, the Constitution also lost, because the force of its authority depends ultimately on the authority of the force wielded in its name. As two law professors recently had occasion to say about the state action doctrine, "formulas tend to catch up with the Court when they are empty. But more serious are the consequences of such a failing of candor for the rule of law. Law does not rule when the motivations behind judicial decisions are kept hidden. Reasoned opinions announce the law only when the stated reasons truly reflect the real reasons for deciding."[10] Though we may wish it to be otherwise, and though it is frustrating to have to acknowledge helplessness in the face of gross miscarriages of justice, it is entirely possible that there are some unjust acts that are not, by that fact alone, unconstitutional. And it is also possible that, finally, there is no remedy in federal law for these injustices, and that the attempt to provide one will lead to other injustices by damaging the Constitution itself.

Acting under the authority of the cumbersome Civil

Rights Act of 1957, the United States Civil Rights
Commission received some 67 formal complaints from
individual Negroes charging Louisiana voting registrars with
having deprived them of their right to vote because of their
race or color, contrary to the Fifteenth Amendment. A
hearing was scheduled in Shreveport during midsummer,
1959, and subpoenas were served on the registrars ordering
them to appear with various voting and registration records.
The Commission refused to disclose the identity of the
persons making the complaints or the specific charges made;
furthermore, it informed the registrars that they would not
be permitted to cross-examine any witnesses at the hearing.
Under these circumstances, the registrars refused to obey the
subpoenas, and filed a complaint in the federal district court
alleging that the Commission had not been authorized by the
Civil Rights Act to adopt such rules of procedure, and, if it
had been so authorized, that the Act was unconstitutional.
The district court, agreeing with the registrars that the
allegations raised a serious constitutional issue, found that
Congress had not specifically authorized such rules. The
Civil Rights Commission appealed.

The issues raised were similar to some of those involved
in cases concerning congressional investigations. Like them,
the proposed civil rights hearing was not an adjudicatory
proceeding; like the typical committee of Congress, the
Commission does not indict, issue orders, punish, or impose
any legal sanction. Both bodies are confined to investigation
and finding facts, although this limited function has not
permitted congressional committees to escape criticism, a
great deal of it from the Supreme Court, and a great deal of
that from Chief Justice Warren. Here, however, he wrote the
opinion of the Court upholding the Commission, citing the
practices of congressional committees as authority! Only
Douglas, with Black, dissented: " . . . important as these civil
rights are, it will not do to sacrifice other civil rights to
protect them."

We live and work under a Constitution. The temptation of
many men of goodwill is to cut corners, take short cuts, and

reach the desired end regardless of the means. Worthy as I think the ends are which the Civil Rights Commission advances in these cases, I think the particular means used are unconstitutional.[11]

Douglas went on to point out that if the charges against the registrars were true, and if they had acted willfully, they were criminally responsible under a federal statute. The Commission is an arm of the Executive, and there is, he said, "only one way the Chief Executive may move against a person accused of a crime and deny him the right of confrontation and cross-examination and that is by the grand jury." The grand jury brings "suspects before neighbors, not strangers," and therefore protects him. "The grand jury, adopted as a safeguard against 'hasty, malicious, and oppressive' action by the Federal Government . . . stands as an important safeguard to the citizen against open and public accusations of crime."[12]

A grand jury, made up of "neighbors, not strangers," was impanelled in Bibb County, Georgia, in 1960 and charged by the judges of the Superior Court of the county with the duty to investigate the "persistent rumors and accusations" of the illegal use of money in connection with the solicitation of Negro votes, and to determine the truth or falsity of them. A man named Wood was the elected sheriff of the county, and the day following the impanelling of the grand jury, he issued a press release denouncing the judges and, allegedly, threatening the jurors. "'It seems incredible,' he said in one part of this statement, 'that all three of our Superior Court Judges, who themselves hold high political office, are so politically naive as to actually believe that the negro voters in Bibb County sell their votes in any fashion, either to candidates for office or to some negro leaders.'" As to the grand jury, he hoped it would "'not let its high office be a party to any political attempt to intimidate the negro people in this community.'" Not content with this, the following day he delivered to the bailiff stationed at the entrance to the grand jury room, an open letter to the grand jury in which he asserted that the judges' charge was false and that the local

Democratic Executive Committee was responsible for the purchasing of votes and that the grand jury "'would be well-advised . . . to investigate that organization.'"[13] For these acts he was cited for contempt, given a hearing, and adjudged guilty. This judgment was affirmed on appeal in the state courts, and he appealed to the Supreme Court of the United States, alleging that he had been deprived of his freedom of speech under the First and Fourteenth Amendments.

Anglo-American courts have long taken a serious view of such publications. In fact, a federal statute provides punishment up to six months imprisonment or a fine up to $1000 for anyone who "attempts to influence the action or decision of any grand or petit juror of any court of the United States [i.e., not a state court] upon any issue or matter pending before such juror, or before the jury of which he is a member, or pertaining to his duties, by writing or sending to him any written communication, in relation to such issue or matter. . . . "[14] And Justice Holmes once said that even publications not sent to, but merely likely to reach the eyes of a jury "would be none the less a contempt" even if containing nothing but true statements. "The theory of our system," he said, "is that the conclusions to be reached in a case will be induced only by evidence and argument in open court, and not by any outside influence, whether of private talk or public print."[15]

There is no question but that the Supreme Court had, even before *Wood* v. *Georgia*, restricted the freedom of a state judge to punish out-of-court comment on pending cases and had, conversely, enlarged the freedom to comment on such cases.[16] Since 1941, the rule has been that the comment must constitute a "clear and present danger," or an imminent, and not merely a likely, threat to the administration of justice before it can be punished as a contempt. (The rule has led to a reversal of the contempt judgment in every case in which it has been applied.) But here the Court went further. The Georgia judges had determined that Wood's publications "presented a clear and present danger to the proceedings of the court and grand jury"; but Chief Justice Warren, along with Justices Black and Douglas, Brennan and Stewart, held that the findings of clear and present danger were unsupported in the trial record, and Warren went on to say that there was no "showing of an actual interference with the undertakings of the grand jury." Now, whatever might be said about the use of the clear and present danger test as a rule governing the issue, it would seem that the test does not require a showing of actual interference, but only of an imminent danger of such interference. Justice Harlan, in dissent, said that the "Court cannot mean that attempts to influence judicial proceedings are punishable only if they are successful."[17] Yet one cannot be sure that the Court did not mean just that, and if it did, then it will have gone a long way toward eliminating entirely the old rule prohibiting out-of-court comment on matters pending in state courts, for it would seem almost impossible to adduce evidence proving the success of attempts to influence or coerce the judgments or decisions of judges or jurors. Would this require a confession from the judge or juror that he had acted out of fear of the likes of Sheriff Wood? Or would a fellow judge be permitted to determine the success of the attempt by evaluating the decision made by the judge or juror?

In its solicitude for Sheriff Wood, who, it must not be forgotten, purported to speak for the Negroes of Bibb County, the Supreme Court extended the rule in still another direction. Prior to this case, the clear and present danger test had not been applied to out-of-court publications addressed to members of *a jury* before their verdict was announced. In each previous case, it was *the judge's* act that was pending. In the 1941 case, for example, the defendants had been found guilty but had not yet been sentenced when the *Los Angeles Times* had editorialized on the case, telling the judge that he ought to send the defendants to the "jute-mill." In the *Wood* case, for the first time, the Court held that attempts to influence a jury are punishable only according to the clear and present danger test. Yet, the distinction drawn, or formerly drawn, between attempts to influence or coerce a judge and attempts to influence or coerce a jury is not fictitious. Justice Harlan spoke to this point in his dissenting opinion in the *Wood* case:

> Of equal if not greater importance is the fact that petitioner's statements were calculated to influence, not a judge chosen because of his independence, integrity, and courage and trained by experience and the discipline of law to deal only with evidence properly before him, but a grand jury of laymen chosen to serve for a limited term from the general population of Bibb County. It cannot be assumed with grand jurors, as it has been with judges . . . that they are all "men of fortitude, able to thrive in a hardy climate." What may not seriously endanger the independent deliberations of a judge may well jeopardize those of a grand or petit jury.[18]

Jeopardizing the "independent deliberations" of a jury is a polite way of saying "intimidating a jury" (and is there not possibility that Sheriff Wood was doing precisely this by issuing his statement?), and an intimidated jury has no place in the fair administration of justice. In fact, the loss of the power to punish out-of-court contempt jeopardizes, under conditions that are by no means rare in this country, the very possibility of a fair trial before an impartial jury; and such a trial before such a jury is a constitutional right.

Almost exactly one year before the *Wood* case, the Supreme Court vacated a death sentence in a murder case coming from Indiana on the ground that the jury was not impartial, and it was not impartial because it was subjected to a tremendous volume of publicity adverse to the accused. As Justice Frankfurter said in his concurring opinion:

> How can fallible men and women reach a disinterested verdict based exclusively on what they heard in the court when, before they entered the jury box, their minds were saturated by press and radio for months preceding by matter designed to establish the guilt of the accused. A conviction so secured obviously constitutes a denial of due process of law in its most rudimentary conception.[19]

More immediately relevant is the problem of "trial by newspaper" in a southern court in which a Negro is on trial, and here the *Wood* decision may have serious and detrimental consequences for the Negro's cause, because it may make it even more difficult for a Negro to obtain a fair trial. In 1949, in Lake County, Florida, a seventeen-year-old white girl reported that she had been raped, at pistol point, by four Negroes. A week later a grand jury indicted Samuel Shepherd and one other Negro for this offense, and a month later they were convicted and sentenced to death. The Supreme Court of the United States reversed without opinion, citing an earlier case holding that the method of jury selection discriminated against Negroes. Justices Jackson and Frankfurter concurred in the result, and they contributed an opinion. The real evil in the case, as they saw it, was the extent to which "prejudicial influences outside the courtroom, becoming all too typical of a highly publicized trial, were brought to bear on this jury with such force that the conclusion is inescapable that these defendants were prejudged as guilty and the trial was but a legal gesture to register a verdict already dictated by the press and the public opinion . . . generated."[20] The presence of Negroes on the jury could not have made this trial a fair one. Mobs had burned the home of Shepherd's parents, and two other Negro houses; Negroes had to be moved out of the community to save them from being lynched, and others fled; the National Guard had to be called out to maintain order; and the newspapers did their best to fan the flames of racial hatred. One of them published, during the "deliberations" of the grand jury, a cartoon "picturing four electric chairs and headed, 'No Compromise—Supreme Penalty.'" As Jackson said: "I do not see, as a practical matter, how any Negro on the jury would have dared to cause a disagreement or acquittal."

> The only chance these Negroes had of acquittal would have been in the courage and decency of some sturdy and forthright white person of sufficient standing to face and live down the odium among his white neighbors that such a vote, if required, would have brought. To me, the technical question of

discrimination in the jury selection has only theoretical importance. The case presents one of the best examples of one of the worst menaces to American justice.[21]

Verdicts of petit juries can be vacated by an appellate court, but this is by no means a satisfactory solution to the problem. The indictment of Leslie Irvin, the accused in the Indiana murder case, was returned on April 21, 1955, more than six years before the Supreme Court vacated the death sentence and remanded the case with instructions permitting a new trial; and some time in the future the Supreme Court of the United States will, almost certainly, be asked once again to review the case, for the press, less restricted now than ever before, will surely have something to say about a person who is said to have confessed to six murders committed back in 1954 and 1955 and who has managed for all these years to "cheat the chair." "Trial by newspaper" is not due process of law, and perhaps the best way to prevent such trials is to put the press—newspapers, radio, and television—on notice that they can be punished for contempt. This was the conclusion in 1961 of two law professors, one from Yale and the other from New York University:

> Perhaps the most effective way to give real meaning to the guarantee of an impartial jury trial in the United States is to restore the contempt power to the courts. Is it possible [however] to draft a narrow contempt statute that would survive American constitutional limitations and still be effective?[22]

Since *Wood* v. *Georgia* in 1962, these judge-made constitutional limitations are more severe than ever.

Since when have Georgia sheriffs enjoyed a reputation that justifies their being made the beneficiaries of new, and potentially dangerous, rules of law? Have we reached the point where legal penalties can be avoided, not only by defending the Negro's cause—one is entitled to doubt that this is what Sheriff Wood was really doing—but merely by purporting to defend it? Suppose this had been a federal grand jury, charged with investigating allegations of the use of violence to prevent Negroes from voting in a federal election; and suppose another Georgia sheriff—Claude Screws, for example—had issued statements similar to Wood's. Are we to assume that the Supreme Court's decision would have been the same? And if the Court is going to assume grand jurors to be immune to threats of intimidation, why should it be so eager to protect the anonymity of witnesses in hearings such as those in Shreveport before the Civil Rights Commission?

It is right that a Negro girl should be permitted to join her classmates in an excursion to Bob-Lo Island; but if, as Justice Stone once wrote, judicial opinions "are not better than an excursion ticket, good for this day and trip only, they...would be much better left unsaid."[23] The Supreme Court has no authority to issue "excursion tickets," or to right every wrong brought to its attention; it is a court of law, deriving its power from the authority that law has in a law-abiding community. Its constitutional decisions are supposed to derive from constitutional principles—not from consideration of the immediate consequences to the parties to the case—and its opinions are supposed to elaborate the applicability of the principles to the facts of the case being decided, and to do so in a convincing manner or not at all. To assume the power of a "kadi under a tree dispensing justice according to considerations of individual expediency,"[24] is to cause its authority to be questioned in a way that is certain to damage the law in general. And with what consequences, finally, for the beneficiaries of its decisions?

This country has had experience with a Court that, in Professor Herbert Wechsler's words, "could not articulate an adequate analysis of the restrictions it imposed on Congress,"[25] which is to say, could not support its decisions in favor of its cause—economic freedom—with reasoned constitutional arguments. Justice Day's opinion for a bare majority of the Court in the first child-labor case[26] is absurd, as Holmes and a generation of constitutional lawyers delighted in demonstrating to more than one generation of students; and the child-labor case was not unique. In fact, great judicial reputations were built on dissents in these economic freedom cases. Did these majority justices not damage the cause they sought to uphold by defending it beyond the point where it was defensible? Did they not succeed in bringing judicial review itself into disrepute, not only with a President who would have "packed" the Court, but with many constitutional lawyers, the men whose job it was, and is, to profess the law of the Constitution? A cause cannot long be sustained by judges alone, and if the attempt to do so leads to judicial fiat, the cause is made to appear unworthy.

THE EXTENTION OF "STATE ACTION"

The Fourteenth Amendment provides that all persons "born or naturalized in the United States, and subject to the jurisdiction thereof, are citizens of the United States and of the State wherein they reside." It also provides that no state shall abridge the privileges or immunities of citizens of the United States, or deprive any person of life, liberty, or property without due process of law, or—and it is this provision that has proved most effective in the struggle for Negro equality—"deny to any person within its jurisdiction the equal protection of the laws." Its concluding section authorizes Congress to legislate in order "to enforce . . . the provisions of this article." Acting primarily under this grant of constitutional authority, Congress enacted the Civil Rights Act of 1875, the purpose of which was to secure to all persons the "full and equal enjoyment of the accommodations, advantages, facilities, and privileges of inns, public conveyances . . . theaters and other places of public amusement." Section 2 of this statute made it a penal offense for *any* person, state official or private citizen, to deny to any citizen, because of his race or color, the privileges secured in the first section of the statute.

In five separate cases, known collectively as the *Civil Rights Cases* of 1883, six persons were indicted for denying Negroes accommodations in inns, theaters, and a railroad car. On appeal, the Supreme Court, with only Justice Harlan dissenting, held that the Fourteenth Amendment prohibits only state or official discrimination, which means that the rights established in that amendment (as well as in the Fifteenth Amendment) can be denied only by states, or by persons acting under color of state law (i.e., in the name of the state). This is known as the "state action" doctrine. By providing for the punishment of private discrimination, Congress had exceeded its authority, the Court held. The statute was declared unconstitutional.[27]

So long as the Supreme Court was dealing with discriminatory state laws, or, so long as it was trying to promote equality in the legal sense, the state action doctrine did not stand in the way of effective judicial action on behalf of the victims of such laws. When West Virginia enacted a statute disqualifying Negroes from jury service, the Supreme Court struck it down as a denial of equal protection of the laws.[28] When, even in the absence of a state law requiring or authorizing his action, a Virginia jury commissioner excluded Negroes from jury service, the Court had no difficulty in finding this too to be state action: "Whoever, by virtue of public position under a state government, deprives another of property, life or liberty without due process of law, or denies or takes away the equal protection of the laws, violates the constitutional inhibition; and as he acts in the name [of] and for the State, and is clothed with the State's power, his act is that of the state."[29] And even when the states became more subtle, by enacting laws that did not expressly discriminate against Negroes, the Court still did not hesitate to carry out the mandate of the post-war amendments. A case in point is a 1910 amendment to the Oklahoma constitution that exempted from a literacy test, imposed as a condition of voting, those persons who, on January 1, 1866, or earlier, were entitled to vote, and the descendants of such persons. Other persons, which of course meant Negroes, were required to take the literacy test, which was then administered with a rigor sufficient to bar them from the polls. The Court unanimously declared this provision to be a violation of the Fifteenth Amendment.[30] As Justice

Frankfurter was to say some twenty years later, the amendment "nullifies sophisticated as well as simple-minded modes of discrimination."[31] The same fate befell a state law forbidding Negroes to vote in primary elections, and a subsequent law that, in effect, authorized the central committees of the political parties to do the same thing was also struck down as a denial of equal protection. But when the parties themselves, acting under no authority from the state, excluded Negroes from the primaries, the Court, in 1935, confronted a form of the issue that characterizes most discrimination today: To what extent, if any, is the discriminatory action that of the state? At first, it found no element of state action present: the exclusion of Negroes from the Texas Democratic primary election was held to be the act of a private organization, and, according to the state action rule, was not a violation of a constitutional right;[32] but nine years later it overruled this decision by holding that when a state entrusts a political part with the selection of candidates for public office, that party is an agency of the state and its actions are state actions.[33] Whereupon South Carolina, in an effort to show that it did not entrust political parties with any public function, proceeded to repeal all its statutory provisions regulating primary elections and party organizations, claiming that the parties were "private voluntary associations" and entitled to conduct their affairs, including their elections, as they saw fit. As might be expected, however, this stratagem did not succeed.[34]

These cases illustrate a few of the variety of ways in which some states attempted, despite the commands of the post-Civil War amendments, to continue the exclusion of Negroes from legal membership in the body known as "the people of the United States." In disposing of them, the Court was not always unanimous, but the decisions rested firmly and easily on principles that are embodied, and are readily seen to be embodied, in the amended Constitution. The same cannot be said of many of the decisions that followed, for it is not easy to adhere to the theory of the *Civil Rights Cases*, according to which private conduct is immune to federal law, and simultaneously to find some principle according to which this conduct is not immune to federal law. The Jaybird case shows why.

Here the Court was dealing with what can best be described as a preprimary election. The Jaybird Association was an organization of white voters in Fort Bend County, Texas, that selected its own candidates to run in the Democratic party primary. The successful Jaybird candidates were not compelled to run in the Democratic primary, but they almost always did so and almost always won, both in the primary and in the subsequent general election. The Court held that it was unconstitutional for the Association to exclude Negroes from its elections,[35] even though it would appear to have been a private organization and its actions, however benighted, not the actions of the state of Texas and therefore immune to federal government supervision.[36] Yet eight members of the Court said it was not really private; that is to say, they agreed that the exclusion of Negroes from the Jaybird election was, somehow, the action of the state of Texas, although they could not agree on why, or in what respect, it was the action of the state of Texas. In fact, there is no opinion of the Court in this case. Black, Douglas, and Burton, who announced the Court's judgment, found state action in the fact that the state permitted the Jaybird election:

> For a state to permit such a duplication of its election processes is to permit a flagrant abuse of those processes to defeat the purposes of the Fifteenth Amendment. The use of the county-operated primary to ratify the result of the prohibited election merely compounds the offense. It violates the Fifteenth Amendment for a state, by such circumvention, to permit within its borders the use of any device that produces an equivalent of the prohibited election.[37]

Frankfurter, alone in his concurrence in the judgment, found the case "by no means free of difficulty," but managed to resolve his doubts by finding state action in the fact that county election officials (state officers) voted in the Jaybird preprimary. Unable to accept either of these rules, Clark, Vinson, Reed, and Jackson asserted that the Jaybird

Association was really the Democratic party in "disguise," or was an "auxiliary" of the Democratic party, or an "adjunct" of it. Only Minton could not find state action anywhere, and he dissented.

It is not easy to see what the Negro beneficiaries of the dubious reasoning will gain by being permitted to vote in the Jaybird election. They were legally free to vote in the party primaries and in the general election, and the local politics of Fort Bend County will not change if they are legally free to vote in the Jaybird election. There is no reason to doubt that it was the only election that "counted in this Texas county," or that the Jaybirds existed for a reason having something to do with the desire of the white population to exclude Negroes from a share in the governing of the county—because, perhaps, this was the most convenient way of excluding them. It is not, however, the only way, and since the white population of the county is four times greater than the Negro population, it is probable that the vote of a Negro, if the whites are united, is no more "effective" now than it was before the decision.

On the other hand, it is easy to see why the members of the Court should have trouble agreeing on the rule of the case and why one highly respected constitutional lawyer should look on the decision as a threat to the freedom of association: " . . . the constitutional guarantee against deprivation of the franchise on the ground of race or color has become a prohibition of party organization upon racial lines, at least where the party has achieved political hegemony."[38] Does the decision mean, since the Constitution surely forbids a denial of the franchise on religious grounds, that religious parties are proscribed? Would not such a proscription "infringe rights protected by the first amendment"?

It is also easy to understand why the Court should believe it necessary to "find" state action in what the Jaybirds did. Unless it is somehow extended, the state action rule constitutes a barrier to judical (and, if Congress were disposed to do something, legislative) action with respect to private discrimination, because it prevents federal law from reaching the source of the discrimination, the private individual or group. When, nevertheless, the Court, believing that its decisions will somehow promote Negro membership in "the people of the United States" in the ultimate sense, began the attempt to reach this private discrimination despite the apparent constitutional barrier, it initiated a threat to more than the freedom of association. It began to threaten privacy itself.

The initial step was taken in 1948 in *Shelley* v. *Kraemer,* a case that opened new vistas in the search for state action. Briefly, the facts are as follows: In 1911, the owners of various pieces of property located in a contiguous area in St. Louis, Missouri, entered into a formally recorded agreement known as a racially restrictive real estate covenant providing that for fifty years from that date the occupancy and use of the property would be restricted to persons "of the Caucasian race." In 1945, a property owner broke the agreement by selling a piece of this property to Shelley and his wife, who were Negroes; a Mr. and Mrs. Kraemer, owners of other property subject to the agreement, brought suit to restrain the Shelleys from taking possession. On appeal, the Supreme Court of the United States acknowledged the legality of the covenant itself, an acknowledgement consistent with the doctrine of state action, but held that judicial enforcement of this legal covenant was state action denying the equal protection of the laws and was therefore contrary to the Fourteenth Amendment.

> State action, as that phrase is understood for the purposes of the Fourteenth Amendment, refers to exertions of state power in all forms. And when the effect of that action is to deny rights subject to the protection of the Fourteenth Amendment, it is the obligation of this Court to enforce the constitutional commands.[39]

The *Shelley* rule, in other words, provides a means whereby the Supreme Court can reach certain kinds of private discrimination, which is the only remaining problem of discrimination today, even while acknowledging the legality (within the terms of the *Civil Rights Cases*) of the private discrimination. It does this by denying the assistance of the courts to private persons who discriminate and, thereby, depriving such persons of any means of effecting their discrimination. This became even more obvious five years later when the Court had a case in which one white convenantor broke the racially restrictive agreement by selling a house to a Negro and was sued for damages by a co-covenantor. The problem in the case was whether the party who had acted "illegally" by breaching a legal agreement could rely on the rights of others in her defense to the breach of contract action. The Supreme Court held that an award of damages by a state court would constitute state action depriving—someone—of the equal protection of the laws. But depriving whom? The Negro purchaser had the house and would not stand to lose it whatever the outcome of the suit; the seller was not being deprived of equal protection— the state had in no way discriminated against her. But an award of damages would affect the ability of other Negroes to persuade other covenantors to breach the "legal" agreements they had entered into. So the Court solved the problem by allowing the seller to rely on the rights of "unidentified but identifiable Negroes." Thus, restrictive covenants are legal, but they cannot be enforced in the courts, either directly or, by permitting collection of damages for their breach, indirectly.[40]

But what, precisely, is the meaning of *Shelley* v. *Kraemer?* The Court said in that case "that restrictions on the right of occupancy of the sort sought to be created by the private agreements in these cases could not be squared with the requirements of the Fourteenth Amendment if imposed by state statute or local ordinance.[41] If this statement contains the essence of the *Shelley* rule, if, that is, a state may not do judicially what it is forbidden to do legislatively, the decisions in the sit-in cases would have seemed to follow as a matter of course, because it is quite clear that a state may not by law require separation of the races in privately owned lunch-counters. Essentially, these cases involved Negroes who, upon being refused service at a lunch-counter because of their race or color, refused to leave the premises when asked to do so by the manager, were arrested by the police for trespass, indicted, tried, convicted, and sentenced to jail. As might be expected, the southern state judges, in the course of rejecting the Negroes' constitutional arguments on appeal, discovered a difference of constitutional proportions between state action that enforces a discriminatory real estate covenant and state action that enforces other kinds of private discrimination; but they did not succeed in demonstrating in what this difference is supposed to consist. Such a demonstration would not be easy, for, if it is solely the enforcement of these acts that is illegal, if the private discriminatory acts themselves are not illegal under the Constitution, then there is no principle in the *Shelley* case that permits the drawing of a distinction among the *equally legal* private acts.

In its decisions of May 20, 1963, the Supreme Court did not even essay such a distinction. It avoided the question altogether, by denying that the cases involved private discrimination, and it was able to do this because Greenville, South Carolina, where the leading case originated, had an ordinance requiring separate lunch-counter facilities for Negroes, and the Court held that the decision to refuse service originated in that ordinance, not in a private decision of the store manager.[42] New Orleans did not have such an ordinance, but the Court placed the blame on the city anyway. Shortly before the incident that gave rise to the case, the mayor and the police superintendent had issued statements condemning and urging an end to the sit-in demonstrations taking place in the city, and the Court held that the store's refusal to serve the Negroes had been "coerced" by these statements.[43] Thus, the Court found illegal state action not in police or judicial enforcement of private discrimination—the *Shelley* situation—but in the discriminatory act itself, and it left the grave question first raised in *Shelley* unanswered.

It cannot go unanswered for long. The ordinances will be repealed, the city officials will remain silent, and the Court will then be confronted with a sit-in case in which the basic question, the question of the extent to which private persons are permitted to rely on the law to enforce their "preferences," cannot be avoided; and the Court will have to define the *Shelley* rule.[44] It will not be any easier then than it would have been this year to limit its application to only some private discriminatory acts if, as Professor John P. Frank once said, "logic is to be maintained."[45] But logic, especially very troubling logic, need not be maintained and there are very good reasons why it should not be maintained in the next round of sit-in cases.

Let us assume that the Court were to apply the *Shelley* rule. This would mean that lunch-counters in states that do not have anti-discrimination laws are legally free to discriminate against Negroes, but that the Fourteenth Amendment forbids a state to enforce the discrimination. Thus, just as a person is within his legal rights when he enters into a restrictive real estate contract, he is also within his legal rights when he refuses to serve Negroes at his lunch-counter; in neither case, however, may he rely on the law to enforce his discrimination. But there is a difference between these two situations that now becomes visible. In the first case, the white covenantor, for whatever reasons (and this is, after all, a pre-condition of the litigation), ceases to discriminate when he sells his property to a Negro. No such event has occurred in the second case; not only is the store manager entitled to discriminate, but so far as we know, or may know, he wants to discriminate against Negroes and will continue to do so in the future. What becomes visible here is the problem of enforcement, and the problem of enforcement cannot be solved within even the expanded state-action doctrine.

To begin with, the lunch-counter manager will be entitled to take the law into his own hands in order to enforce his acknowledged right to discriminate against whom he pleases—that is, to resort to what the law calls "self-help." It is sometimes assumed that racial discrimination cannot exist without the help of the law, and that the store owners and managers will not resort to the use of force, even if the states give them—as they probably will give them—a greater latitude to do so. Against this optimistic assumption, and the evidence from places like Durham, North Carolina, that supports it, must be placed such events as those of Oxford, Mississippi, and the possibility of similar events in other parts of the South. Will white southerners acquiesce or will they, as they are relentlessly pursued by the federal law, turn vengefully on Negroes when that law gives them the opportunity? In either case, there is surely something wrong with legal principles whose application may provoke violence and that, at the same time, regard that violence as perfectly legal. Yet the meaning of the *Shelley* doctrine as applied to sit-in cases in this manner is that the manager may, under the Constitution, discriminate against Negroes, and may, under both the Constitution and local law, authorize thugs or "bouncers" to use physical force to remove Negroes from his premises.

The way to avoid this possibility, and it is likely that the Court will avoid it, is to forgo a reliance on the *Shelley* rule and to expand the state-action doctrine in another direction, that is, by ruling that the owners or managers of businesses open to the public are acting under color of state law when they discriminate against some members of the public. Then it would not be legal for them to discriminate on the basis of race or color, and they would not be entitled to utilize "self-help." This would solve one aspect of the enforcement problem, for the criminal statute[46] under which Claude Screws, the brutal Georgia sheriff, was indicted would be available to federal prosecutors, and, in addition, there is a civil statute permitting an injured party to bring a damage suit against any "person who, under color of any statute, ordinance, regulation, custom, or usage of any State" deprives him of a right secured by the Constitution or by federal law,[47] including, if the Court adopts this approach, the right to service at a nonsegregated lunch counter open to the public.

The difficulty is that in both criminal and civil actions enforcement of the right will depend on the co-operation of local juries. Even assuming, however, that these juries will act in the worst possible manner and simply refuse to convict or award damages, or even to return an indictment, there is still another way to enforce a federal law against discrimination: an injured party can always petition a federal court for an injunction against the offending lunch-counter manager, and failure to obey an injunction is punishable as a contempt of court, a judgment in which juries play no part. This leaves the problem of what to do with the white customers—for example, the high school students at the favorite soda fountain, or their older brothers at the favorite tavern—who violently object to Negroes joining them at the counter or bar. It is difficult to see how they could be enjoined (unlike the managers, they would not be acting under color of state law and, therefore, would not be acting in violation of a federal law), nor is there a federal statute under which they could be punished.[48] Perhaps the answer to this is to be found in the words of Justice Holmes: "the law does all that is needed when it does all it can,"[49] and that the Court will have reached the point where it must rely on the demonstrated willingness of most Americans, under most circumstances, to obey the law (or, in this case, the spirit of the law).

It should be understood that this approach to the sit-in cases involves the reversal of the holding in the *Civil Rights Cases* of 1883, for the Court held in these cases that the discrimination practiced by inns, theaters, and railroads was not state action. The Court does not casually reverse its constitutional decisions, especially those of such long standing and on which so much depends. Yet, so grave are the implications of *Shelley* v. *Kraemer*, that the Court would nevertheless be adopting the less radical approach if it were to hold that businesses open to the public exercise a public responsibility, and that their acts are state acts.

It is the consideration of what lies beyond the sit-in cases if they are eventually settled on the basis of the *Shelley* rule that is surely troubling more than one of the justices of the Court,[50] just as it has troubled more than one legal commentator. For courts are needed to enforce not only the law of contracts, as in *Shelley*, or the law of trespass, as in the sit-in cases; they are needed to enforce all the laws, including the laws of wills and of charitable trusts. A state may not by law forbid white testators to dispose of their property to Negroes, nor may it forbid the creation of a charitable trust that includes Negroes among its beneficiaries. Does this mean that a court may not enforce a will that draws a racial line or appoint trustees to administer a trust the benefits of which are limited to a particular racial or religious group? Even Professor Louis H. Pollak sees the need to draw a line beyond which *Shelley* should not be extended.

> The line sought to be drawn is that beyond which the state assists a private person in seeing to it that others behave in a fashion which the state could not itself have ordained. The principle underlying the distinction is this: the fourteenth amendment permits each his personal prejudices and guarantees him free speech and press and worship, together with a degree of free economic enterprise, as instruments with which to persuade others to adopt his prejudices; but access to state aid to induce others to conform is barred.[51]

Applied to concrete cases, Pollak's argument means that the host may rely on the police to remove undesired guests, that the lunch-counter manager may rely on the police to remove undesired customers; but that a testator may not rely on a probate court to enforce a provision in a will barring any share in the estate of a child who *in the future* marries outside the testator's faith,[52] because the enforcement of this provision would be to "induce compliance by others with the . . . testator's prejudices."[53] With all respect, I cannot find *in the Fourteenth Amendment* a recognition of a difference between enforcing a will that disinherits a son who has already married outside the faith, and enforcing a will that threatens to disinherit the son if he should, later on, marry outside the faith.

More immediately relevant, however, is the way in which Professor Pollak's distinction works in practice: the father is not permitted to "coerce" his son[54] with respect to a matter of obvious, perhaps even overriding importance to him, but the Kress lunch-counter is permitted to call the police to enforce its discrimination against an entire class of citizens.[55] Yet to me, the latter act is more reprehensible, for, unlike Professor Pollak, I am unwilling to say that the father who attempts, even by using his money, to perpetuate the faith of his father is prejudiced; and I am unwilling to say this in part (but only in part) because I do not think I possess the knowledge that allows me to refer to religious belief as prejudice. Beyond this, can we not say that there *is* a difference between behavior based on a love of one's own and of one's own faith, and behavior based on a hatred or dislike of others? Can we not agree that in most cases the perpetuation of religious belief is not contrary to the common good of the United States? Even Justice Douglas once said that Americans "are a religious people whose institutions presuppose a Supreme Being."[56]

Finally, what would be the effect on charitable trusts of the use of *Shelley* in the sit-in cases? Trusts abound in this country,[57] and most of them restrict their benefits to a particular group. What would be the status of a trust endowing an orphanage for poor Methodist children, for instance, or a "senior citizens' home" for Episcopalians, or, for that matter, a school for poor Negro children? This is discrimination. Is it therefore illegal for the state to allow them to exist, or for a probate court to appoint a fiduciary, or, having determined that they are truly charities, for the state to grant them tax immunities? The Court resisted the temptation, or at least, refused the request, to so rule when the *Girard College* case came up for the second time;[58] but it is difficult to see how the Court could apply the *Shelley* rule to the discrimination involved in the sit-in cases and withhold it from the discrimination involved in charitable trusts. Nor do recent cases provide any confidence that the Court will restrain itself again. In *Burton* v. *Wilmington Parking Authority*, a Negro petitioned for a court order forbidding racial discrimination by a privately-owned restaurant located in space leased from a parking authority that was an agency of the state of Delaware. With three dissenters, and with Mr. Justice Stewart concurring separately, the Court managed to find the required element of state action by "nimbly fetching enough connections to treat the state as the culprit,"[59] while resolutely continuing to insist that private discrimination "does no violence to the Equal Protection Clause" of the Fourteenth Amendment.[60] This prompted Mr. Justice Harlan to protest:

> The Court's opinion, by a process of first undis-criminatingly throwing together various factual bits and pieces and then undermining the resulting structure by an equally vague disclaimer, seems to me to leave completely at sea just what it is in this record that satisfies the requirement of "state action."[61]

It seems obvious that this is a Court that will not easily be satisfied to strike down discrimination only when it is the action of the state, especially when, as time passes, it becomes ever clearer that private discrimination can in fact exist without the support of state laws, and even in the face of state laws, and when the achievement by Negroes of legal membership in the American community is not followed by membership in the ultimate sense.

LAW AND SENTIMENT

Where is the least student of the law who cannot erect a moral code as pure as that of Plato's law? But this is not the only issue. The problem is to adapt this code to the people for which it is made and to the things about which it decrees to such an extent that its execution follows from the very conjunction of these relations; it is to impose on the people, after the fashion of Solon, less the best laws in themselves than the best of which it admits in the given situation. Otherwise, it is better to let the disorders subsist than to forestall them, or take steps thereto, by laws which will not be observed. For without remedying the evil, this degrades the laws too.[62]

Whichever approach the Court adopts in the sit-in cases*—

---

*In the event, Congress came to the Court's rescue when it was passed the legislation referred to in note 71, intra, the Civil Rights Act of 1964. Title II of this Act forbids discrimination by hotels, restaurants, etc., engaged in interstate commerce. This was upheld in *Heart of Atlanta Motel* v. *United States*, 379 U.S. 241 (1964).

the mechanical application of what appears to be the *Shelley* rule or the expansion of state action to include managers of businesses open to the public[63]—the Court will have effected profound changes in American institutions and will threaten more. To rule that the local police and courts may not enforce private discrimination is to jeopardize the privacy of clubs, of wills, of trusts, and theoretically, but so remotely as not to deserve more than a mention, of homes; and to rule that a local lunch-counter manager is, even if only in some respects, an official of the state whose conduct in the course of his business is subject to federal control is drastically to affect the character of the federal system. Changes of this magnitude are not unprecedented, but, except in other cases involving Negro rights, school segregation being the best example, such changes have not in the past been made by courts. Surely Professor Robert A. Horn is correct in saying that the *Civil Rights Cases* rest "upon a theory of American federalism which cannot be reconciled with that developed and accepted by the Supreme Court in the great series of cases interpreting national powers" since 1937,[64] and now that the justice who was least willing to upset the "federal balance," Justice Frankfurter, is no longer on the bench, it may be possible for the Court to abolish this anachronism; but the reference to the vast national powers in other areas— labor relations, for instance, and agriculture—is misleading. The assertion of national power in these areas was made by the national legislative and executive authorities, organized by a national political party, and supported by popular majorities—an overwhelming majority in 1936: the Court did not initiate these massive changes; it merely accepted them, after first resisting them. These changes were made, and made successfully, with the consent of the governed, expressed in the constitutionally prescribed manner. It is by no means obvious that all of what the Court is trying to do for the Negro has such consent, and to proceed without strong evidence of consent is to ignore, or at least to challenge, the limits of the law.

The law has surely demonstrated its ability to "alter race relations"—indeed, the evidence produced by Jack

Greenberg, now director counsel of the NAACP, supports his thesis that "in many places law has been the greatest single factor inducing racial change." But there is little evidence that the law, by working on the "underlying attitudes," can bring about these changes with the "willing consent" of the white persons affected.[65] There is no reason to doubt that the desegregation of the armed forces has led to Negroes being accepted by white soldiers, sailors, and airmen (the complaints of discrimination are lodged mainly against officers); but in the civilian world, the world affected by the school and restrictive covenant decisions, the old attitudes are unchanged, or if changed, only for the worse. According to Morton Grodzins, "racial passions are on the rise and find less community restraint" among the white groups on the fringe of Negro neighborhoods in the large metropolitan areas in the North. This is true even though "segregation is more complete than it ever was for Negro rural residents in the South." There is evidence of some progress, but the preponderant evidence points in the other direction. "The larger evidence is not that of integration [or] intra-community social gains. Rather it is in the direction of more uncompromising segregation and larger Negro slums."[66] Progress cannot be measured by the number of favorable Supreme Court decisions; we deceive ourselves if we think it can. Indeed, in the case of decisions attempting to promote full Negro membership in the American community, the opposite may be true.

In November, 1962, more than eight years after the school desegregation decisions, the number of Negroes in schools with whites in the southern and border states, including Washington, D.C., was 255,367, or 7.8 per cent of the total Negro enrollment; the comparable figure for May, 1960, was 181,020, or 6 per cent. But these figures conceal a significant element of the situation. More than one-third (87,749) of the total number of Negroes in schools with whites are in Washington, where Negroes constitute 83.4 per cent of the total public school enrollment. This means that one-third of the Negroes in "schools with whites" attend schools that, in fact, are almost wholly Negro.[67] Of the remaining two-thirds, the vast majority are in schools in the border states where the situation is similar to that in Washington. Legal desegregation is not desegregation in fact. In the eleven so-called deep South states, containing most of the Negro school population (2,803,882 students), only 12,217 students, or .44 per cent, are in school with whites.

What is worse, segregation among the inhabitants of Washington and the other cities directly involved in the restrictive covenant suits is probably more pronounced now than it was in 1948, when the decisions were handed down. Whites have simply moved out of the cities; in Washington, for example, the white population declined from 66 per cent of the total in 1948 to 46 per cent in 1960. This exodus is not the result solely of the school and restrictive covenant decisions—various factors having nothing to do with racial problems are at work here—but the decisions certainly contributed to it. If the NAACP's purpose in bringing the covenant suits was to make more housing available to Negroes, it succeeded (although the demand still exceeds the supply by a wide margin, because the "Negro population always increases faster than the living space available to it"[68]), but it certainly did not succeed in integrating the neighborhoods. In St. Louis, the white population of the area surrounding and including the Labadie Avenue district, the district involved directly in *Shelley* v. *Kraemer*, declined from 82.2 per cent of the total in 1950 to 28.1 per cent in 1960, and Labadie Avenue itself is apparently 100 per cent Negro. In Detroit, the white population of the affected area declined from 77.6 per cent to 12.5 per cent in the same decade, and the 4600 block of Seeboldt Avenue is 100 per cent Negro. The restrictive covenants were replaced at first by "evasionary agreements," but these were short-lived and "of only limited effectiveness," as Jack Greenberg put it. "By and large they leave the housing market subject to other forces."[69] They do indeed, and the result is Negro "ghettos." "The only interracial communities in the U.S., with the exception of a few abject slums, are those where limits exist upon the influx of nonwhites."[70]

The nationwide discrimination against Negroes, manifested in so many ways, does not, of course, preclude a nationwide consent to decisions according Negroes a legal membership in the body known as "the people of the United States." Except in places like Mississippi, Negroes vote with the consent of the governed, their right to a fair trial is acknowledged, as is their right to decent treatment at the hands of the police. What does not appear to have that consent are decisions attempting to force whites to go to school with Negroes or to live in the same neighborhoods with them. The law certainly altered race relations in this country, but it has not been able to abolish racial hatred, distrust, prejudice, or whatever it is that underlies the racial problem.

Yet it might be argued that the law's inability to overcome racial prejudice has not been demonstrated, that what has been demonstrated is the inadequacy of the law available to federal courts, that these courts have been inhibited by the limited scope of national constitutional rights inherited from the post-Civil War Supreme Court. The solution, for those who continue to argue in this fashion, is new law, a new decision by the Court that authorizes Congress to punish manifestations of racial discrimination wherever it occurs.[71] But racial prejudice is not in itself unconstitutional, and it will manifest itself at least in those places where it is not reached by the law. More to the point is the probability, for which there is some evidence, that, as those places become fewer and fewer, as the Court flushes it from one cover after another, expanding the public sphere as it contracts the private, the prejudice will turn on the Court and on the law itself. The means are available to it; the bigoted have the ballot and the voting booth is still private, and must remain so in a free country. In Alabama, George Wallace is elected governor over the liberal Jim Folsom; in Louisiana, Jimmy Davis defeats de Lesseps Morrison;[72] and in Arkansas, the decent Orville Faubus becomes a racist within a few years, while Dale Alford (on a *write-in vote!*) replaces Brooks Hays in Congress. In Alabama again, the veteran New Dealer Lister Hill is re-elected over the extreme racist, James D. Martin, but only by a margin of less than one per cent—even though Martin ran as a Republican. Meanwhile, Ross Barnett has indicated his intention of opposing John Stennis for the Senate in the 1964 Mississippi primary. It may indeed prove to be as true now as it was, or probably was, when Justice Brown said it for the majority in *Plessy* v. *Ferguson* in 1896, that the attempt to eradicate racial prejudice by means of law will "only result in accentuating the difficulties of the present situation," especially when that law is court-made law, made in the absence of support from the legislature, and made with materials—the constitutional words and phrases—that do not readily lend themselves to the solution of the problem, and therefore much of it unable to withstand a sustained search for principle.

"Courts," writes Professor Pollak, "are not all there is to law."

> It is imprudent—and it is even nondemocratic—to rely solely on judicial mechanisms. The time has come—it is long since overdue—for our other legal institutions, at every level of government, to assume greater and greater responsibility for the affirmative ordering of a democratic community.
>
> But these other legal institutions are precisely those which—unlike the courts—are intended to be directly responsive to popular will. If they fail to assume responsibility, it is because the majority of the people of the United States have not yet come to terms with the national commitments made in their name.[73]

One recalls Lincoln's words in the First Inaugural:

> The fugitive slave clause of the Constitution, and the law for the suppression of the foreign slave trade, are each as well enforced, perhaps, as any law can ever be in a community where the moral sense of the people imperfectly supports the law itself. The great body of the people abide by the dry legal obligation in both cases, and a few break over in each [section of the country]. This, I think, cannot be perfectly cured. . . .

There is support among the majority of the people of the United States for the Court's efforts to promote the Negro's legal membership in the body known as "the people of the United States," and if it is lacking in the case of the effort to promote full membership in this "democratic community," as it certainly appears to be, and as Professor Pollak seems to think, what are we to conclude? How are we to proceed, this country whose government was instituted to secure the rights with which all men are equally endowed by their Creator, *and* whose just powers are derived from the consent of the governed? Do we continue to make commitments? No matter what we do to the law in the process? "With public sentiment," Lincoln said, "nothing can fail; without it, nothing can succeed. Consequently he who moulds public sentiment, goes deeper than he who enacts statutes or pronounces decisions. He makes statutes and decisions possible or impossible to be executed." Lincoln knew that the Supreme Court can mold public sentiment as well as pronounce decisions, and perhaps the contemporary Court is doing so. What it does not appear to be doing in every case, however, is molding the sentiment necessary to the execution of the decisions it pronounces, and one reason for this is to be found in the character of those decisions. Too many of them are "unprincipled," some of them supported by clearly specious arguments, with ostensible reasons that simply cannot be believed. If this is true, its decisions will have to be executed without the consent of the governed, and that, according to the Declaration of Independence, is unjust and, according to the experience of all history, impossible except by terror and violence.

What is true of the Court may also be true of militant Negro leadership. The time is near at hand when it will have won all the legal victories, and it is not impossible that it will then find itself confronted by the same massive, stubborn problem, changed but essentially unchanged, unaffected, or if affected, only for the worse. For, we have it on the authority of James Baldwin that the situation of the Negro in Harlem, which, with continued Negro migration north, will swiftly become the situation of most Negroes in this country, is worse, is more demoralizing, than the situation of the Negro in the South where he started. This is the cruelest aspect of all.

CHAPTER 16

LET ME CALL YOU QUOTA, SWEETHEART

It was said of the late Justice William O. Douglas, and it was said by way of praising him, that more than any other judge in our time he dared to ask the question of what is good for the country and to translate (or, at least, to try to translate) his answers to that question into constitutional law. In this respect he was the very model of the activist judge, and it is the activist judge who has come to characterize the federal judiciary, especially the federal judiciary in Washington.

Not everyone, of course, agrees that this should be so. Some thirty years ago Justice Felix Frankfurter registered his disagreement with one of Douglas's judgments by reminding his colleagues that a Supreme Court Justice does not (or is not supposed to) "sit like a kadi under a tree dispensing justice according to considerations of individual expediency," or, he might have said, according to his private judgment of what is good for the country.

The general public would probably agree with that, especially since a kadi is rather like a mullah and Americans have learned something about mullahs recently. Nevertheless, it has been Douglas's view of the role of the judge that has won out in the prestigious law schools and in the influential press—our "greatest living jurist," pronounced

Reprinted from *Commentary*, May 1981, by permission; all rights reserved.

Bob Woodward and Scott Armstrong in *The Brethren* just before Douglas died—which is one reason we now have a surfeit of kadis on the federal bench, and at every level. Even lower-court judges now do casually what Douglas was praised for daring to do. For the same reason, there is also a surfeit of kadis among lawyers generally, and particularly among lawyers in the various departments and agencies of the federal government.

This disposition to disregard the authority both in and of law represents the triumph of legal realism, the school of thought which, throughout most of the 20th century, has been trying to persuade us that the essence of the judicial process does not consist in interpreting law, whether statute or constitutional, but in making it. Of necessity, legal realists insist, judges make law, and if this makes them kadis, so be it. Besides, they say our judges are usually better qualified than our legislators to know what is good for the country.

In some circles this idea enjoys the status of self-evident truth, but the very fact that it has been iterated and reiterated for so many years is proof enough that the average person is not yet convinced. As he sees it, laws are supposed to be made by legislators, whom he elects, and applied in individual cases by judges, whom, at the federal level, he does not elect. If he is at all reflective, he will concede that, for example, given an ordinance forbidding vehicles to be driven in public parks, it will be necessary for someone—a policeman, perhaps, and ultimately a judge—to decide whether a tricycle ridden by a six-year-old child is a vehicle. But he is not ready to concede that, to take another example, when Congress makes a law *forbidding* discrimination, it is open to federal judges, even if they sit on the Supreme Court, to remake it into a law *permitting* discrimination. And whatever the *New York Times* might say (a way "to atone for past discrimination"), he is likely to stamp an angry foot when a federal judge tries to persuade him that a system of racial quotas is not discriminatory.

Unfortunately, while this typical citizen has been immersed in his private world, emerging occasionally to cast a ballot for those he wants to represent him in the public, there have been others who have come to understand that what really matters under our present system of government is not voting but suing: suing in the federal courts, suing the federal government, and best of all, suing the federal government in the federal courts in the District of Columbia. Their favorite statute is Title VII of the Civil Rights Act of 1964.

Congress forbade employers to discriminate on the basis of sex; Title VII flatly forbids it. But it was not Congress that forbade sexual harassment; the idea that sexual harassment is a form of sexual discrimination could only have been conceived by someone with a fertile imagination and no respect for statutory language. After all, the employer who demands sexual favors of a particular woman, even if he demands them in exchange for a job, will surely be astonished—or would once have been astonished—to be told that this is proof of his bias against women as a class. (His trouble, he is likely to protest, is that he finds women irresistible.) Even when disabused on this point, he would protest his innocence (or the innocence of his company) by showing that whereas some of his supervisors demand sexual favors of women, there are others who demand them of men, and, though reprehensible when considered as individual acts (he might point to a company policy strictly forbidding them), this catholicity of sexual preference is proof of the absence of discrimination on the part of the company.

By now, however, every major employer in the country ought to know that the federal courts have held otherwise. Not only that, but the Court of Appeals for the District of Columbia Circuit has now ruled, in a case by the name of *Bundy* v. *Jackson*, that an employer can be held to have discriminated on the basis of sex without a showing that he had discriminated on the basis of sex.

This truly inspired reading of the statute was offered by Chief Judge J. Skelly Wright, a judge made in the mold of Douglas and not given to acquiescing in Congress's decision as to what is good for the country. As he wrote in the *Harvard*

Law Review a few years ago, the Warren Court especially must be praised for teaching us that there is "no theoretical gulf between the law and morality," by which Judge Wright meant that the law must be made to conform with morality—someone else's law and his morality.

With the help of the Equal Employment Opportunity Commission, one of Washington's most zealous agencies, Title VII plaintiffs began, foolishly as it turned out, by filing their sexual harassment charges against private companies—Bausch & Lomb, the Bank of America, and the Public Service Electric & Gas Company. Unlike government agencies, private companies have reason to offer more than a token resistance. Furthermore, because these companies were located outside Washington, the suits were tried by federal courts outside Washington. These two factors may explain why the plaintiffs did not prevail.

Not until similar charges were brought against the Environmental Protection Agency and the Community Relations Service, both agencies of the federal government, and tried or heard on appeal in Washington, was sexual harassment held to be a form of discrimination forbidden by Title VII. This was in 1977.

Still, even after the EPA case, employers could assume that since Title VII forbids discrimination, and forbids sexual harassment only insofar as it is part of a discriminatory act, any plaintiff would have to prove not only that she (or, in principle at least, he) was the victim of a sexual advance but, by refusing to submit, that she had been denied some tangible employment benefit, whether in the form of a job, promotion, or salary increase. Not so, said Chief Judge Wright for the three-judge panel in *Bundy* v. *Jackson.* That may have been true at the time of the EPA case, but, said Wright, unless the court reads Title VII to forbid the sexual behavior in and of itself, employers might engage in such behavior with impunity. (In saying this Wright conveniently overlooked the possibility that local lechers might be dealt with under local law.) So saying, and admitting that the plaintiff had not contended her resistance had caused her to be deprived of any "tangible job benefits," Wright sent the case back to the trial court with instructions to hold hearings on the plaintiff's claim to deserve a promotion.

If the law of this case becomes the law of the land—Wright's opinion was issued only in January of this year—private as well as public employers can be held to have discriminated if, like the city of Washington here, they permit their female employees to be subjected to unwelcome sexual advances. These "demeaning propositions" poison the work environment, Wright said, and a poisoned environment is a discriminatory environment. It would be the job of EEOC to clean it up.

Interestingly enough, not even the EEOC had dared to claim the authority that Wright would give it. In its so-called Interim Guidelines on Sexual Harassment, published in the spring of 1980, it had hinted it was toying with the idea, but in its Final Guidelines the EEOC noted that there had been a good deal of opposition from outside the agency, and the idea was abandoned, at least temporarily. And why should there not have been opposition? The prospect of the EEOC becoming a kind of Sexual Environmental Protection Agency is one to strike fear in the heart of any employer. To protect himself, he would have to impress on his employees that any on-the-job or even job-related sexual banter (so easily mistaken for the real thing) would cost them their employment. The consequence might be a clean working environment but not one that many of us, man or woman, would like to work in. ("Where none admire, 'tis useless to excel;/Where none are beaux, 'tis vain to be a belle.")

These suits (most of them arising under Title VII) bear the names of their nominal plaintiffs—Williams, Barnes, Bundy, Simer, or Luevano—but in practice they are brought or instigated by public-interest law firms and the EEOC. With the assistance of federal judges, these plaintiffs have fashioned an extremely effective institution of unrepresentative government, which now threatens to entrench itself alongside the government we know from the Constitution.

This is government by consent decree, a development of, if we may so call it, the sweetheart suit.

In the *Simer* case, a sweetheart suit if ever there was one, a couple of public-interest law firms acting nominally on behalf of Elsie Simer and eight other plaintiffs, sued the federal government's Community Services Administration. At issue were some $18 million of unexpended emergency energy funds appropriated by Congress to help poor people cope with rising fuel costs. With grants from still another federal agency (YOUR TAX DOLLARS AT WORK, as the signs at highway construction sites used to say), the law firms sued to force the expenditure of those funds. What resulted was a "negotiated" settlement, a consent decree, according to which Elsie Simer and her eight co-plaintiffs were each awarded $250, the maximum allowed under the statute, and the law firms pocketed a lion's share of the remaining $17,997,750.

Nice work if you can get it, as the old song says. Unfortunately for them, the *Wall Street Journal* got wind of this last August, and in a detailed story pointed to the possible collusive aspects of the case. Armed with this information, the Capital Legal Foundation, an organization that actually deserves its designation as a public-interest law firm, intervened and forced the federal judge who had signed the consent decree to vacate it. He had, the judge confessed later, been "lulled by the appearance of an adversarial situation," misled by the parties "both as to the facts and the law." Perhaps he had been. At least he and CSA's General Counsel had the decency to be embarrassed by the revelations, which is more than can be said for the principals in the *Luevano* case.

Luevano v. *Campbell* began when some public-interest law firms combined with civil-rights lawyers to file a class-action suit against the director of the Office of Personnel Management (or Civil Service Commission, as it used to be called), alleging that the Professional and Administrative Career Examination (or PACE), the principal entry-level test administered to candidates for positions in the federal government's executive branch, discriminated against blacks and Hispanics.

Acting on behalf of those blacks and Hispanics who had failed the test (Angel Luevano being one of them), the lawyers asked the judge (1) to declare that OPM, by using the test, had deprived the plaintiffs of rights secured by Title VII of the Civil Rights Act of 1964; (2) to enjoin the further use of the test; (3) to enjoin the defendant from acting in any way to deprive plaintiffs of their Title VII rights; (4) to award plaintiffs back pay for the work they had not had the opportunity to perform; (5) to award plaintiffs the costs of their suit, including attorneys' fees; and (6) to provide "such other and further relief as the Court may deem just and proper."

This is what the plaintiffs wanted and, we are asked to believe, what the defendant, the federal government, did not want to give them. For two years, with lawyers from the Department of Justice acting for the OPM, the parties "negotiated," so to speak, and then, in January 1981, in order to resolve the dispute "without the time and expense of contested litigation," they agreed to settle.

Some settlement. The government not only gave the plaintiffs everything they asked for; by giving them a hiring quota system, the government actually gave them more than they asked for. This did not deter the judge, Joyce Hens Green of the U.S. District Court for the District of Columbia, from giving the agreement her preliminary approval. On the same day, even as he packed his private papers and marched off to join a Washington law firm, the outgoing Associate Attorney General, John H. Shenefield, announced his pleasure with the agreement and denied that it would require the imposition of a quota system. There being no "absolute numerical requirement," he said to the press, there is no quota.

The *New York Times* agreed: "The fact is that the government undertook no numerical obligation. And when the promised remedial action is completed, hiring will again be totally color-blind." This is, at best, wishful thinking;

there is no reason to think that we shall ever see the end of this "remedial action." Even so, what the *Times* finds convenient to conceal is that the statute which is said to require remedial action in fact forbids it.

Title VII of the Civil Rights Act of 1964, which was amended in 1972 to cover employment by the federal government, declares it to be an unlawful employment practice for an employer "to fail or refuse to hire or to discharge any individual, or otherwise to discriminate against any individual with respect to his compensation, terms, conditions, or privileges of employment, because of such individual's race, color, religion, sex, or national origin."

As statutes go, this one would appear to be a model of clarity and precision. To make it even clearer that its purpose was to forbid what the *Times* calls remedial action, or reverse discrimination, Congress went on to declare that nothing in Title VII should be interpreted to require employers "to grant preferential treatment" to any individual or group because of race, color, religion, sex, or national origin, not even to correct "an imbalance which may exist with respect to the total number or percentage of persons of any race [etc.] employed by any employer."

Not only did Congress forbid reverse discrimination, but, in still another section of Title VII, it made it clear that employers would continue to be permitted to screen job applicants by means of professionally developed ability tests, provided the tests were not "designed, intended, or used to discriminate because of race, color, religion, sex, or national origin."

Remedial action, as the *Times* calls it, is permitted today not because the Supreme Court could not understand this language but because it ignored it, and because Congress has permitted the Court to ignore it. The Court knew very well that the Kaiser Aluminum Company was violating the statute when it reserved half the places in a training program for its black employees. But, said Justice Brennan in the *Weber* case, to read the statute as written would bring about an end completely at variance with the purpose of the statute.

Congress's express purpose was to eliminate discrimination against persons with specified characteristics: but Brennan said Congress's real purpose was to provide jobs for such persons, even if this required employers to discriminate against persons with other characteristics. Besides, he added, the statute does not say that employers are not *permitted* to prefer one race over another, at least blacks over whites.

Moreover, whereas Congress had made it clear that employers would be permitted to use general ability or aptitude tests, the Court said in another case that only job-related tests would be permitted: "What Congress has commanded," it said, despite substantial evidence to the contrary, "is that any tests used must measure the person for the job and not the person in the abstract." With this the way was paved for the Carter administration's agreement to impose racial quotas.

Here, summarized from some forty pages of convoluted text, are the main provisions of that agreement:

(1) Within three years following Judge Green's final approval of it, the government will phase out the PACE and replace it with job-related "alternative examining procedures," procedures that have no "adverse impact" on blacks and Hispanics; (2) examining procedures are understood to have an "adverse impact" not when blacks and Hispanics do not pass the tests at the same rate as non-Hispanic whites, but when they are not *hired* at substantially the same rate; (3) if there is "adverse impact," the government must make "all practicable efforts" to eliminate it; (4) all practicable efforts must include the following: (a) appointment without testing of anyone with a college grade-point average of 3.5 or better, or of anyone who stands in the top 10 percent of his class; (b) appointment without reference to test score of anyone who speaks Spanish or has the "requisite knowledge of Hispanic culture" (where the job to which the appointment is made is one where performance would be enhanced by these skills); (c) appointment without testing of anyone who successfully completes a work-study program organized by a federal

agency and a college, including a two-year college; (d) establishment of special programs designed to enable blacks and Hispanics to pass the PACE during the period it is still in use; and (e) in the event that adverse impact is not yet eliminated, a willingness to adopt whatever measures the plaintiffs or the court should require; (5) the government may cease these efforts to eliminate adverse impact when— the Reagan administration managed to eliminate this provision—blacks and Hispanics comprise "at least 20 percent of all incumbents at the GS-5 level and higher levels in the entire job category on a nationwide basis" *and* when— the Reagan administration did not succeed in eliminating this one—an agency can demonstrate the "validity" of its alternative examining procedure.

In addition to these substantive provisions, the Justice Department agreed to pay the plaintiffs sums of money ranging from $6,250 to $12,500; to help two of the plaintiffs find government jobs; to search OPM records for the names of other blacks and Hispanics who took the PACE but did not get jobs, and, if they filed charges of discrimination, to pay each a sum of $3,000 as "back wages," and assist each of them to find a government job; to compile records of the racial composition of the federal work force; to pay plaintiffs' attorneys (and expert witnesses) for the work already done, and for the work they will do in connection with monitoring compliance with the decree, and for the work involved in any future judicial proceedings instituted under provisions of the decree.

On one point only was the Justice Department seemingly adamant: it refused to admit that the government's use of the PACE violated Title VII or that it had not been properly validated in accordance with the appropriate guidelines; it therefore refused to concede that the government was "subject to any liability." What was withheld in principle, however, was given up in practice: the government scrapped the test and doled out the money. In exchange for all this, the plaintiffs graciously agreed to accept what the government gave them.

This drastic measure, controlling the method by which, annually, hundreds of thousands of applicants for federal jobs will be examined, was adopted not by the OPM, the agency in charge of examining and hiring, but by Justice Department lawyers working in the context of a lawsuit. Many of the agencies that would be immediately affected were not even informed that there was a lawsuit or, indeed, until one week before it was signed, that there was an agreement. The agreement was signed over the objections of the OPM, the agency most vitally concerned; it was signed even though officials in the OPM had thought that, after the November 1980 election, the whole scheme had been shelved. It was signed even though the Reagan transition team had been told that nothing would be done until the new administration had had the opportunity to study it. It was signed without consulting private employers, although it is clear that both the plaintiffs and the government lawyers had them in mind when they negotiated the agreement. (Title VII applies to private employers as well as to the government, and the Uniform Guidelines on Employee Selection Procedures which speak openly of the necessity to take affirmative action, are written primarily with them in mind.) It was signed simply because some lawyers in the Department of Justice and the EEOC arrogated to themselves the authority to decide what was good for the country, and it mattered not at all to them that they represented a repudiated administration.

Shortly after taking office, the new Attorney General, William French Smith, was quoted as saying that in view of the legal difficulties of withdrawing from an agreement to which the government had given its consent, the Reagan administration would, with amendments, abide by its terms. The blatant quota provision was removed, and that is surely significant, but the government is still obliged to eliminate adverse impact, and its efforts to do so must continue until it succeeds in devising examining procedures which have been validated. And this presents a problem.

There are rules for determining the validity of an

examining procedure, which is to say, for determining whether it accurately measures the qualities or skills required for successful job performance; they are set down in the Uniform Guidelines on Employee Selection Procedures, a document written by the EEOC and other affirmative action agencies. It should surprise no one familiar with the Guidelines or the agencies to learn that no examining procedure has yet been validated. Nor is it being unduly cynical to suggest that, so long as the Guidelines are in place, none ever will be.

The purpose of the Guidelines is, quite clearly, to prevent the validation of any examining procedure that does not produce a racially balanced work force; and the purpose of the consent decree, as signed by the Carter Justice Department, was, equally clearly, to see to it that any validating be done according to *those* Guidelines and not guidelines written by the new administration. Fortunately, the Reagan team managed to amend the agreement to allow it to follow the Guidelines as set down in the Code of Federal Regulations, "or as subsequently modified." If the government can change the Guidelines (which will depend on its ability to impose its will on the zealots in the bureaucracy), this change might prove to be significant.

But the Carter people set still another trap. The plaintiffs may challenge an agency's claim to have validated an alternative examining procedure, but the agency may not meet that challenge unless it gains the consent of the Justice Department. "No agency," reads section 12(f) of the agreement, "may assert in Court the validity of an alternative examining procedure . . . unless it has first obtained a written statement from the Attorney General or his or her designate that he or she will defend the validity of the agency's use of the alternative examining procedure." So the issue—hiring by merit or quotas—will turn on who is Attorney General, or more likely, who is Associate Attorney General, someone like John H. Shenefield or someone who knows what is going on.

Then, to make it virtually certain that the OPM (or any

agency) will not be able to escape its obligation to hire blacks and Hispanics at the same rate that it hires non-Hispanic whites, even if it succeeds in demonstrating the validity (the job-relatedness) of its new procedures, the parties to the agreement cleverly included the following provision (and the Reagan team was not clever enough to have it removed): "Once an agency has demonstrated the validity of an alternative examining procedure in accordance with this Decree, it has no obligation under the Decree to modify the procedure or the use of the procedure, or to replace it, *unless there is another selection procedure for the same job having at least substantially equal validity and less adverse impact*" (emphasis added). This means that the OPM will be required to set aside its procedures in favor of procedures designed by the plaintiffs (with the help of the EEOC) unless it can prove to Judge Green that their validity is not "substantially" equal.

So, finally, we have reached the end. In the absence of validated *and* acceptable tests, the OPM will be obliged to continue to make all practicable efforts to eliminate adverse impact until the point is reached where the work force comprises X percent black, Y percent Hispanic, and Z percent non-Hispanic whites. This is not a quota—we have the word of John Shenefield and the *New York Times* on it—because there is not an "absolute numerical requirement." If quota means fixed number or even fixed proportion, they are right: the number or proportion of blacks and Hispanics to be appointed will depend on how many of them apply for jobs and on the relation of that number to the number of non-Hispanic white applicants; and these numbers can change. In fact, they can be changed radically: one or another group can flood the applicant pool.

It must also be pointed out that the success of this bold new program of hiring will depend on the ability of the government accurately to identify, classify, and count the individual members of each group. There will have to be rules for this; the government cannot allow applicants to define themselves, as the Commerce Department learned when it began to administer the Minority Business Enterprise program. In these matters at least, our government is getting better all the time.

With the founding of the United States, it was hoped that government and, indeed, the whole public sphere, would become merely instrumental. The great political questions had been settled in principle, and in America, with the Declaration of Independence and the subsequent establishing of the Constitution, they had been settled in practice as well. For example, it was thought that there could be no further disputing the issue of who should rule, or who is entitled to rule: to the Founders it was a self-evident truth that just government is government to which the governed give their consent. Nor would there be further disputing of the issue of government's purpose: government is instituted to secure the rights with which all men are by nature equally endowed. Beyond that, government was to leave men alone. As the late Herbert Storing put it in his last published work, government was seen by the Founders to have the narrow but still indispensable function of "facilitating the peaceful enjoyment of private life." No longer political in the larger sense, government would be reduced to administration.

We have, however, never lacked dispute as to how that administration should be organized or, more particularly, how its members should be chosen. The original "administration by gentlemen," as Leonard D. White called it in his history of administration, gave way in time to President Jackson's more democratic principle of rotation of office and, when that principle was corrupted, to the principle of "to the victor belong the spoils." Then came civil-service reform and eventually Woodrow Wilson's science of administration: how rights were to be secured became a question of scientific management (and not one to be answered by political spoilsmen). But the story does not end here.

White, who, at the University of Chicago, taught many of the political scientists of my generation, had a good deal of influence in the design of the procedures by which the members of the public service, as he called it, would be chosen. A scientist, yes, but he was too much a gentleman in the older sense to think that public administration was a job for narrow specialists or technical experts. His model was the British public service, and especially its highest level and the system by which its members were chosen. There, recent honors graduates of the few best universities were selected by competitive examination, with a view not to their ability to perform a specific job but, rather, with a view to their ability, because of their education and intelligence, to perform well in increasingly responsible positions. Public service was understood to be a lifetime career. When President Roosevelt appointed him a Civil Service Commissioner in 1934, White was instrumental in inaugurating an American (and therefore more democratic) version of this British system.

The Junior Professional Assistant Examination, as it came to be called in 1939, was a "broad-band" examination, administered to college graduates; it assessed both verbal ability and capacity to perform a specific job. In 1955, for various reasons, it was replaced by the Federal Service Entrance Examination; differing in certain respects, the FSEE still tested for verbal, quantitative, and abstract reasoning ability. Entering at the GS-5 or GS-7 level, the successful applicants began what the Civil Service Commission hoped would be a lifetime of public service.

In 1974, the FSEE gave way to the PACE, but again there was no essential difference among the three tests. The officials who designed them dared to hope that in time the tests would gain the prestige once enjoyed by the Foreign Service Examination, and that the best of the country's young persons—fairly selected by competitive examinations—would choose lifelong careers in the public service.

The PACE asks the sort of questions that students who have taken the College Boards would recognize. It is not an easy test; in a given year only about 40 percent will pass it, and fewer than 8 percent will pass it with a score of 90 or above, and it is from this small group that the successful applicants will be chosen. In recent years, approximately 150,000 persons annually have taken the test and 7,000 have been appointed. Unfortunately, few of these have been blacks and Hispanics. The majority of the white applicants fail the test, but as a group the whites do better than blacks as a group or Hispanics as a group. In 1978, to cite specific figures, of the blacks taking the test, only 5 percent passed, and only 0.3 percent passed with a score of 90 or better. (The corresponding figures for Hispanics are 12.9 percent and 1.5 percent.)

These are terrible statistics; they cry out for remedial action of some sort. But they also suggest the price that we are likely to have to pay if the government is required to abandon the merit system and replace it with a system of racial quotas or, in deference to Mr. Shenefield and the *New York Times*, a system of remedial or compensatory hiring. That price will be heavy, and the parties to the *Luevano* decree seem to acknowledge this even as they deny it. They know that hiring ought to be done on the basis of merit—both principle and the efficient running of the government require it—which is why, in one section of the agreement, they say that "nothing in this Decree shall be interpreted as requiring any federal agency to hire any person for a job who is unqualified to perform the job...." But their commitment to affirmative action requires them to add, "under qualification standards that have been properly validated in accord with the Uniform Guidelines." Both merit and a racially balanced work force. Unfortunately, as those terrible statistics suggest, it will be some time before the two prove to be compatible.

CHAPTER 17

VOTING RIGHTS AND WRONGS

The Voting Rights Act of 1965 is surely the most successful civil-rights measure ever enacted by the national government. Everybody—or, at least, everybody who has publicly offered an opinion on the subject—agrees with this judgment, and there is good reason why they should. Among civil rights, that of voting is fundamental because the enjoyment of other rights is likely to depend on it; prior to 1965, however, and despite the Civil Rights Acts of 1957, 1960, and 1964, it was a right denied to most Southern blacks. In Mississippi, for an egregious example, only 6.8 percent of voting-age blacks were then registered to vote; thanks to the Act, that proportion is now almost 70 percent, and in 1980 almost 60 percent of them actually voted. What is more, not only do white candidates for public office throughout the South now actively and publicly solicit black support at the polls, and Southern Senators and Congressmen legislate with a view to the interests of their black constituents, but major Southern cities have black mayors (Atlanta being the most conspicuous of these). Indeed, there are now almost 2,000 black elected public officials in the six states of the Deep South.

So successful has the Act been in achieving its objective

(which, as then Attorney General Nicholas Katzenbach put it, was the removal of barriers to black voter registration), that even some of its devoted supporters began to question whether its "Draconian" pre-clearance provision in Section 5 was needed any longer. Under this provision, some nine states (mostly Southern) and political subdivisions of thirteen others are required to submit all proposed changes in their voting laws and procedures to the U.S. Attorney General for his approval. For states accustomed to referring to themselves as sovereign commonwealths, this is an ignominious position to be in, especially since, in practice, their appeals are made not to exalted political officials, such as Attorneys General Griffin Bell or William French Smith, but to anonymous persons—who knows their names? and who can bring them to account?—in the Civil Rights Division of the Department of Justice. That great civil libertarian, Justice Hugo L. Black, protested that Section 5 treated the states as "conquered provinces" and was unconstitutional. (More recently, the usually soft-spoken Thad Cochran, Republican Senator from Mississippi, put it this way: "Local officials have to go to Washington, get on their knees, kiss the ring and tug their forelocks to all these third-rate bureaucrats.") What, these states ask, are they *now* doing to deserve this treatment? And why single them out? Is there no voting fraud up north, in Chicago, for example? It may have been in response to this question that Henry Hyde of Illinois, the ranking Republican on the House Judiciary Committee's Subcommittee on Civil and Constitutional Rights, asked, "Shall we extend the mandatory pre-clearance for these 'selected areas' another ten years ... or is seventeen years in the political penalty box enough?"

Hyde's question was asked last summer when the House was debating proposals to renew or extend the Voting Rights Act. Unless Congress acts before August 6, 1982, some of these states and political subdivisions will be eligible to petition the U.S. District Court for the District of Columbia to be removed from this Section 5 preclearance coverage; in the words of the phrase coined to describe this procedure, they will be able to "bail out." Rather than permit this, some members of the House proposed that the pre-clearance provision be extended to cover all 50 states and all their political subdivisions; this, at least, would meet the complaint of unequal treatment. At this, Henry Hyde, for one, balked. What is significant, however, is that he ended up voting for the extension. He did so, he explained, because of what he learned during committee hearings on the proposals: "Witness after witness testified to continuing and pervasive denials of ready access to the electoral process for blacks."

Any fair-minded person would have to agree with this assessment. Despite the progress made since 1965, there are still more or less remote areas where state and local officials continue to resist according voting rights to minorities. Without federal supervision, there is no assurance that these practices would not continue or be resumed in other voting districts in some of the states. The price of liberty, as Tom Paine said, is eternal vigilance, and it is unfortunate, but the time has not yet come when we can rely on every local official to provide it.

The House agreed. It passed a bill extending the Act by the overwhelming margin of 365 votes (389–24); and when, on December 16, an identical bill was introduced in the Senate, 61 members of that body, including 8 Republican committee chairmen and several Southern Democrats, immediately indicated their intention to support it. Its easy passage would seem to be assured when it reaches the floor of the Senate, probably in April; as its sponsors, Senators Edward Kennedy and Charles Mathias, were quick to point out, a majority of this size is sufficient to defeat any attempt to filibuster on the bill. It is almost sufficient to overturn a presidential veto, not that there is much likelihood that the President would dare to cast one. Opposition to this bill, even White House opposition, has been conspicuous by its absence, so much so that some Senate staff members have complained of difficulties in finding witnesses willing to testify against it.

This is unfortunate because the bill in its present form is

much more than an extension of the current law. Unless it is amended it deserves to be defeated.

II

What is new in this bill is not to be found in Section 5's pre-clearance provision, on which most of the debate has been focused; that section is unchanged. What is mostly objectionable in this bill is not to be found in the new bail-out section, even though its effect will be to make it almost impossible for any jurisdiction to take advantage of the bail-out privilege. What is new and profoundly objectionable is the seemingly innocuous amendment to the text of Section 2 which, by general agreement, was not one of the Act's "key sections." (In one compendium of significant civil-rights laws, this section was omitted from the text of the 1965 Act precisely because, in the editor's view, it was no one of the "key sections.")

In its original form, Section 2 was a mere declaration, or a restatement in statutory form, of the Fifteenth Amendment to the Constitution. Where the Amendment says the "right of citizens of the United States to vote shall not be denied or abridged" on account of race or color, Section 2 says, more explicitly, that no "voting qualification or prerequisite to voting, or standard, practice, or procedure shall be imposed or applied [so as to] deny or abridge" the right to vote. Not suprisingly, unlike other sections of the Act, this one has given rise to very little litigation, and in the current debate over extending the Act very little attention has been paid to it. Yet its language was altered in a significant way. The words "to deny or abridge" the right to vote were deleted: in their place were put the words "in a manner which *results* in a denial or abridgment" (emphasis added) of the right to vote. This new language will make Section 2 the key section of the Act, one that will affect the electoral laws and practices of every state and political subdivision in the nation. There is reason to doubt that this was understood by all the Congressmen and Senators who lined up quickly in support of the bill.

The new language is intended to express the difference between the right to vote and what the federal courts, in voting-rights cases, have made of the right to vote. (It was placed in Section 2 of the bill because that section, unlike Section 5, applies to the entire country, and applies to existing voting laws and practices as opposed to voting changes.) Voting, Chief Justice Warren pronounced in a 1969 case, includes "all activities necessary to make a vote effective," and the effectiveness of a vote is now measured by its results. Thus, a vote can be "diluted"—that is, made less effective—if a city annexes its surrounding territory with the consequence that the proportion of black voters declines from 56 percent to 47 percent of the population; or if, as a result of reapportioning its voting population, a state reduces the percentage of black voters in a district below 65 percent, the proportion calculated by the Justice Department and certain federal District Courts to make it relatively certain that a black will be elected; or if, when changing from a system of plurality to one of majority voting, a city cannot prove that the change will not "dilute the effectiveness of the Negro vote." This last reference is to a 1980 case, *City of Rome* v. *United States,* and a consideration of it and *City of Mobile* v. *Bolden,* decided the same day, will help to explain what Congress is up to.

Rome, Georgia, had a commission form of government, the commissioners being elected on an at-large basis and by a plurality of the vote. (As the Supreme Court noted, "literally thousands of municipalities and other local government units throughout the nation" have such a system.) In 1966, the state of Georgia enacted new laws affecting municipal governance, among them one providing for election of commissioners by majority vote. Since Georgia was covered by Section 5 of the Voting Rights Act, it had to "pre-clear" this electoral change with the Attorney General. He refused his approval and Rome went to court. The trial court found no discriminatory purpose in the new law, but it ruled against the city because the law was discriminatory in effect. As the Supreme Court repeated in its affirmance of the lower court's decision, the law would deprive "Negro voters of the opportunity to elect a candidate of their choice," by which it meant, a candidate of their own race. More precisely, the city had *not* proved that the new law would *not* have the effect of depriving Negro voters of the opportunity to elect a Negro candidate.

On the same day, the Supreme Court reached the opposite conclusion in a case presenting starkly similar facts. Mobile, Alabama also had a commission form of government, the three commissions being elected every four years by majority vote in at-large elections. *City of Mobile* v. *Bolden* began when black citizens of the city challenged the legality and constitutionality of the at-large election procedure, alleging that their vote had been "diluted" because, while blacks comprised more than 35 percent of the population, no black had ever been elected a city commissioner. Although the trial court found that Mobile blacks registered and were able to vote without hindrance, it nevertheless held this "dilution" of voting power to be an abridgment of the right to vote in violation of the Fifteenth Amendment, and ordered the replacement of the commission system by a mayor-council system, with council members to be elected from nine single-member districts. A sharply divided Supreme Court reversed, holding that an election law that is racially neutral on its face can be said to violate the Fifteenth Amendment only if it can be shown to have been motivated by a discriminatory purpose and that there was no such showing in this case. A plurality of the *Mobile* Court held that Section 2 of the Act is coextensive with the Fifteenth Amendment, and, therefore, does require proof of discriminatory purpose.

What accounts for the discrepancy in these judgments? The Mobile case was tried not under the Voting Rights Act but, rather, under the Fifteenth—and, to some extent, the Fourteenth—Amendment. Alabama, like Georgia, was covered by Section 5 of the Act, but Mobile, Alabama, unlike Rome, Georgia, had not changed its election law—it had been in effect since 1911—and, therefore, was not required to "pre-clear" it with the Attorney General under Section 5.

Thus, as the situation stands after these two 1980 cases, anyone challenging old election laws, or new laws in jurisdictions not covered by Section 5 of the Voting Rights Act, must sue under Section 2 of the current Act or under the Fifteenth (or Fourteenth) Amendment, and to prevail he must show discriminatory purpose; to prevail under Section 5, it is the city or state that bears the burden of proof and it must show no discriminatory effect.

The amended Section 2 is intended to reverse the Supreme Court's decision in *City of Mobile*. By making it clear that, in its judgment at least, proof of discriminatory purpose or intent is not required in cases brought under the Fifteenth Amendment (by way of Section 2), the House Judiciary Committee, as it frankly admitted in its report on the bill, intended to do away with the discrepancy between the law of *Mobile* and the law of *Rome*.

If enacted, it would permit voting-rights suits to be filed by the Attorney General or any private litigant against every state, city, county, or other electoral jurisdiction in the country. It would put every jurisdiction on notice that it might have to appear in a federal court to defend its election laws—any law affecting elections—against the charge that they "dilute" the votes of blacks and a few other minority groups. And it would, of course, make these federal courts the country's electoral lawgiver.

III

At the end of his dissenting opinion in *City of Mobile*, Justice Thurgood Marshall said that if the Court "refuses to honor our long-recognized principle that the Constitution 'nullifies sophisticated as well as simple-minded modes of discrimination'... it cannot expect the victims of discrimination to respect political channels of seeking redress." Such minatory statements are singularly out of place in judicial reports— after all, judges are not supposed to provoke or even to excuse lawlessness—but, except in the context in which it appears, Marshall's point concerning sophisticated modes of discrimination has considerable merit. There are ways of abridging the right to vote without apparently denying it.

The paradigm case of this occurred some twenty years ago when Alabama, without removing a single white voter, managed to exclude all but a fraction of Tuskegee's black voters from the city (all but 4 of a total of 400) by redrawing the city's boundaries, transforming its shape from that of a simple square to "an uncouth twenty-eight sided figure," as Justice Felix Frankfurter put it. The Supreme Court was unanimous in its judgment that this was a violation of the Constitution, with all but one member agreeing that it was an abridgment, if not a denial, of the Fifteenth Amendment's right to vote.

But in *City of Mobile* the Court was not retreating from its position in the Tuskegee case; it was refusing to join Marshall in his insistence that the Constitution requires that "the votes of citizens of all races shall be of substantially equal weight." To the Court—or, actually, to the plurality of Justices who joined in Justice Potter Stewart's opinion—this was a call for proportional representation. "The theory of this dissenting opinion . . . appears to be that every 'political group,' or at least every such group that is in the minority, has a federal constitutional right to elect candidates in proportion to its numbers." This, said Justice Stewart, is not the law of the Constitution.

Marshall angrily denied that he was calling for proportional representation; this charge was, he said, a "mischaracterization" of his position. There is, he went on, a clear distinction between a requirement of proportional representation and the discriminatory effect or vote-dilution test. "The vote-dilution doctrine can logically apply only to groups whose electoral discreteness and insularity allow dominant political factions to ignore them." In like manner, the amended Section 2 of the Voting Rights Act contains this disclaimer: "The fact that members of a minority group have not been elected in numbers equal to the group's proportion of the population shall not, in and of itself, constitute a violation of this section."

Despite these assurances, however, one from Marshall and the other from Congress, the distinction between the vote-dilution test and the proportional representation of at least some minority groups is likely to be no clearer than that between racial goals and racial quotas.

Those words in the amended Section 2—"in a manner which results in a denial or abridgment"—will derive their meaning in part from the Supreme Court's decision in *United Jewish Organizations* v. *Carey,* and according to Justice William Brennan, "the one starkly clear fact of this case is that an overt racial number was employed to effect petitioners' assignment to voting districts." In equally stark fact, race was the *only* criterion employed in the redrawing of district lines. Yet the Court, with Brennan concurring, approved it by a vote of seven to one.

At issue in this case was the New York reapportionment statute enacted after the 1970 census, and more precisely, the district lines drawn in three metropolitan counties, Kings, New York (Manhattan), and Bronx. In one of the newly-drawn districts, the nonwhite majority was *only* 61 percent, and the Justice Department, from whom Section 5 pre-clearance was required,* concluded from this and other facts that the state had *not* shown that the district lines had *not* been drawn with the purpose or effect of diluting the voting strength of nonwhites (blacks and Puerto Ricans). Faced with the necessity to have its reapportionment plan in place in time for the 1974 primary and general elections, the state revised the plan as it affected the districts in these counties, increasing the size of the nonwhite majority from 61 percent to 65 percent. This satisfied the Justice Department in

---

*These counties were subject to the pre-clearance provision of the Voting Rights Act because New York then had a literacy test for voting and, given a choice between Richard Nixon and the candidate of a badly discredited Democratic party, fewer than 50 percent of the state's voting-age population had gone to the polls in the 1968 presidential election. In combination, these factors were presumed to be evidence of disfranchisement of some sort.

Washington but not everyone in the local district, for, in order to find the number of nonwhites needed to achieve the required 65-percent proportion, the state had to reassign to other districts some members of what had been a consolidated Hasidic community. The Hasidim went to court and, as one might expect, lost. They lost because, as Brennan put it in his separate opinion, they had "not been deprived of their right to vote" (which, of course, could also have been said of the nonwhites in the country), and because while their vote may have been diluted as a result of their being divided into separate districts, they do not constitute a group explicitly protected under the Voting Rights Act. Congress at its pleasure has reserved this status for blacks and so-called language minorities: American Indians, Asian Americans, Alaskan Natives, and persons of Spanish heritage. The Hasidim were expected to take their chances along with the rest of the whites, and in this case at least there was no evidence of "cognizable discrimination against whites." Whites could elect their representatives—that is, they could elect whites—in those districts where they were in the majority. *UJO* v. *Carey*, like some cases before it, stands for proportional representation, not, admittedly, for every group—the Court did not join Marshall by saying that "the votes of citizens of all races shall be of substantially equal weight"—but proportional for some groups.

One of Chief Justice Earl Warren's legacies to American politics was the aphorism, "Legislators represent people, not trees or acres," and, that being so, states were forbidden by the Constitution to apportion seats in either house of their legislatures on any basis other than population. Now it turns out that legislators represent not undifferentiated people— people defined only as individuals living in districts of approximately equal size—but groups of people defined by their race, and they can be said to represent them only if they are of that race. As the Court said, the votes of blacks will be diluted when the number of blacks in a district is not sufficient "to insure the opportunity for the election of a black representative." How many black representatives?

That depends on the number of blacks in the county. How many are required in a district to insure the election of a black representative? If one takes it for granted that blacks vote as a bloc, at least 50 percent, and beyond that the number would seem to depend on voter turnout. In Kings County, turnout tends to be low, so 61 percent was deemed insufficient. Why 65 percent? "A staff member of the legislative reapportionment committee testified that in the course of meetings and telephone conversations with Justice Department officials, he 'got the feeling... that 65 percent would be probably an approved figure' for the nonwhite population in the assembly district in which the Hasidic community was located...."

Of course, as any well-informed student of voting behavior could have told these anonymous Justice Department Solons (and told them over the phone), 65 percent may not be sufficient to insure the election of nonwhite representatives. In the first place, voters can (and sometimes do) look to factors other than race when casting their ballots, and it is an insult to assume this to be untrue or even uncharacteristic of "nonwhite" voters. In the second place, in some areas (and Kings County is one of them) nonwhite voter turnout is so low that, even if nonwhites voted as a solid bloc, districts on the order of 80 or even 90 percent would be required to insure the election of their candidate. Voter turnout is related to education—the more education, the higher the turnout—and not at all to race, a fact that ought to be pondered by the ideologues in the Justice Department and federal judiciary. Since the nonwhites in these Kings County (which is to say, Brooklyn) districts tend to be very poorly educated, it is not surprising that, judging from the returns in the 1980 congressional elections, their turnout may be as low as 10 percent and surely is as low as 20 percent. Whatever the reason, four of the five districts the Justice Department presumed to be safely nonwhite after the 1974 reapportionment proceeded to elect white representatives in the ensuing local elections.

What, then, can we make of Congress's assurance that

Section 2 does not require a group's representation to be equal to its proportion of the population—or that disproportionality does not "in and of itself" constitute a violation of the section? If we assume, surely correctly, that this language is not intended to be a repudiation of *UJO* v. *Carey* and the other vote-dilution cases, Congress means that some factor in addition to disproportionality must be present before it can be said that a group's vote has been abridged by being diluted. What factors? Well, for example, the fact that a group's "discreteness and insularity [has allowed the] dominant political factions to ignore [it]"; or the fact that, after a city annexed additional territory, the number of black seats on the council declined; or the fact that there is evidence of racial bloc voting. Where there is "underrepresentation," the presence of any one of these additional factors, or any one of what Justice Stewart in the *City of Mobile* case referred to as "gauzy sociological considerations," will continue to trigger a violation. So much for the "not-in-and-of-itself" disclaimer.

Besides, whatever Congress's intention in making this disclaimer, the courts are likely to treat it the way they treated a similar disclaimer in the Civil Rights Act of 1964. There Congress said specifically that nothing in Title VII of that Act should be interpreted to require employers "to grant preferential treatment" to any person or group because of race, color, sex, or national origin, not even to correct "an imbalance which may exist with respect to the total number or percentage of persons of any race [etc.] employed by any employer."

Clear enough, one would think, but the Supreme Court paid it no heed. To read this as written, said Justice Brennan in the *Weber* case, would bring about an end completely at variance with the purpose of the statute, by which he meant the purpose of the Court. Congress's disclaimer should be taken with a grain of salt. If the amended Section 2 is adopted, minorities whose voting power has been "diluted" will be able to file suits against jurisdictions throughout the country, and the remedy for vote dilution will prove to be minority representation in proportion to the size of the minority group.

In trying to achieve this, however, the federal courts will encounter a few problems. Where nonwhite voter turnout is as low as it is in Kings County, New York, will the amended Voting Rights Act require districts with populations 80 or 90 percent nonwhite? Some Republicans hope so; they know that the more blacks they can pack into a district, the more Democratic the vote of that district, and, consequently, the better will be their chances to win in surrounding districts. From their partisan point of view, as many districts as possible should be 100-percent nonwhite.

Then, is it not a violation of the Voting Rights Act to combine Puerto Ricans and blacks in the single category, nonwhite? Both are explicitly protected groups and, according to the principle of *UJO* v. *Carey*, each is entitled to representation in proportion to its numbers. (Interestingly enough, the Puerto Ricans of Kings County objected to the 1974 redistricting plan precisely because it did not establish a Puerto Rican district.) Perhaps in future cases the nonwhite group will have to be split into its component parts and each part given a district it can call its own. If so, the redefined Tuskegee (that "uncouth twenty-eight sided figure") will, by comparison, look like a perfect ellipse. And, for one more example, it will be interesting to witness the situation where a city is ordered by the U.S. District Court for the District of Columbia to concentrate blacks in voting districts in order to "undilute" their voting power at a time when the local U.S. District Court has ordered the city to annex surrounding territory in order to integrate the schools.

IV

A genuine system of proportional representation, of the sort sometimes employed in Western Europe, is one where each political group—*Union socialiste et républicaine, Gauche indépendante, Jeune Republique, Rassemblement du peuple francais*, etc.—is guaranteed a share of seats in the legislature equal to its share of the popular vote. Since these groups are defined by their interests or the opinions they hold, and the popularity of these opinions cannot be known until they are elicited, there have to be elections. But one can learn how many blacks there are in the country simply by consulting the census reports. Why, then, bother to hold elections? Why construct these elaborate election districts to insure that black voters will elect, say, a Charles Diggs rather than, say, a Peter Rodino (chairman of the House Judiciary Committee)?

And indeed, one of the unintended consequences of this enactment of the amended Section 2 would be that the other sections of the Voting Rights Act would, in effect, be made superfluous. Who needs statutes providing Attorney General pre-clearance, or bail-outs, or federal election examiners and observers, when, with a few seemingly innocuous words, the judiciary can be authorized to do everywhere what the Justice Department has been doing only in the few "covered" jurisdictions, such as Houston, where it called off a general election, or New York City, where, merely because it thought it had not been given sufficient information, it prevented the holding of a primary election, or Kern County, California, where it ordered the printing of Spanish-language ballots—67,430 of them, of which number only 174 were actually used—in a 1978 primary election? Government by judiciary can be more efficient— think of school busing, abortion, prison reform—than government by administrative agency, to say nothing of government by local election officials.

PART V

RELIGION AND POLITICS

CHAPTER 18

THE IMPORTANCE OF BEING AMISH

~ ~

The Amish have won from the Supreme Court of the United States a special exemption allowing them and so far only them, to ignore an otherwise valid statute. It is not part of my purpose here to speculate about the reasons for their unprecedented success—and it is unprecedented, for although many groups have tried, none before the Amish has ever succeeded. But if it were my purpose, I would attribute their success to the fact that when it comes to culture there is no group more counter than the Amish, and in this day of bourgeois diffidence, that sort of thing matters.

The facts of the case, *Wisconsin v. Yoder*, decided by the Court on May 15, 1972, are these: Wisconsin's school attendance law requires parents to cause their children to attend school, either public or private, until they reach the age of sixteen; Yoder, a member of the Old Order Amish religion, refused to permit his daughter Frieda, fifteen at the time, to attend school beyond the eighth grade, and specifically refused to permit her to attend high school. There was no disagreement (or at least none that appears on record) between him and his daughter on this score; both agreed that it would be profoundly contrary to the Amish religion and way of life for her to attend the public high school, and no doubt they are right about that. (Indeed, if I credit half the stories I hear, what goes on in the high schools is profoundly contrary to my way of life too, and mine is a long way from being Amish.)

Yoder and his Amish colleagues had made an effort to settle the dispute before it reached the courts. They had asked the State Superintendent of Public Instruction to consider the kind of accommodation Pennsylvania has made with the Amish. In that state Amish children are permitted to satisfy the high school attendance requirement by attending an Amish vocational school and, during the balance of the week, to perform farm and household duties under parental supervision, keeping a journal of their daily activities. But the Wisconsin officials would have none of so sensible a compromise. So it was, a complaint having been filed with the local county court, that Yoder, after trial and conviction, was fined $5.00. Under the statute he could have been sentenced to jail.

The court was not unsympathetic to his claim, finding that the compulsory school attendance law did interfere with his freedom to act in accordance with his sincere religious belief, but concluding nevertheless that the requirement of school attendance until age sixteen was a "reasonable and constitutional" exercise of governmental power. The circuit court affirmed, but the Wisconsin Supreme Court reversed, holding that the conviction violated the free exercise clause of the First Amendment. This decision was affirmed by a divided Supreme Court of the United States, the Court's opinion being written by Chief Justice Warren Burger, usually the most sober of men; the lone dissenting vote, paradoxically, was cast by Justice William Douglas, usually the most liberal if not radical of men. So the Amish will be permitted to pursue their traditional, pious, gentle, yet industrious ways; and that is good. But the rule in Yoder's case is not good.

Jews especially will have no difficulty being sympathetic with Yoder's plight. It is similar, for example, to the plight of the Jewish merchant unable to work out an accommodation with the local officials who insist on enforcing Sunday closing laws. And the question Yoder fought through the courts is also similar to the question litigated, not so long ago, by just such a Jewish merchant. A few states make an exception to their Sunday closing laws for persons who, because of religious conviction, observe a day of rest other than Sunday, and the Supreme Court has suggested this may well be "the wiser solution to the problem." Pennsylvania, however, where Abraham Braunfeld had his place of business, was not one of these states. He was in the habit of closing his retail clothing and home furnishing business "from nightfall each Friday until nightfall each Saturday"— as the former Chief Justice, Earl Warren, put it in his 1961 opinion for the Court in *Braunfeld* v. *Brown*—and he sought a court order permitting him to remain open on Sunday. Like Yoder, he hoped to be exempted from a law because of its peculiar impact on him. But at this point there appears a difference between the two cases, and presumably, it was this difference that proved to be material and accounts for the fact that Braunfeld lost his case. "The impact of the compulsory attendance law on respondents' practice of the Amish religion," said Chief Justice Burger, "is not only severe, but inescapable, for the Wisconsin law affirmatively compels them, under threat of criminal sanction, to perform acts undeniably at odds with fundamental tenets of their religious beliefs. See *Braunfeld* v. *Brown*. . . . "

Presumably he referred to Braunfeld's case in order to make the point that whereas Yoder was being affirmatively required to do something that violated his religious beliefs, Braunfeld was merely being asked to refrain from something. While the law imposed a financial burden on him—or, at a minimum, put him at a competitive disadvantage—it did not require him to act in a manner forbidden by Jewish law. It did not—and this, one assumes, would be the equivalent case— require him to open his shop on the Jewish Sabbath. To sum it up, the state may sometimes make piety expensive, but it may never require impiety.

That sounds reasonable enough, but one is left with the lurking suspicion that the distinction is not all that clear.

What of the case of a person firmly persuaded that salvation requires him to go out onto the highways and byways (or at least onto the streets of Brockton, Massachusetts) and preach the gospel by selling or giving away copies of a religious publication—indeed, a person persuaded not only of the necessity to do this but of the consequences of a failure to do it, namely, punishment by "everlasting destruction at Armageddon"? What of such a person being confronted by a child labor law that forbids him to engage in this kind of activity?

The Court had such a case in 1944, and the person involved, a Mrs. Sarah Prince, made it sufficiently clear to the officer who told her to take her nine-year-old niece, Betty Simmons, off the streets that she would not have been satisfied with the distinction drawn in the *Yoder* case. Mrs. Prince told him that neither he nor anyone else could stop her. "This child," she said, "is exercising her God-given right . . . to preach the gospel, and no creature has a right to interfere with God's command."

Here, clearly, is the case where the requirement that one must refrain from an activity (preaching on the streets rather than, as in *Braunfeld*, remaining open on Sunday) has the affirmative effect of requiring one to act in what is understood to be an impious fashion. Not only was Betty Simmons being required to act in an impious fashion, but if she was right about the divine consequences of failing to preach on the streets—Armageddon and all that—she had had it, for the Supreme Court upheld the law.

The problem is this: may a person, because of his religious beliefs, be entitled to an exemption from a valid law? Pennsylvania may require merchants to close their shops on Sunday. Are Jews, because they are Jews, entitled to keep their shops open? The Court said no. In effect, it would be a denial of the equal protection of the laws for Pennsylvania to assess a fine against, say, Ryan, a Roman Catholic, and not against Braunfeld, a Jew, for the same act. Massachusetts may forbid children to engage in commercial activity on the streets. Are Jehovah's Witnesses, precisely because they are Jehovah's Witnesses and required to sell copies of *Watchtower* on the streets, exempt from this requirement? The Court said no. The law is a reasonable health measure, and no one can claim an exemption from it. Wisconsin may require parents to send their children to school until the age of sixteen. Are the Amish, because they are Amish who see nothing but iniquity in the high schools of the community around them, exempt from this requirement? For the first time in its history, the Court said yes to this question.

No doubt it is a difficult question, and no doubt the Justices, silently cursing the Wisconsin school officials for their refusal to find some way of accommodating the Amish without resorting to the courts, would have preferred to avoid it. Indeed, one wonders why they did not avoid it; they would have had a precedent for that. Back in 1944, and again in 1946 in the same case, the Court refused to answer what was probably the most radical formulation ever given this question in American law: does the constitutional guarantee of religious freedom afford immunity from criminal prosecution for the fraudulent procurement of money through the United States mails?

The Court, speaking through Justice Douglas both times, refused to answer, first by sending the case back for retrial and then, on its return, by reversing the conviction on the ground that the indictment had been handed down by a grand jury from which women had been improperly excluded.

It is easy to understand the Court's reluctance to grapple with the issue involved in this one. The defendants were members of the so-called "I Am" movement who claimed to be Saint Germain, Jesus Christ, George Washington, and Godfre Ray King among others, and to possess miraculous powers, including the power to make the sick well and, less generously, the well sick. The Ballards (the name under which they had been indicted and tried) had passed a collection plate through the mails, so to speak, and the government, refusing to credit their miracles, indicted them for mail fraud. They could be convicted, however, only by proof that they knowingly made false representations, and it is said to be no business of any public official in the United States to say what is or what is not a false religious representation. "The religious views espoused ... might seem incredible, if not preposterous, to most people [but] if those doctrines are subject to trial before a jury charged with finding their truth or falsity, then the same can be done with the religious beliefs of any sect."

So said Justice Douglas, although, having decided to send the case back for retrial, it was unnecessary for him to say it. All he accomplished with it was to provoke Harlan Stone, then Chief Justice, to reply that freedom of worship does not include the "freedom to procure money by making knowingly false statements about one's religious experiences." Stone thought the government should be allowed to try to prove the falseness of some of the claims made, at least the claim to have "physically shaken hands with St. Germain in San Francisco on a day named" and have cured "hundred of persons" by means of their special "spiritual power."

In any event, the Ballards escaped punishment, and they escaped it not because a special exemption was carved out of an otherwise valid statute but because almost everyone except Stone was anxious to avoid the trial of such questions, and they should not be criticized for that.

Unlike the Ballards, whom the Justices to a man probably regarded as scoundrels of the worst sort, Yoder and his Amish friends escaped punishment precisely because they were held to be decent, "law-abiding," "productive," "sincere," and—viewed from a world beset with a sense of guilt for what is understood to be its ecological sins and its psychological madness—living "in harmony with nature and the soil," the closest thing possible to the virtuous "sturdy yeoman" of the Jeffersonian "ideal." Pervading Burger's opinion for the Court is a muted admission that the Amish (and others similarly situated, to use the legal phrase) may well have been right all along. It is no wonder Wisconsin could not prevail against them; neither could the gates of hell.

Of course, the Court would have us believe that there is nothing novel about the decision or the rule on which it rests. As Burger put it in his opinion, only state interests "of the highest order ... can overbalance legitimate claims to the free exercise of religion"; or again, while "religiously grounded conduct must often be subject to the broad police power of the State [this] is not to deny that there are areas of conduct protected by the Free Exercise Clause of the First Amendment and thus beyond the power of the State to control, even under regulations of general applicability." But this is not the rule that had been applied in earlier cases, including the ones Burger cites; and it surely is not the rule of the case most apposite to Yoder's, the second flag-salute case (1943), which he does not even deign to mention.

West Virginia required school children to salute the flag and recite the pledge of allegiance. Children who refused to comply were expelled and treated as delinquents; and their parents were made liable to prosecution and, upon conviction, a fine and jail sentence. Jehovah's Witnesses refused to salute the flag, on the ground that to do so would constitute worship of a graven image, and their parents brought suit to enjoin enforcement of the regulation.

Here, in every material sense, is the compulsory school attendance case: in each case children and their parents are being compelled, by a statute carrying criminal penalties, to perform acts contrary to their religious beliefs. The Court ruled in favor of the Jehovah's Witnesses, but it was very careful to avoid making them the special beneficiaries of its decision. The flag-salute requirement was held to be unconstitutional, a violation not, however, of the free exercise of religion clause of the First Amendment but of the free speech provision. Stated otherwise, the Court held that no one, pious sectarian or militant atheist, could be required to salute the flag. In the school attendance case, on the other hand, the Court held that the statute was constitutional, except as applied to Yoder and the other Amish.

The court has never before held that one's religious convictions entitle him to an exemption from the requirements of a *valid* criminal statute. This is new law, and of a dangerous sort. It is dangerous because if one is entitled to disobey a law that is contrary to his religious beliefs, and entitled as well to define his own religious beliefs, the proliferation of sects and of forms of worship will be wonderful to behold: drug cultists, snake worshippers, income-tax haters—why, in Shelley's words, the sense faints picturing them all. But there will be no stopping this religious revival (or what, for legal purposes, will be labeled a religious revival), short of permitting public officials, and ultimately the judges, to do precisely what the Supreme Court has insisted they may not do, namely, get in the business of distinguishing the honest from the dishonest, the genuine from the spurious. The principle was stated best by Justice Robert Jackson in the second flag-salute case: "If there is any fixed star in our constitutional constellation, it is that no official, high or petty, can prescribe what shall be orthodox in . . . religion, or other matters of opinion or force citizens to confess by word or act their faith therein."

But in Yoder's case the Court took the first step in this heretofore prohibited direction by drawing a line between the religious and the secular; it did this by emphasizing that the exemption being carved out for this religious group could not be claimed by other kinds of groups, "however virtuous and admirable" may be their "way of life." No assertion of "secular values" will do, chief Justice Burger insisted in his opinion. Even Thoreau, who, like the Amish, "rejected the social values of his time and isolated himself at Walden Pond," would not have been entitled to the privilege, because, unlike the Amish, his "choice was philosophical and personal rather than religious."

This, inevitably and with very good reason, proved too much for Justice Douglas. He agreed that the Amish could not be compelled to go to high school, but he insisted that the privilege could not be restricted to those whose objection to a law rests on religious belief in a formal sense. So what's wrong with Thoreau's philosophical position? he wanted to know. And the "philosophy" of the conscientious objector who figured it out for himself that "human life is valuable in and of itself"? Douglas wants it known that he adheres to "these exalted views of 'religion,' " and we can expect him to send battalions of his favorite cultists—flag-burners, not-this-war-I-won'ters, and the like—through the gap that will inevitably be blown in that line.

Finally, is it not strange to be told now—after eighteen years of effort to integrate the public schools, when one of the principal political issues appears to be whether there shall be busing to achieve a balance between races; when the decision that gave rise to all this in 1954 held that "education is perhaps the most important function of state and local governments," that "compulsory school attendance laws...demonstrate our recognition of the importance of education to our democratic society," that, indeed, it is "the very foundation of good citizenship," that, in the famous statement that so troubled the logicians, "separate facilities are inherently unequal"—is it not strange to be told now that it is unconstitutional for a state to require children (or, at least, some children) even to go to high school? Is it not strange that they be permitted to segregate themselves from the rest of the American community? That they cannot be forced to attend other schools or, presumably, to accept other children in their schools? Is this not inconsistent with the law of school integration? Or shall we see the day when a suburban school district, asked to show cause why it should not be integrated with an inner-city school district, will reply with the following words:

Said counsel for schools suburbanish:
    "Sure, we admit that we're clannish;
But there's no use your fussing for court ordered busing,
    'Cause there's no one out here but us Amish."

CHAPTER 19

THE "ESSENTIAL SOUL" OF DAN BERRIGAN

> "...Father Dan is reported to have confided to a press conference [at the Cannes Film Festival] that he liked the movie and thought the actor who played him...had 'caught my essential soul.' "
>
> Vincent Canby, *New York Times*, May 28, 1972.

In the old days at Cornell nobody paid much attention to the religious community on campus. It existed; it had its own chaplains—its "livings," so to speak—but not on the university payroll; it even had its own building, thanks to the generosity of Myron C. Taylor, Franklin Roosevelt's special ambassador to Pope Pius XII, but nothing much went on there beyond the simply devotional or ceremonial. Occasionally one of the chaplains, in a forlorn bid for a larger congregation, would suggest that academic credit be given for some Bible study course he was giving, or wanted to give, hoping that this additional enticement would do for Bible study what it had for Naval ROTC; but that sort of thing could, in those days, and however unjustly in some cases, be rejected with little more than an indulgent smile. A chaplain's lot was probably not a happy one on any college campus, but at Cornell, with its anticlerical background, it seemed an especially unhappy one. One of the best of the chaplains, a man dearly loved by some students for his wisdom and goodness, was not displeased when his bishop reassigned him to a parish church in town. Cornell's business was—well, if not business, certainly not Biblical studies, and unlike almost every other private university in the country, never had been. James Perkins, president of the university for a time, knew what he was asking when, during the planning for the centennial, he suggested that the university chorus sing something appropriate to Cornell, and not that "religious stuff." The chorus ended up singing Beethoven's *Missa Solemnis*, not in a spirit of defiance, but because no one except Perkins could imagine two hundred voices belting out in a concert at New York's Lincoln Center the "Cornell Even' Song" (sung to the tune of "O Tannenbaum"), or even the well known "Far Above Cayuga's Waters."

On the whole, the only religious facility that enjoyed much custom was the chapel (destined to be destroyed by arson during the Troubles in 1968–69, although no one could figure out why or by whom): here the faculty could marry off its children and bury its dead, without having to serve as wardens, ushers, lay readers, deacons, or on fundraising committees, or even pretend to any particular form of piety (the altar revolved, displaying at the touch of a button a choice of faces: Christian or very Christian, Jewish, and another that might be described as "none of the above"). To paraphrase the familiar aphorism known to generations of students of public administration, Cornell's clerics were on tap, but not on top, available for ceremonial occasions, like striped trousers and tailcoats, but otherwise playing no role in what was understood to be the serious daily life of the university.

This situation had changed considerably by the time Father Daniel Berrigan, S.J. (who asks everyone to call him Dan) arrived in the autumn of 1967. John Kennedy was dead and, for college students at least, so was the Peace Corps. Overseas service had come to mean service in Vietnam, which had the effect of reminding the young men in the student body that duty is not necessarily compatible with self-interest. With the assistance of an eager and suddenly relevant clergy, the more selfishly disposed young men promptly rechristened self-interest Moral Conscience, and civil disobedience became a way of life at Cornell: draft-card burnings, confrontations with chemical company representatives and military recruiters, disruptions of public meetings and ROTC commissioning ceremonies—in fact, almost the full range of events that would shortly characterize the extracurricular life on most campuses. All this was done with the blessings of the clergy; in March 1967, six months before Dan arrived on the scene, they issued a public statement "affirming the moral right of these students to engage in such civil disobedience" and pledging their help in the event some retaliatory action be threatened against the students, especially "disciplinary action by the University." Anabel Taylor Hall, the campus religious center, took on a new life, teeming with students and jubilant clergy pledging to each other, if not their lives, fortunes, and sacred honor, at least their approbation of whatever they might contrive to do next in the name of their newly discovered moral purpose. In their way, the clergy had declared war on the United States Government.

One might have thought that sending Dan Berrigan to this place at this time was like sending coals to Newcastle or William Sloane Coffin to the Woodstock Festival, but Dan was no ordinary opponent of the war and no ordinary priest, a fact that those who have experienced the intensity of his antiwar passion and have been charmed by the soft music of his voice will eagerly confirm. Why should Cornell be unique and resist him who has in abundance that special charm we associate with the Irish? Yeats set it down for us:

> *There was a green branch hung with many a bell*
> *When her own people ruled this tragic Eire;*
> *And from its murmuring greenness, calm of Faery,*
> *A Druid kindness, on all hearers fell.*

It charmed away the merchant from his guile,
    And turned the farmer's memory from his cattle,
And hushed in sleep the roaring ranks of battle:
    And all grew friendly for a little while.

He had insisted that the time was past "when good men can remain silent," and his quiet but compelling voice had been heard in the church as now it would be heard on campus, among the poor and meek as well as the rich and the proud, the nameless as well as the famous: Gregory Peck, who was so moved by the idea of a "group of people [putting] their freedom on the line ... breaking the law, knowing they'd be arrested," that he devoted a rather large sum of his own money to the task of filming Dan's play, *The Trial of the Catonsville Nine,* so that it might be seen by a wider audience; and Leonard Bernstein held one of his famous fund-raising evenings for him and his brother Philip, thereby indicating that in Radical Chic circles Dan ranked right up there with the Panthers.

There are those who say Dan Berrigan is not popular with the higher officials of the Roman Catholic Church and his Jesuit order, that he is the sort of priest "who causes the lights of the Vatican to burn through the night," but there is little evidence of this. On the contrary, he seems to have had a profound effect on the younger clergy, and on some older ones too, giving them a new sense of mission and a greater zeal in its performance; nor has he encountered anything like the opposition that Arthur Terminiello and Charles Coughlin, radical priests of a generation ago, had to contend with. Terminiello was suspended by his bishop, and Coughlin was silenced by his superiors while his magazine, *Social Justice,* was barred from the mails as a violation of the Espionage Act; whereas, when Dan began serving his sentence in the federal institution at Danbury, Connecticut, the Jesuit Provincial of New England went to the trouble of welcoming him to the province as "a suffering and prophetic brother," and expressed the hope the prison authorities would permit them to celebrate a Mass together.

Well, Dan did not initiate the antiwar movement at Cornell, but it was inevitable that he should take command of it almost as soon as he set foot on campus. The others lacked his flair and his poetic gifts, and, of course, his notoriety. They might preach civil disobedience, but Dan engaged in it—dramatically—and even the priest who went to the trouble of getting himself reclassified precisely to get hold of a draft card he could burn with some reason, got less mileage out of it than Dan got by taking a glass or two, or something, with the boys. He preached, he debated, he counseled, he read his poetry, he lent a soulful presence to a campus not accustomed to it, he served as faculty sponsor of the Homophile Society, he celebrated Mass daily, and he heard an occasional confession. A familiar figure on his edge of the campus, in his beret and turtleneck sweater festooned with medallions of one sort or another, he was constantly surrounded by numbers of admiring students and "nonstudents."

He talked then as he still talks of doing "an unfashionable thing," but actually he was among the most popular figures on campus, increasingly the cynosure of most eyes. The Catonsville affair took place after he had been at Cornell for about a year, and while it would lead to his arrest, trial, conviction, and, after unsuccessful appeals and a four-month period leading the FBI on that merry chase, an eventual imprisonment, none of this was calculated to make him unpopular. In fact, it would appear to have enhanced his status among the people he was trying to reach. The night he debated a professor from the Government Department on the subject of civil disobedience (his prepared remarks that night appear now as Chapter Four of his book, *No Bars to Manhood*), he arrived 15 to 20 minutes late, strolling down the central aisle of the Moot Courtroom of the Law School with his retinue strung out behind him like some inspecting officer's staff. There was a delay while he carried on and lost an argument with the professor of law who was chairing the meeting concerning the failure on the part of someone to set aside space for this retinue, and then still another delay while they found their way to the room set aside for the overflow. But of course no one left. The promise of his presence ensured that.

He made his first Cornell mistake that night and was hissed for it, which came as something of a shock to him, presumably because it had never happened to him before. During the question period he was asked whether he and the eight others at Catonsville had considered the possibility that some harm might come to the defenseless and probably terrified clerk in the draft board office when she saw these grim and uniformed ecclesiastics descend upon her like avenging angels, wrest the card files from her care, and proceed to the parking lot there to burn them with home-made napalm. It must have been a Mephistophelian scene. "It would have scared me half to death," the questioner concluded.

"Yes," Dan replied after a moment's thought, "we gave that *prayerful* consideration. But we decided the protest was so important that we had to run that risk.... Besides," he concluded after a short pause, probably recalling that they had not bothered to solicit the clerk's views as to whether *she* wanted to run that risk, "anyone who works for the draft board deserves no more consideration than the guards at Belsen and Dachau."

And for this remark he was hissed—not roundly, not generally, but, I think it would be fair to say, generously. Of course, it ought to have been greeted with a roar of outrage, especially by the Christians in the audience, as a way of dissociating themselves from a remark so grossly antisemitic, but this was a season at Cornell when roars of outrage were reserved for admonitions to obey the law, and for Averell Harriman and Dean Rusk (what a reception *he* received from our enlightened community).

The meeting broke up at this point because his opponent refused to continue, and it was left to a Jewish Professor of Government, a refugee from Nazi Germany, to make the appropriate response. He had recently injured a foot and it took him some time to hobble up to the platform on his crutches, but, having been seated near the front, he managed to get there in time to block Dan's exit. "That remark," he began in a voice just barely in control, although he was usually the must gentle of men, "that remark is either blasphemous or you are a fool...." " I confess to being unable to hear the rest because Dan had begun to back away and my temporarily crippled colleague was pursuing him, trying simultaneously to keep his finger under Dan's nose and to manage his crutches, and solving that problem finally by hobbling forward a step, then pointing a crutch instead of a finger, then hobbling forward another step. It was a marvelous thing to watch, but for Dan it was obviously an unsettling experience: Surely it had been a long time since he had come face to face with so intense a demonstration of so genuine a moral fervor. He was backed halfway out of the room, managing occasionally, apparently, to indicate with a word or two—and sometimes merely a gesture—that he realized his mistake, that he had been ill-advised to make that remark. And surely he could agree that it is blasphemous to usurp the divine right of judging who is worthy of living and who is not. One wonders whether he would also agree that it is a profanity to trivialize the most horrible experience in the long history of a people who know what it is to suffer horrors. And what can be said of it as a political judgment? Suppose we reverse the terms of the comparison, as grammatically as we are entitled to do, and say this: "The guards at Belsen and Dachau deserve no more consideration than the clerk at the Catonsville, Maryland draft board." Would such a remark have been greeted by a greater volume of hissing, or by expressions of incredulity, or by a roar of the sort of laughter reserved in better days for the egregiously foolish and ugly things? What would Leonard Bernstein say to it? And Gregory Peck, and the rest? It was a bad time in America, a time when to be opposed to the Vietnam war seemed to win immunity for whatever else one might care to say or do.

The Cornell phase of Dan's career came to a sudden and wholly unexpected end when in April 1969 the black students, who never did dance to his pipe, took over the university with real guns which they gave every indication of being willing to use, and Dan became as irrelevant as, on that occasion, President Perkins was invisible. His gospel of peace seemed out of place, inadequate; and in the blink of a frightened eye, and there were lots of frightened eyes at Cornell during that period, the priestly Peter Pan looking so much younger than his years was transformed into the middle-aged *enfant terrible*, ignored and, one is bound to say, properly so, for he had been upstaged. His later comment on this time seems to concede as much in the somewhat petulant note it sounds: "The students who traveled to Baltimore by the hundreds in October [for the trial of the Catonsville 9] put us down sharply a few months later: our style, our nonviolence, our religion." By June 1969, two months later, he was, he said, "old hat."

Well, not quite. His finest hour at Cornell was yet to come, and it may prove to have been the finest hour of his life, for nothing that preceded it and nothing thus far that has succeeded it can match the moment in April of the next year, April 19, 1970, the first anniversary of the seizing of Willard Straight Hall by the blacks, when his fame as a fugitive from the FBI led to his being given a featured role in a Cornell student extravaganza given the name "America Is Hard to Find," supported by a cast of thousands—fifteen thousand, according to the local press. They were on hand from schools all over the East, sitting or lying on, or other wise covering, every inch of floor space in that huge field house, when at just the right moment—exactly the right moment—Dan, rising from the midst of that great throng like some trident-bearing Neptune breaking the surface of the sea, dramatically announced his presence and his determination to remain a fugitive. Then Arthur Waskow asked the crowd if it was ready to give Dan sanctuary from the FBI and "was answered by a thunderous yes." That, *that* was the moment: That was better than Catonsville, better even than the trial at Baltimore, even though the former had been immortalized by the camera's eye and the latter by the poet's word (his own).

Will you give Dan Berrigan sanctuary? "He was answered by a thunderous yes." Surely, surely Dan could be forgiven for wondering whether anyone present could possible forget that night. Or should be allowed to forget it.

Convicted of burning paper to protest the burning of children ("Americans who can bear equably with the sight of burning children," he wrote at the time, "are enraged and baffled by the sight of burning draft files"), he had refused to turn himself in to federal authorities ("I don't have any real yen to be put on the federal happy acres"); yet he had caused the word to be spread that he would return to Cornell, FBI or no FBI, that he would Come Again. And he had. He had been smuggled into the field house disguised as a motorcyclist, and just as Waskow, who was conducting the Freedom Seder, had symbolically opened the door for the prophet Elijah, who is to herald the coming of the Messiah, Dan rose from the crowd, stripping the motorcyclist's helmet from his head, and they had roared, I mean, simply roared. Clenched-fists-thrust-in-the-air roared. Right on! That's telling it like it is Dan baby! Will you give Dan Berrigan sanctuary? "He was answered by a thunderous yes." It was a night they had put it all together, as they say in those circles.

Things began to fall apart shortly thereafter. Before the summer was out he had been apprehended by FBI agents posing not as motorcyclists but as bird watchers, of all things, and he was packed off to the Danbury Federal Correctional Institution. This had to happen; he must have known that he could not spend the rest of his life accepting the sanctuary or even the hospitality of friends (and probably not the ones who had done the shouting in the field house), running from spare bedroom to Castro Convertible to Simmons Hide-a-Bed to plain living room sofa. After a while there was nothing to be gained by that, nothing whatever, and there was a good deal to lose: Really to go into hiding would be to risk being forgotten.

No, he was no more hiding during those four months than in 1958 General Charles de Gaulle was hiding in Colombey-les-Deux Eglises. The only reason to pretend to go into hiding was to remain in the spotlight, and, at this stage of his career, the only way to remain in the spotlight was to go into hiding, so-called. How else do you get to play Elijah at the Freedom Seder? Under what other conditions is it a reportable event to preach a sermon at the First United Methodist Church of Germantown, Pennsylvania (the television people having been advised in advance in order to give them time to set up their cameras)? Or give interviews or contribute articles to *Saturday Review, Commonweal,* the *New Yorker,* the *New York Review of Books, Christian Century,* the Sunday *New York Times Magazine,* and the *Village Voice*? Or cocking a snook at the FBI, make television network appearances and manage to get a play produced? And all this within a period of a few months of so-called hiding? Elizabeth Taylor can burst pendulously into the news with a 50-carat diamond dangling from her forehead, but priests need something else going for them.

Things began to fall apart after that last Cornell weekend not because he would shortly be in jail, but because he had exhausted the dramatic possibilities of his priestly office. It is news when a priest burns draft cards by the drawers full, especially when he does it with homemade napalm; but you can only do that once (and, besides, his brother Philip had already done the lamb's blood *shtick*). It is news when a priest, especially an Irish priest, openly defies the FBI; but then that game is caught too, as Lincoln used to say. It is news when a priest writes a play in which he himself is given the leading role, thereby writing the account of his own martyrdom; but it would really be overdoing it to subject oneself to double martyrdom, so to speak, simply to write another play. Of course, it can be filmed, and one can give press conferences at Cannes; that is good for a while. It would be news to blow up the government heating system and kidnap Henry Kissinger. That would be a terrific gesture—brilliant even if a bit grandiose, as his brother put it in that letter to Sister Elizabeth McAlister—terrific, sure, but hardly a priestly gesture, and certainly not seriously entertained by these priests. And so you reach the point where being a priest becomes a handicap instead of an advantage, when your "brothers and sisters" in the Weathermen are busily engaged in bomb-construction or trashing the banks or blowing up washrooms in the Pentagon, and your profession requires you to administer the sacraments or celebrate a Mass, or quietly teach the perplexed or counsel the troubled or comfort the bereaved, or, in some cases, simply study. And there is no news in that; not nowadays, at least.

In the old days—one might even say, the good old days—when in certain countries the entire church was "underground," there was news to be made in the mere fact of celebrating a Mass. There is something to be said for those countries: a clever priest can use a government that persecutes him and, if he does not have one, the next best thing is to be able to invent one. Essentially, that is what Dan has done. He was duly convicted of having committed a crime that he admits having committed, he was given a sentence not out of line with those given others for similar offenses, he enjoyed the right of appeal—all the way to the Supreme Court, where not even Justice Douglas voted to hear his case—and then he chose to avoid jail by refusing to turn himself in to the authorities. At this point the FBI was given the task of finding him. Nothing special about this. Nothing vindictive, nothing persecutory. But listen to Dan's account: "Undoubtedly the FBI comes after people like me with guns because deeper than their personal chagrin and their corporate machismo, which is a kind of debased esprit de corps since they always get their man, there was that threat that the Panthers and the Vietnamese had learned so well as a reality. The threat is a very simple one because we are making connections, political connections, religious and moral connections, connections with prisoners and Cubans and Vietnamese, and these connections are forbidden under the policies which J. Edgar Hoover is greatly skilled both in enacting and in enforcing. They know by now what we are about, they know we are serious. And they are serious about us."

Beware the Jabberwock, my son!
   The jaws that bite, the claws that catch!
Beware the Jubjub bird, and shun
   The frumious bandersnatch!

II

He owes his fame in part to the fact that he is a priest. Countless other men and women, and not all of them unknown by any means, have burned draft cards, stormed the Pentagon, counseled resistance to the draft, and made highly critical statements about Mr. Nixon (and, lest we forget, Mr. Johnson too); but somehow they have not made anything like the impact on the public's consciousness that Dan has made, even if they have been tried in the courts in well-publicized trials. He and his brother Philip are priests, and America is not accustomed to seeing priests challenge the law. An older Jesuit, writing in the special edition of the *Holy Cross Quarterly* devoted exclusively to the Berrigans, says that their achievement consists in having "challenged in the public mind the automatic identification of American Catholicism with the status quo [and] its alliance with prevailing patriotic causes," thereby raising a doubt that "American Catholicism can be counted on to supply acolytes for *all* shrines of the civic religion that is the American Way of Life." Well, yes, Father Duff may be right, but there have been priests in the past who insisted that "Christianity has a social message," and who discerned some difference between that message and "the American Way of Life," and who tried to lead a moral crusade against it. One thinks again of Father Coughlin, the antiwar priest of the late Thirties, who called Franklin Roosevelt a "scab President," and who, with the help of the even more disreputable Christian Front, succeeded in getting American Catholicism identified for a time with extreme isolationism and, in some quarters, with the native fascism making the rounds then. Father Duff is old enough to remember this. Still, he has a point: despite the Coughlins and the Terminiellos, the prototypical American priest remained Pat O'Brien, kind to children at the settlement house, sure, but also, saints be praised, a helluva good man to have in the trenches with the rest of the Fighting 69th. The Berrigans may have put an end to that.

But Dan is more than a priest. Unlike his brother Philip, to say nothing of the nameless thousands of other priests in America, Dan is a personality. He has a marvelous talent for publicizing himself, a talent shared, in the priesthood, only by Father Coughlin again, and Coughlin's appeal was to an entirely different audience. Dan is no rabble-rouser; he is too quiet, too thoughtful, too educated a man for that. If Coughlin came out of the isolationist Middle West and appealed to the worst passions of the readers of the *Chicago Tribune* and the Hearst press, Dan comes out of the internationalist East and, paradoxically, appeals to the very decent passions of Mr. Spiro Agnew's "effete snobs" of the Establishment. They love him in Long Island—and in Westchester and Fairfield County, Connecticut.

Time, a part of the Establishment by any man's standards, ran a cover story on him, suggesting that he might very well be a martyr, and comparing him along the way with Thomas More, even though More had to lose his head and suffer the posthumous indignity of having it displayed on London Bridge (still in London at the time), and even so did not achieve beatification until 1886, 351 years later (he was canonized only in 1935). It is Dan's talent for publicity that accounts for the swiftness of his elevation to the ranks of the exalted. Unlike More, Dan has written a play about his own martyrdom—probably the first to do so—in which he is likened to Jesus Christ and Socrates. Thus he serves as his own chronicler, being unwilling, the times being what they are, to wait for an apostle or a Plato or Xenophon, or to trust them with the nuances of the material. *The Trial of the Catonsville Nine* has been a smash hit in theaters in Europe and Canada, as well as in the United States; and now, thanks to Gregory Peck and the actor who plays Dan, and managed to catch his "essential soul," there is the film, capable of bringing the message to millions. The third act is the important act; here the nine defendants speak to the court and, through the agency of Dan's poetry, to Gregory Peck and the rest of mankind. Dan sees to it that his brother Philip speaks first and that he himself speaks last, sort of wrapping it up for the defense, and not only last, but longest, getting 14 and a half pages to John Hogan's one and a half, for example, or Mary Moylan's three and a half. Anyone can burn a draft card, but only a poet can be trusted to immortalize the event, because only the poet or someone like him, can see its full significance. Only the poet will know what to say in the dramatic presentation of the trial, because only the poet can see the significance of The Trial.

Some of the most famous literary events have been trials. Socrates was tried. Jesus was tried. Jesus suffered before Pontius Pilate and, in the manner of his suffering, as we learn from Dan in the fifth chapter of *No Bars to Manhood*, "added a cubit to His stature," and Dan, we learn in the same chapter of the same book, added a cubit or two to his at Catonsville. Catonsville is a story one simply does not trust to other pens. Because of Catonsville he can "claim a certain sorry advantage over most of those who have yet to choose the place and time of their response to American violence, a response that will embody their existence and carry their lives captive, in bonds to a choice, in a direction they cannot yet know." (Dan's carried him to the Cannes Film Festival, for instance.)

It is not the profundity of his political thought that accounts for his fame and the esteem in which he is held. Even *Time* admits that when he is talking politics "he often sounds commonplace [grinding] on mechanically about 'national illness ... madness ... the latest American idiocy.' " Even Father Duff gently chides him for certain hyperbole. The decent young man who faced the terrible question of whether to obey the law that required him to participate in a war he profoundly believed to be an evil and immoral abomination, could, I think, be moved by the example of this apparently tormented priest and refuse to serve; but I do not understand how anyone can be persuaded in this direction, or be attracted to Dan, by the political thought that accompanies the example and by which he tries to justify it. The fact is, it does not make sense; there was no relation between his analysis of the political situation and the action he proposed by way of remedy or solution. The American government, he said, is utterly and hopelessly corrupt, "fearful of change, racist, violent, a Nero abroad in the world," committing terrible crimes which it tries always to conceal, teaching the best of its youth to be murderers, directing its considerable powers knowingly to the "grinding under of human beings"; so corrupt that in order "to join the heart of man" it is necessary for him to "resign from America."

So goes the analysis. And what should be done? "Let me say as plainly as I know how, I don't see as a political tactic that anything that might be called 'useful' is left to us, except civil disobedience." Civil disobedience! The situation is hopeless, he says, and he proposes the "desperate" remedy of a ceremonial breaking of the law. As if Count von Stauffenberg, instead of placing that bomb at Hitler's feet, had set fire to a Third Reich draft card and said, "Take that, mein Führer!"

What sort of sentimental nonsense is it that tells a man to be *civil* in his disobedience to a government he regards as absolutely corrupt? Jefferson and his colleagues at the beginning were not being civil in their disobedience to British authorities; they were killing British soldiers, and they knew what would happen to them if they lost the war, which is why they pledged to each other their lives, their fortunes, and their sacred honor. Civil disobedience is a different thing; Martin Luther King defined it as "an open and loving breaking of the law with a willingness to accept the consequences." No *just* man would lovingly break a Nazi law. Whom or what would he be loving? Lovingly to break a law, as Herbert Storing has made clear in the best of the essays on civil disobedience, is to acknowledge that there is something in the regime that deserves to be loved; that there is some justice in the regime, and it is to this justice, or sense of justice in those comprising the government, that one appeals when he lovingly breaks an unjust law of that fundamentally just regime. As Storing shows, the case for civil disobedience breaks down even under these conditions, but that is beside the point here. Here there really can be no argument as to the inadequacy of civil disobedience in the context for which Dan prescribes it. If he is right about the utter corruption and evil of American government, what ought to follow is revolution, not draft card burnings. His "brothers and sisters" of the Weathermen appear to know this even if he does not; if they wanted to be whimsical, they could appropriately quote Scripture to him, saying that having become a man, he should put away childish things.

But, of course, Dan's analysis is absurd. To say that the American government "stifles dissent" is ridiculous; to call the United States a Nero is to disclose an ignorance of tyrants and of the nature of tyranny; to say that Americans "can bear equably with the sight of burning children" is to utter slander of hideous proportions; and to charge the clerk at Catonsville with crimes the equal of those committed by the guards at Belsen and Dachau is, as I said earlier, blasphemous and profane.

The Trial of the Catonsville Nine may be a dramatic and propagandistic triumph, but its poetry, and the license enjoyed by poets (in general and by this one is particular), conceals the absurd or, alternatively, the pernicious character of the doctrine it espouses. The judge, nameless and the object of ridicule in the play, refuses to charge the jury that they may take into account the purity of the motives that led the defendants to burn those draft cards. The defendants claim not to understand this, and the following exchange takes place:

> *George Mische:*   But was the jury told they could not use their conscience in determining—
>
> *Judge:*   I certainly did not tell them they could disregard their oath and let you off on sympathy, or because they thought you were sincere people.

Daniel Berrigan: Your honor, we are having great difficulty in trying to adjust to the atmosphere of a court from which the world is excluded, and the events that brought us here are excluded deliberately, by the charge to the jury.

Judge: They were not excluded. The question—

Daniel Berrigan: May I continue? Our moral passion was excluded. It is as though we were subjects of an autopsy, were being dismembered by people who wondered whether or not we had a soul. We are sure that we have a soul. It is our soul that brought us here. It is our soul that got us in trouble. It is our conception of man. But our moral passion is banished from this court. It is as though the legal process were an autopsy.

Judge: Well, I cannot match your poetic language.
      (*Applause from the audience*)

That is how it goes in the play. Now I propose to rewrite the last part of this scene, this time giving the good lines to the judge.

Judge: Yes, Father Berrigan, I must insist that "moral passion" be kept out of this trial, your moral passion, the jurors' moral passion, and my moral passion—and please extend us the courtesy of acknowledging that we too are capable of feeling it.

Daniel Berrigan: I am sure you are, your honor, all of—

Judge: Thank you. Now I want you to understand, if possible, why what you call your "moral passion," or conscience, or the purity of the motives that led you to Catonsville, is irrelevant. I will ask you whether this right to follow conscience rather than the law is a right belonging to everyone or only to you and your friends?

Daniel Berrigan: "Everyone" is not on trial here. My friends and I—we, made sick by this war and by the government that wages it—are on trial. Your question is too abstract; I can't answer it until some flesh is put on its bare bones.

Judge: Well, I'll put some flesh on them for you. I'll bring "moral passion" into these proceedings! I'll begin by charging the jury that they can take account of their moral passion, if they like, and disregard the evidence, if they like, and bring in a verdict of guilty, if they like. And how do *you* like that?

Daniel Berrigan: We never doubted that we would be convicted.

Judge: All right. Then when it comes to sentencing you, I'll pay no attention to the statute and send you up for as long as it pleases me.

Defense Counsel: I object, your honor!

Judge: You? Be quiet or I'll cite you for contempt. Under the rules, of course, you don't deserve to be cited; but the rules have now given way to moral passion, you know.

Defense Counsel: You do that, your honor, and I'll file an appeal so fast. . . .

Judge: Ah! You'll file an appeal, will you? You'll appeal to the rules because I have broken them, is that it? Your clients may do as they please—after "prayerful consideration," no doubt—but the rest of us must abide by the rules. Tell me, Father Berrigan, what makes you so special?

Daniel Berrigan: Well, I . . . ah . . .

Judge: Oh, never mind. I am bound to say, however, and I think most of the people in this courtroom will agree with me, that no country dedicated as Lincoln said, to the proposition that all men are created equal, can officially acknowledge that some people are purer in heart than others and therefore deserve a special immunity from the rules that bind everyone else. . . . I also suspect that most of the people in this courtroom will agree with me when I say that you have not even begun to think about these matters, Father Berrigan.

(Tremendous applause from the audience)

Judge (languidly tapping his gavel): Order, order.

There, we can be fairly certain, is a scene that Gregory Peck will not film or Leonard Bernstein set to music.

What used to set Dan apart from the other leaders of the Movement—Jerry Rubin or Abbie Hoffman, for example, or even Dr. Spock and the old-time pacifist, Dave Dellinger—was not the profundity of his political thought (or the banality of it), or the depth of his despair, the degree of his anger, or his capacity for finding ways of expressing it. What used to set him apart and make him so appealing to the student Left, especially, was his nominal authority to sanctify what the others could only justify or recommend. The act committed in his name or in his presence took on a significance it lacked when done by or with the others. Burning a draft card with Dan was doing God's work. Unlike the Yippies, Crazies, the simply angry, and those who give no fancy name to their crime, Dan provided a spiritual presence in the lives of his young, and not-so-young, followers. I suppose President Nixon would say he provided that extra dimension. Even with the Chicago 7 (or was it 8?), the young resister merely had the sense of Crossing-a-State-Line-with-the-Intent-to-Incite-Promote-Encourage-or-Participate-in-a-Riot, or something equally banal in the end; but with Dan he was making a spiritual odyssey into the "dark night of resistance." And who does not want to explore the hidden depths of that "dark socket of existence" or live it up during the "dark night of resistance"? You're only young once. But then people grow up, and graduate, returning only for class reunions. Some people, the Weathermen, for example, never do return.

Politically, the Weathermen seem to have traveled a long way beyond the draft card burning with which they began, some of them with Dan at Cornell, and to be utterly uninterested in exploring sockets of existence, light or dark, with him. In fact, they seem to have traveled well beyond the range of his voice, as he learned when he tried to reach them with that famous Open Letter. "Dear Brothers and Sisters," it begins, "this is Dan Berrigan speaking...across the underground." But there was no response, even though he was quick to point out that there was no difference between them respecting the destruction of property (other people's, that is); destroying property is all right, as "a means"; he draws the line only at the taking of human lives. "No principle is worth the sacrifice of a single human being"— apparently, now, not even the life of that clerk at Catonsville or of the guards at Belsen and Dachau. Why not? Because God has commanded us not to kill? Well, no, as a matter of fact, he does not quote the Bible to them. Instead of a divine commandment Dan offers them a "rule of thumb" that he "came upon ... somewhere," and here it is: "do only that which one cannot not do." Which is to say, do the irresistible. (And wouldn't Cole Porter have had a good time setting that to music?) Sure people are going to apply that rule differently; that is the trouble with an ethics that is wholly formal and abstract. Dan knows that, and he offers the name of a man who can be trusted to apply the rule correctly and can therefore be accepted as a model. Dan is a Jesuit priest, right, so the model man is Jesus Christ? Well, no, as a matter of fact; instead of Jesus Christ he offers Che Guevara: "I hope you see your lives as Che saw his, that is to say mainly as teachers of the people, conscious as we must be of the vast range of human life that still awaits liberation and education and consciousness."

I suspect they do indeed see their lives as Che saw his; that has been obvious for some time. As I had occasion to write a few years ago, Che was the hero of such people because he was not a theorist but a committed man of action whose life acquired its "meaning" only on the barricades, whether in Cuba or in the wilds of Bolivia. For the angry adolescents of the world he was a perfect model because he himself was the perpetual adolescent, going so far as to give up a cabinet post, an adult job, in Castro's revolutionary government in order to return to the barricades. The Weathermen certainly do not need to be enjoined to follow the example of Che Guevara, nor do they need the help of a middle-aged priest to interpret his life and teaching. They show every sign of having mastered his teaching.

III

Dan's greatest admirers would agree, I think, that he is not, finally, a political man, and that it is unfair to judge him by the standards appropriate to the political world. He is essentially a religious man, a mystic, his friends say, "a man of God risking all to grasp what that means in the secular '70s." His latest book, *The Dark Night of Resistance*,* won the Thomas More Medal as the "most distinguished contribution to Catholic Literature in 1971," and it will not do for an Episcopalian political scientist to question this award or to suggest that 1971 must have been a particularly poor year for Catholic literature. Dan recounts in this book how in Hanoi, where he had gone to assist in the repatriation of the first American fliers released by the North Vietnamese, he experienced one of his rather frequent spiritual awakenings, this one brought on when he encountered Buddha, the "many faces of Buddha," at a time when "the United States of America was taking an Infant Jesus to its religious heart, changing His underpants on major feast days. A culture of infancy savored and prolonged: a religion for infants."

One might have thought that the Thomas More awards committee would be put off by such talk—I mean, it certainly does not *seem* very Catholic, or even very Christian, not, at least, to someone brought up on the Book of Common Prayer; but in the day of *Godspell* and *Jesus Christ Superstar* and *Hair* and *Oh! Calcutta!* one must be prepared to acknowledge the possibility that there is some truth in the old saying that all roads lead to Rome. Still, Christianity a "religion for infants"? Nowadays you get Christian prizes for that?

We know of course what he thinks of Americans, so we are somewhat prepared to read that they are divided into two contemptible types: The first wants "the Ten Command-

---

*Since this was written he has published one or two more. As he said in *No Bars to Manhood* (pp. 7-8), after a certain point in time, publishers would "take almost anything [he] chose to compile...."

ments tattooed on his bung hole, in ten colors," so he can "back into eternity, doubled over...like a New Eastern slave"; the second "wants the American flag tattooed in three colors, on his prick's round," so he can—well, never mind. Whereas in his vision there is a Paradise Park with "a free zone [erogenous?], laughter, released stays and buttons and zippers [I guess so], a few lovers or many [where] the people enter, grow, run, fly, perambulate, consume, pull corks from, spread jams and peanut butter on, swim and sun in, etcetera as the day is long...." Terrific. (But would Thomas More have liked it?)

There are undoubtedly profundities here that escape the lay mind; we know from his friendly journalists that his religious thought is profound. We cannot expect easy answers to the hard questions he raises, and since we are told by the friendly journalists that the strength of his thought consists in his "mysticism" we must be prepared to follow him up peaks lost in Himalayan mists or down the winding back alleys of transcendental meditation; everything we know about him confims his reputation as a radical priest, so we cannot expect a traditional answer, even though he insists he is "unrecognizable" to himself apart from the Christian tradition. "In spite of all," he cries out, "what are we to do with our lives?" It is the best of questions and, given the nature of our times, the most urgent of questions. And the answer—or rather, his answer? It is not easy to find, but every now and then we catch sight of Dan drifting along with the prevailing winds of doctrine blowing through the not-so-nether regions of the American counterculture, trailing the familiar banner: do your own thing!

Do it the way of Guru Gandhi, if that's your bag, or Guru Socrates, or Guru Buddha—or even Guru Jesus; or learn what you can from R.D. Laing or Herbert Marcuse; they are all here, a "plethora of riches," the complete pantheon of today's deities, including, of course, everybody's favorite guru, Che Guevara. Che? A gunman? Can a "gunman" be a guru? Yes, "provided he is first of all a peaceable man, a man of his people [such as] Guevara, Ho, Castro." "*Disciple:* How do I attain ultimate reality? *Master:* It is May. Seek a tulip in hell, and bring it back." (Deep, man, like real deep.)

Dan has a dream, a "dream of every resisting commune with a guru (Christian, Jewish, Hindu, Zen) in roving residence." (*Perplexed Disciple:* But Master, whose word do I follow when they tell me conflicting things? *Guru Dan:* The scriptures are the "word of god in whatever language or tradition"; therefore, there can be no conflict. Or if there is, take your choice, because "it is neither useful nor inevitable that our lives be stuck fast in moral stalemate.") He himself has "no stake in Church or state, as currently in evidence; their aims, their values, their mutual transfusions of comfort. . . . [He is] dead to all that." The important thing is to be—guess what?—"authentic," to work out "new ways of getting connected," as he told the Weathermen, new ways "of getting married, of educating children, of sharing goods and skills, of being religious, of being human, or resisting." "We are trying to get reborn," and, it should be stated for purposes of clarification, lest it be thought that this rebirth will require too much effort and discipline on our parts—too much of the "hard and bitter agony" that T.S. Eliot speaks of in "The Journey of the Magi"—reborn in any way and into any thing we choose. "What are we to do with our lives?" Jerry Rubin said it all in two words, and said it without the cant: "Do it!"

IV

Several of his friends who sheltered him in the fugitive days of 1970 have explained what it was like then to be with Dan, to share his sorrows and joy, his excitement, his plans, and even, as one of them put it, the exhilaration of defying the government. But it was not all that sort of game. Dan would also arrange marvelous weekends in the country when entire families would come together with him to consider how they could build a new society, and end racism, and war, and things like that. "Dan had a vision that in an atmosphere of retreat from the world, into ourselves, we would awaken to a new life and new possibilities." So what happened? Well, what with the "whining mosquitoes" and the "yappings of family dogs" and the "tedious demands of children," there could be no peace for "ideological contemplation, no atmosphere for mystical transformation." Imagine the star of Catonsville, Peck's good boy himself, the Elijah of the Freedom Seder and the fugitive from the FBI, having to compete with family dogs and children! It surely is not difficult to understand why "Dan's self-restraint became increasingly visible," or why he took on such a look that his friends "withered in his gaze."

But damn it! Was it really wrong to love the children, to carry on jobs, to be well-meaning? Could they be expected to transform themselves immediately into Dan's vision of them? Of course not. They had been "seduced by the man and by [their] own romanticism"; he was not their pastor and it was wrong for him to pretend to be. Nor was his way, however right for him, necessarily the right way for them. They had their integrity too. Well, these things got said, and having been said, relations were a bit difficult for a while—there was even some "guarded hostility" (although nothing approaching the war they were assembled to end); then they went for a swim. They met again in the evening, but, unfortunately, things were not the same as they had been before their spat.

Not all his friends reacted in this way. The wife in another of the families that sheltered him explains how she and Dan were baking a pecan pie one day. I gather from her account that this must be a nerve-wracking experience under the most propitious of pie-baking conditions, what with those nuts to be shelled, and the shells getting all over the floor, and the syrup bubbling on the stove, threatening constantly to boil over, and what a mess that would be; but to find oneself simultaneously up to one's intellectual neck in philosophical dialogue with America's most famous theologian, and then to be interrupted by the "shrill intrusion of children's voices," well, that makes it the kind of experience that will strain the strongest of constitutions. Dan left the kitchen, but she did not get angry with him. Instead, she got a bit angry with the children and sent them out of the room. She then records that Dan did not eat any of the pie at dinner that night and she wondered why. She "was puzzled," she says, and "he never explained."

Well, of course, it had nothing to do with the pie; she can rest assured on that score at least. His mind was on other things; more exalted things: He was writing the Thomas More Medal-winning *Dark Night of Resistance* at that time. "I want to do an unfashionable thing," he writes on the first page of the book,

> in a time which is not so much fashionable—as simply mad. So mad that it has become a wearying stereotype to speak of its madness. Since the admission hangs choking on the air, is part of the daily burden. You young resisters, what of the madness to which we have delivered you, like a sour ration at the cell door? You fervent apostles of war normalcy, you hunted Panthers, you police, you political big-stick wielders, you few men and women faithful to suffering and the long haul, you, my friends, concocting ways of keeping me uncaged, you students pondering a future in the shadow of Dame Liberty violated (your future closing like a vise). For all of you, resisting, resisting resistance, keeping it heated, keeping it cool, you great self-spawning disease, you nation, you of the nation within the nation, still unrecognized, still in bondage—for you. Something unfashionable; one man's spiritual journey. The delayed journey, into light; or more exactly into a light forever quenched, delayed, snuffed out.

"[Alice] puzzled over this for some time, but at last a bright thought struck her. 'Why it's a looking-glass book, of course! And if I hold it up to a glass, the words will all go the right way again.'

> "This was [how it came out to] Alice . . .
> "*Twas brillig, and the slithy toves*
>   *Did gyre and gimble in the wabe;*
>   *All mimsy were the borogoves,*
>   *And the mome raths outgrabe.*"

CHAPTER 20

THE NATION AND THE BISHOPS

Nothing is settled yet—a final decision won't be reached until a meeting scheduled for next May—but there is reason to fear that the National Conference of Catholic Bishops may have put its church on a collision course with the U.S. government. Last month in Washington the bishops adopted the second draft of a pastoral letter on war and peace, and it is vital that we all be clear about its implications and, assuming its adoption as a statement of church policy, its probable consequences.

At issue is the peace that has characterized relations between church and state during most of our history, and, beyond that, the peace of the world and the perpetuation of liberal democracy in at least a part of it. The bishops are playing for very high stakes.

Not the least of the probable consequences is that lay Catholics will be put in the position of having to choose between obeying either their spiritual advisers or the law of the land. The letter reiterates an earlier episcopal pronouncement that conscription is immoral, "except in the case of a national defense emergency," and that, even in such an emergency, any conscientious person may refuse to serve in the armed forces.

Moreover, like Archbishop Raymond G. Hunthausen of Seattle, who has advised Catholics not to pay what he regards, incorrectly, as the defense portion of their income taxes (50%), the letter reiterates the bishops' support for "selective conscientious objection." Whether a person "participates in a particular war" should depend on his judgment—or more likely, the bishops' judgment—"of the ends being pursued or the means being used" in that war. The bishops know that this—Dial a War?—is not now a legal right, but they are insisting that Congress make it one.

Then, those Catholics who don't exercise their option to refuse military service are warned that they may not deliberately use their weapons, or join in the use of weapons, against civilian populations. If obeyed, this is certain to have ramifications affecting this country's second-strike deterrence policy. Beyond this, young Catholics in the civilian population are advised to seek careful guidance as to their civic responsibilities in this nuclear age, and while the bishops do not—"at this time"—forbid Catholics to work in nuclear weapons plants, we can be fairly certain that debate on this question hasn't ended. Bishop Leroy Matthiesen of Amarillo, Texas, who has already advised his flock to avoid such employment, will see to that.

The letter is grounded on two premises: that nuclear war must be avoided at all costs and that, once begun, such a war couldn't be contained. Thus, the letter continues, no nation *could* be excused for first using nuclear weapons, and no nation or alliance (that is, NATO) *can* be excused for adopting a policy that depends on or contemplates their first use. Finally, except under conditions that are unlikely ever to be met, no nation or alliance can be excused for adopting a policy of second use.

This means that deterrence—preventing a nuclear attack by threatening to retaliate in kind—cannot be justified except insofar as it is temporary expedient, a tactic whose purpose is to set in motion the process leading to complete disarmament. The bishops acknowledge that nuclear weapons haven't been used since World War II, but they refuse to credit deterrence with this happy, but in their eyes fortuitous, fact. Besides, even if deterrence has played some part in maintaining peace between the superpowers, there is no guarantee that it will continue to do so. Deterrence is not, they say, an "infallible way of maintaining real peace," and, perhaps out of habit, they will settle for nothing less than infallibility. They therefore demand that all nations divest themselves of all nuclear weapons.

Having reached this point in their analysis, it seems to have occurred to the bishops that the Soviet Union is less likely than the U.S. to accept their counsel on this (or any other) matter. At any rate, although it isn't directed to anyone in particular, their final policy suggestion seems to be addressed principally to us Americans: "non-violent means of resistance to evil should be carefully weighed." Gandhi's tactic may not "always" succeed, but, weighed in the balance with the "almost certain effects of a major war," it is, say the bishops, worth considering. It may even be worth a try. (And if it doesn't work, we can always go back to the drawing board—if we are still around, and if we are permitted to have a drawing board.)

Much has been made of the bishops' right as citizens to speak out on public affairs, even on those matters (and defense policy is acknowledged to be one of them) on which they are not experts. So prevalent is this view of what the bishops are entitled to say that anyone who questions it is likely to be attacked by liberal editorial writers and ridiculed by cartoonists. (It is remarkable how popular the bishops have become since they shifted their attention from abortion to nuclear weapons.)

But there is a difference between, say, McGeorge Bundy, whose authority, if any, depends altogether on the power of his argument, and the bishops, whose authority derives from their offices: We may all, even the Catholics among us, ignore Mr. Bundy, but the Catholics among us may not so readily ignore the bishops. And when the bishops preach civil disobedience, neither may the rest of us.

With only slight exaggeration, it can be said that the

bishops claim to speak not in their capacity as citizens, but in the name of God. Father Timothy S. Healy, S.J., Georgetown University president and probably Washington's most popular Catholic, affirmed this in a recent piece in the *Washington Post*: to nonbelievers the bishops are merely men, speaking as other men speak, but to Catholics "the bishops speak with another voice [and] it is fascinating that even the nonbelieving world has grown edgily conscious that the voice it hears is more than the voice of men."

As one might expect, the pastoral letter itself is quite frank on episcopal authority. The church is "the instrument of the Kingdom of God in history," and every one of its members is required to be not merely a believer but a "doer of the Word." This means that Christians must now move "from discussion to witness and action," and the bishops must take the lead by educating their communicants on the issues of war and peace, urging them "to make the moral decisions required."

The letter is less than frank, however, as to what is expected of Catholics who hold public office, especially those with responsibility to formulate foreign and defense policies. (What would have been the response of President Kennedy when told that, in the opinion of his church, his first strike and deterrence policies were immoral?) Like all Catholics, they are expected to be good citizens, but they are also expected to "hold to the universal principles proclaimed by the Church"; and if this puts them or any other Catholic in conflict with the civil law, the bishops' attitude is: So be it. They, at least, are willing to risk "persecution," and as for "the possibility of martyrdom," that, they assure us, is the "normal" way of a priest.

But it has not been the normal way of an American priest. As Washington said in 1790, the U.S. government would give "to bigotry no sanction, to persecution no assistance," and the government has kept that promise: the clergy have run no risk of being persecuted and have been given no reason to become martyrs. In return, Washington continued, the government "requires only that those who live under its protection should demean themselves as good citizens, in giving it on all occasions their effectual support."

And, on the whole, the clergy of all denominations, in exchange for a freedom of conscience and worship that is constitutionally guaranteed, have acknowledged their duty to obey the laws. Willingly or not, they have agreed with Jefferson that "the acts of the body," unlike the operations of the mind, "are subject to the coercion of the laws." Which is to say, they have agreed with the principle that under a government instituted to secure the rights with which nature endows all men (whether pious or impious) no man (however pious or impious) may put himself above the law. To Jefferson this was a principle derived from the self-evident truth that all men are created equal. The bishops are coming perilously close to denying that principle and that truth, and we may all suffer the consequences.

CHAPTER 21

A NEW FLOCK OF SHEEP

As the Catholic "Peace Bishops" are about to learn, it is not possible to be both an American and a martyr. Christian "witnesses" have been known in other times and places to endure unspeakable torments rather than abandon their faith, and there must still be Americans (perhaps these bishops) who would cheerfully audition for that role, but, alas for them and fortunately for the rest of us, our civil authorities refuse to cooperate by casting them in it. They don't ask anyone to "testify" to his faith; the Constitution forbids them to ask such questions. They ask only that everybody obey the laws, which explains why our potential or passive martyrs are reduced to going to court. There, instead of being tortured, they are rewarded. Like almost every other American profession or, indeed, activity, what passes for martyrdom here is likely to prove profitable. It surely was for Eddie C. Thomas and it is likely to be for the bishops and their flocks.

A Jehovah's Witness, Thomas was initially hired by his employer to work in a roll foundry which produced sheet steel for a variety of industrial uses; when the foundry was closed down, he was transferred to a department engaged solely in the fabrication of military tank turrets. Citing religious scruples against any kind of military weapons work, Thomas quit his job and—apparently setting aside whatever scruples he might have had against receiving aid from a

Reprinted, with permission, from *The American Spectator*, September 1982.

government that has a use for tank turrets—applied for unemployment compensation. Here he was opposed by the Indiana law that recognized voluntary terminations of employment but only those for "good cause in connection with the work." His administrative appeals proving fruitless, Thomas went to court, eventually all the way to the Supreme Court where, as any cynical (and not so cynical) observer of that august body could have predicted, he won. By refusing to award him unemployment compensation, the Court said, Indiana had deprived him of the free exercise of religion in blatant violation of the First Amendment. Only Justice William Rehnquist dissented.

At this point, it might be useful to be reminded of what the Constitution (as opposed to the Supreme Court) has to say on this subject of religion and the military. The religious provisions of the First Amendment read as follows: "Congress [and by judicial construction, the states] shall make no law respecting an establishment of religion, or prohibiting the free exercise thereof." It used to be understood that nothing in this language prevented the government from requiring military service of every citizen or from punishing anyone who, for whatever reason, refused to serve. Since the United States has never seen itself as a modern Sparta, the apparent severity of this principle has always been moderated by the practice of allowing people with religious scruples against bearing arms to claim exemptions as conscientious objectors. But this was understood to be a matter of legislative grace, not constitutional right. As someone said during the Bill of Rights debates in the First Congress, and no one contradicted him, "no man can claim this indulgence by right," and so long as these issues were governed by the Constitution, no man could claim any lesser indulgence by right. Jefferson stated the principle embodied in the free exercise clause when he wrote that, unlike the operations of the mind, the acts of the body "are subject to the coercion of the laws," and he would have scoffed at the idea that the operations of Thomas's mind were being coerced when, by Indiana law, he was being deprived of a share of the state's money.

None of this carries any weight with the modern Supreme Court; it has long since abandoned any idea that it might learn something of importance from the Constitution itself or from the men who framed and first explicated its provisions. The *Thomas* case provides an example of this. The only issue to be decided, said the Court, was whether Thomas refused to make tank turrets "because of an honest conviction that such work was forbidden by his religion." Since it was clear from the record that he had "terminated his employment for religious reasons," the Court forbade the state to deprive him of compensation, for to do so would prohibit him freely to exercise his religion. Formulated in Jefferson's terms, this means that the law may not coerce or "punish" an act of the body (quitting a job) that is induced by an operation of the mind (a religious opinion), a proposition which would have astonished Jefferson and the framers of the First Amendment.

This new principle of religious freedom would permit a person to disobey a criminal statute if, in his "honest" opinion, to obey it would require him to act contrary to a religious belief. So it was in *Wisconsin v. Yoder* (1972), a case much relied on by the Court in *Thomas*. Yoder, a member of the old Order Amish sect, refused to allow his children to attend high school, public or private, and was convicted of violating the state's compulsory school attendance law. He and his co-defendant were fined the sum of $5 each. The Supreme Court, ruling in his favor, did not declare the law unconstitutional—after the school segregation case especially, who would dare to say that it is not important that children be required to go to school?—it simply said that Yoder did not have to obey it. Although it had ramifications that extended far beyond this particular religious group, the case illustrated the importance of being Amish: Alone among all the people of Wisconsin, Yoder and his fellow sectarians do not have to obey a valid criminal statute.

In one respect, however, the *Thomas* decision departs even more than *Yoder* from the original understanding of the free exercise clause. It is an article of faith with the Old Order

Amish that their communities, and beyond a certain age their children, be isolated from the influences of the world around them. God, they all believe, has forbidden them to render unto Caesar what, in this case, Caesar had demanded. But there is no equivalent consensus among the Jehovah's Witnesses concerning employment in weapons factories; indeed, Thomas had a friend and fellow Jehovah's Witness in the plant who said it was not "unscriptural" to work on weapon parts. Thomas's opinion was idiosyncratic even within his church, yet he was permitted to rely on it when he claimed compensation. As the Court put it, "the guarantee of free exercise is not limited to beliefs which are shared by all of the members of a religious sect."

While acknowledging the possibility that someone might come forward with a claim "so bizarre, so clearly nonreligious in motivation, as not to be entitled to protection under the Free Exercise Clause," the Court was unwilling to make that judgment here and, moreover, suggested that it would be reluctant to make it in any case. Such judgments, it said, are not within "the judicial function and judicial competence." Here, at least, it was correct, but legions of dissenters, each asserting an "honest" religious opinion—it must be a religious opinion—will be able to march through the door opened by the *Thomas* decision.

So far, only the name of Eddie C. Thomas is inscribed in our *Book of [Minor] Martyrs*, but there will soon be many more eligible for inclusion. Jehovah's Witnesses are not the only sectarians with religious scruples, and our factories produce lots of weapons in addition to tanks. Some produce nuclear warheads, for example, and it may not have been a coincidence that, within a few weeks of the Court's decision in the *Thomas* case, the Bishop of Amarillo was calling upon his diocesan Catholics to quit their jobs in the nearby warhead assembly plant. He suggested that they find life-saving rather than life-destroying jobs, and, thanks to the Court, Texas will be under a constitutional obligation to tide them over until they succeed (or, at least, until their periods of eligibility run out). Since the so-called "Peace Bishops" (and their Protestant coadjutors) are at work all over the country, the time will soon arrive when all the states will be under a similar obligation. Under the threat of being inundated by such claims, their unemployment compensation boards might decide to get tough. "What," they might ask, "after all these years, makes you now think that making nuclear weapons is forbidden by your religion?" And the response will be, "my bishop told me so," and that will be that.

Another bishop, this one from Seattle, is advising his people to withhold half their federal income taxes as a way of protesting the arms buildup. When brought before a court, they too will say, "my bishop told me that it is forbidden to pay for life-destroying weapons, and that to be forced to pay for them would deprive me of the free exercise of my religion." And if the Court is consistent, that, too, will be that.

Rather than fight the issue in the courts, the states would be better advised to ask Congress to dust off that old Roosevelt Court-packing plan. Then, assuming the President makes the right appointments and the law is brought back in conformity with the Constitution, our potential martyrs will have a chance to demonstrate the real depths of their convicitons.

CHAPTER 22

THINKING ABOUT THE CITY

Cities express an ambivalence in the American soul: we like cities and wish to live in them—or at least to visit them—but we also dislike cities and wish to avoid them, and live instead on farms or in suburbs, and wish we could redesign the whole country along the lines of the Berkshires, in western Massachusetts—with the Turnpike for rapid transit but to a different kind of Boston. Cities are the home of commerce— business and industry we now say—and therefore of the inequality that naturally arises out of commerce—some men become richer than others—whereas this country was founded on the proposition that all men are created equal, and it seems to follow, for some of us at least, that equal we should remain. Originally, then, we opposed the city in the name of democracy. Yet we know, when we think about it, we would be hard pressed to name a purely agrarian society that was at the same time democratic—outside Rousseau's books that is, and Jefferson's imagination. The latter, as a wise man has reminded us, "did not seem to realize the extent to which, in constantly seeking to strengthen agriculture, not *with* other elements making for a balanced economy but *at the expense of* other elements, he was acting to strengthen slavery." At any rate, our ambivalence toward the city has one of its roots in Jeffersonian democracy, which retains its vitality among us even though the sturdy yeoman farmer has long since been replaced by the suburban homeowner fighting crab grass with a bad back.

The great cities, the ones we visit on holiday or are whisked to in ever-increasing numbers by the charter flights, were once the homes of kings and emperors, who built the palaces that are now the museums and the grounds that are now the public parks, and who won the battles memorialized in the squares and fountains and obelisks and columns constructed out of captured cannon melted down for the purpose. We love Paris, it is not a bit like Chicago, Milwaukee and St. Paul; the trouble is, we cannot imagine Paris without Louis XIV and Napoleon, neither of whom we could abide for a moment if he were to offer himself on or off a party ticket; or Rome without the emperors and popes, or Vienna without the Hapsburgs, or London without Elizabeth and the Georges and the others. Again, much of what attracts us to the city has an undemocratic element in it. At the very minimum it reminds us of what Tocqueville told us: justice, or at least democratic justice, and that cultivation of the human spirit that produces beautiful things are not compatible.

> Do you wish to give a certain elevation to the human mind and teach it to regard the things of this world with generous feelings, to inspire men with a scorn of mere temporal advantages, to form and nourish strong convictions and keep alive the spirit of honorable devotedness? Is it your object to refine the habits, embellish the manners and cultivate the arts, to promote the love of poetry, beauty, and glory? Would you constitute a people fitted to act powerfully upon all other nations, and prepared for those high enterprises in history? If you believe such to be the object of society, avoid the government of the democracy, for it would not lead you with certainty to the goal.

This is a harsh judgment, palliated only slightly by the virtues of democracy, which he delineates in his following paragraph.

We admire Venice for its color and variety: it is an exotic place, with vestiges of an earlier meeting of the East and

West. We admire Amsterdam, rather similar to Venice in its canals and especially in its sights, scents, and flavors brought from the exotic East by generations of Dutchmen. And the London of the first Elizabeth, and of the East India Company and the East India Docks; of ship chandlers, spice shops, coffee importers and coffee houses, and Ceylonese tea merchants; the London through whose port came the world and through whose same port one went out to the world, literally and imaginatively. We admire, in short, the cosmopolitan city—the *cosmos polis*, the world city; but we suspect, having been taught by Jefferson, that it is precisely the *cosmo*politan character of the city that makes government difficult and community impossible; and some of us—Lewis Mumford, for example—have such a yearning for community that we come to hate the city, and dream of new places in the countryside—call them Garden Cities if you must—surrounded by green belts and featuring the Community Center, the contemporary substitute for self-government. Of course there is a connection between free government and community (if not the community center), which is why the town meeting occupies so prominent place in our democractic pathos. And of course cosmopolitanism is a threat to community, because the *cosmos polis* destroys homogeneity; it brings in foreigners with strange ways and strange religions. The anti-Federalists at our beginning opposed the ratification of the Constitution most of all because free republican government could exist, they insisted, only in small, homogeneous places, where, as one of them said, "the manners, sentiments, and interests of the people [are] similar." Mercy Warren, one of the 18th-century founders of American isolationism, wondered if it might be possible to preserve the "pure republican spirit of the Americans" by building some sort of wall around the country, cutting them off from European luxury, on the one hand, and Western empire, on the other. She and the other anti-Federalists opposed the Constitution precisely because it would lead to the replacement of the small, homogeneous and *therefore*, they insisted, self-governing communities by the large, impersonal, commercial, eventually urban country which, they also insisted, could only be governed despotically. George Clinton, governor of New York and writing under the name of Cato, the greatest of Roman republican names, put it this way: "The progress of the commercial society begets luxury, the parent of inequality, the foe to virtue, and the enemy to restraint, [and also] ambition and voluptuousness," and eventually despotism. "Those who labor in the earth are the chosen people of God," said Jefferson, "if ever He had a chosen people," and we all know what he had to say about the city:

> While we have land to labor then, let us never wish to see our citizens occupied at a workbench, or twirling a distaff. Carpenters, masons, smiths, are wanting in husbandry; but, for the general operations of manufacture, let our workshops remain in Europe. It is better to carry provisions and materials to workmen there, than bring them to the provisions and materials, and with them their manners and principles. The loss by the transportation of commodities across the Atlantic will be made up in happiness and permanence of government. The mobs of great cities add just so much to the support of pure government, as sores do to the strength of the human body. It is the manners and spirit of a people which preserve a republic in vigor. A degeneracy in these is a canker which soon eats to the heart of its laws and constitution.

But *our* ambivalence stems from his, because he probably formulated that statement about the city on his way to Philadelphia and a meeting of the American Philosophical Society. Jefferson was, for all his rusticity, among the most urbane of Americans, the man who thought Bacon, Newton, and Locke were the three greatest men who ever lived—and there was nothing rustic about Bacon, Newton, and Locke, and nothing bucolic about the world their thought helped to build.

I am contending that the American ambivalence toward the city has its roots in the dispute that took place at the beginning, the dispute between the men we call Federalists and those we call anti-Federalists. Residual elements of that original dispute are reflected in the later struggles between Hamilton and Jefferson, and the Hamiltonians and the Jeffersonians, and later in those between Nicholas Biddle and the friends of the Bank, on the one hand, and the Jacksonians, the sturdy yeomanry, on the other; and still later in those between the Gold Republicans from the East and the William Jennings Bryan Democrats from the West, the descendents of Jackson. Bryan became famous for his imprecations against the cities: "Burn down your cities and leave our farms, and your cities will spring up again as if by magic; but destroy our farms and the grass will grow in the streets of every city in the country. . . ." And, of course, one can hear echoes of it still, beating in the heart of the Republicans, once again located in the Middle West, even if the Republican body comes from California or Maryland. These men dislike the effete East, or the Eastern Establishment, as much as Bryan and Jackson ever did. America may be the first new nation, the first to be established on the basis of the modern principles delineated by Hobbes and Locke, but there has seldom been a time without a significant body of opinion that distrusts modernity, its principles and its works.

Our ambivalence toward the city arises out of our acceptance and our simultaneous rejection of modernity. I mean by this, and without here elaborating it, we built on the Hobbesian-Lockean principle of self-interest, but we yearn for a good we can share in common, a common good, a community, which the younger generation has called a participatory democracy, an idea coming from Rousseau. But it is no easy task to define a common good for a civil society whose organizing principle is self-interest, whether that principle is accepted eagerly, which is more or less the case with the authors of the *Federalist Papers,* or reluctantly, as was true of such anti-Federalists as Melancton Smith, and true also, I think, of the greatest of the commentators on America, Tocqueville. Brotherhood cannot be willed (Tom Hayden and the New Left to the contrary notwithstanding), and the authors of the *Federalist* knew this very well, which is why they eschewed reliance on "moral and religious motives," and accepted instead the Lockean corollary of the Hobbesian-Lockean premise: the pursuit of wealth will solve the political problem, and wealth will flow naturally from the unrestrained greed of men. In less pejorative terms, the society that attains what *Federalist* Number 10 calls the first object of government—that of protecting the unequal faculties of acquiring property—will be one that directs the energies of its people into wealth-getting. It will not be a society of good Samaritans; it will, however, be a society whose members are not so likely to fall among thieves when they travel the road from Jerusalem to Jericho, or Boston to New York, because the passions of men will be directed into activities that do not lead to bloodshed and do not threaten the peace. The passion for acquisition—greed—will assume first importance under this new, this modern dispensation, and it is a passion that can be satisfied in peaceful ways. Scarcity will be overcome and, in fact, wealth will abound. The Gross National Product will assume astronomical proportions, just as Locke said it would. In this way self-interest will be served. Acquisition will be a substitute for morality; that is, acquisition will replace the morality that formerly constituted the community, the cement that bound men into a community. Acquisition becomes the substitute for brotherhood. The modern world will have less need of Samaritans, which is all to the good, Hobbes, Locke, and their epigoni would say, because there were never many *good* Samaritans anyway.

The anti-Federalists opposed this arrangement, and some of them knew exactly what they were opposing. Nevertheless, it can be said that however much the anti-Federalists talked of sturdy yeoman and republican virtue and small communities of brothers, in the end they too took their stand with Lockean acquisition. And so too did their lineal descendants of the next generation, the Jacksonians. The Jacksonians may have yearned for something in addition—Marvin Meyers shows this most perceptively in his book, *The Jacksonian Persuasion*—but they proved unwilling to pay the price for it, and in this respect too they resembled their ancestors. John Adams taunted the anti-Federalists with this unwillingness. You want republican virtue? he asked them. You want rustic simplicity? You want the small virtuous, agrarian republic? If so, what you want is San Marino:

> A handful of poor people, living in the simplest manner, by hard labor upon the produce of a few cows, sheep, goats, swine, poultry, and pigeons, on a piece of rocky snowy ground, protected from every enemy by their situation, their superstition, and even by their poverty, having no commerce or luxury....

In fact, they did not want it. Not at that price. But this has never prevented us Americans from yearning for imaginary San Marinos.

Tocqueville is the man to read on this subject. No one since Rousseau has better articulated the problems and the costs of modernity. It was one thing to share a good in common, to live in a community with a common purpose, when all men and all classes were bound to each other by the laws and the institutions of the place, sharing the tenets of a faith held in common; when the organizing principle of the regime embodied an articulation of the ends that men individually and collectively were to seek; when the principles of the regime were derived from an understanding of the human soul that placed it in an ordered universe; or to say this in more familiar language, when the civil law was patterned after the natural law and the natural law, in turn, was grounded in God's eternal law. In such a world, men and societies derive comfort from their opinion that they are living according to divine providence, or according to the natural law, and it was understood in that world that self-preservation was merely the lowest in the natural hierarchy of ends. The trouble was, there were disputes as to what that common faith would be, leading to religious wars, civil and international, and countries tended to resemble the Northern Ireland of today. But when self-preservation becomes the totality of the law of nature, as it does for Hobbes and Locke, and when the law of civil society comes to be based on *this* understanding of the natural law, promoting the materialism that would relieve man's estate even as it corrupted his soul, it is not strange that the common good becomes an elusive thing. Nor is it strange that Tocqueville was forced finally to define the common good in terms of self-interest, "the only immutable point in the human heart," he said. As to what happens generally to the soul of the man who is only told to preserve himself, Tocqueville has no solution at all. He can only regret what he foresees: the desuetude of nobility, of refined habits and embellished manners, or poetry and of philosophy itself.

In Tocqueville's *Democracy in America* is to be found a comprehensive understanding of the problems of modernity. Nevertheless, he understood as well the fundamental justice of the modern principle, that gave rise to the modern liberal-democratic state, namely, the principle that all men are created equal. It is quite clear that he was passionately attached to various aspects of life in an aristocracy, but it is equally clear that he acknowleged the fundamental injustice of aristocracy. In democracy there is justice, but in democracy there is also the danger that those things that make life worth living are endangered. He may have hoped that somewhere within the new civil society there could be founded a citadel in which these things could continue to exist, if not to flourish, or from which they could be defended; a place (perhaps the university, but certainly not the modern city) relatively impervious to the onslaughts of egalitarian public opinion, but he know enough not to be sanguine about this. These things—let us simply say, the arts and the life of the mind—were formerly a part of aristocracy. They were a part of the aristocratic city, and they would be jeopardized in the modern world built on equality and self-interest. Tocqueville, one might say, appreciated the justice of modernity, but he knew the price that would have to be paid for it.

When we complain of our cities we do so on the ground of their alleged inhumanity, or their inhuman scale and pace; on the ground that they are not suited for a truly human life.

When we, in the American context, start asking the question—what is the city?—we are in fact asking the larger question of what is the purpose of human life. The one is reflected in the other, but this is partially concealed from us nevertheless. It is concealed because we are out of the habit of asking that larger question, and we are out of the habit of asking it because it was the intention of modernity to suppress that question, or at least to suppress the *public* asking of it. For, when that question was *asked* publicly, it was *answered* publicly, that is to say, officially; and there were religious wars, and inquisitions, and censors, and, generally, no liberty, and life too often resembled the life in Hobbes's state of nature: "solitary, poor, nasty, brutish, and short." So, as I say, Hobbes and Locke intended that that question no longer be asked, and, on the whole, they were successful.

The question was asked at our beginning by the anti-Federalists, most of whom knew very well that their small, homogenous, virtuous republics of sturdy yeomen would have to be built on the foundation of an official church; but that question was not asked or answered by the republic we did build. This republic was the large commercial republic whose first object, Madison said, was the "protection of [the] different and unequal faculties of acquiring property." We build our cities with this purpose in mind, to facilitate the making of money, which, in turn, would preserve human liberty. To this we have added only an amusement park here and there. But the great old cities we admire are admirable precisely because they reflect an official concern with the question of what is the purpose of human life. That is a noble question, capable of being answered in a noble manner. The answer given may be wrong, but it is not likely to be banal. The greatest monuments in these old cities are of course religious monuments: The Parthenon in Athens, St. Peter's in Rome, Notre Dame in Paris, Westminster Abbey in London, to say nothing of Jerusalem. They, and their adornments—the pictures, the sculpture, the frescoes, the music, the poetry—these are the things present in the old cities, built before modernity, built before self-preservation and self-interest became the sole ends of civil society. In such cities are to be found expressions of the nobler aspects of the soul, the poetic rather than the prosaic. The modern city is prosaic because modern life is prosaic. The question—what is the city?—is a reflection of the recognition of the fact that modern life is prosaic, and of our dissatisfaction with that fact in our day.

NOTES

CHAPTER 1

1. 96th Congress, second session, July 1980.

2. Ibid., p. iii.

3. *Barron v. City of Baltimore*, 7 Pet. 243 (1833).

4. *Gitlow v. New York*, 268 U.S. 652 (1925).

5. *Dred Scott* v. Sandford, 19 How. 393 (1857); *Hepburn v. Griswold*, 8 Wall. 603 (1870); *Knox v. Lee*, 12 Wall. 457 (1871).

6. *Lamont v. Postmaster General*, 381 U.S. 301 (1965); *Tilton v. Richardson*, 403 U.S. 672 (1971).

7. *Boyd v. United States*, 116 U.S. 616 (1886).

8. The exceptions were *The Justices* v. *Murray*, 9 Wall. 274 (1870) (Seventh Amendment); and four Sixth Amendment cases: *Kirby* v. *United States*, 174 U.S. 47 (1899); *Wong Wing v. United States*, 163 U.S. 228 (1896); *Rassmussen v. United States*, 197 U.S. 516 (1905); and *United States v. Cohen Grocery Co.*, 255 U.S. 81 (1921).

9. Madison to Jefferson, October 17, 1788. *Writings*, ed. Gaillard Hunt (New York: Putnam, 1900-1910), vol. 5, pp. 271-275.

10. Article I, section 8, #8. So far as I know, Robert A. Goldwin was the first person to remark this, in a paper presented in 1979 to The Hastings Center, Institute of Society, Ethics and the Life Sciences, and to be published as "Rights versus Duties" in *Ethics in Hard Times*, ed. Arthur L. Caplan and Daniel Callahan (New York: Plenum Publishing Corporation, 1981).

11. Jonathan Elliot (ed.), *The Debates in the Several State Conventions, on the Adoption of the Federal Constitution....* (Charlottesville, Va.: Michie, 1937), vol. 3, p. 137.

12. Ordinances Passed at General Convention...of Virginia...(Williamsburg, 1776), pp. 100-103.

13. See Herbert J. Storing, "The Constitution and the Bill of Rights," in M. Judd Harmon (ed.), *Essays on the Constitution of the United States* (Port Washington, N.Y.: Kennikat Press, 1978), pp. 32-48.

14. *Federalist* 84.

15. *Calvin's Case*, 77 Eng. Rep. 377, 392 (K.B. 1609). As quoted in Edward S. Corwin, *The "Higher Law" Background of American Constitutional Law* (Ithaca: Cornell University Press, 1955), pp. 45-6.

16. Ibid.

17. Thomas C. Grey, "Origins of the Unwritten Constitution: Fundamental Law in American Revolutionary Thought," *Stanford Law Review*, 30 (May 1978), 843–893.

18. Hobbes, *Leviathan*, ch. 30.

19. Locke, *Essays on the Law of Nature*, ed. W. von Leyden (Oxford: Clarendon Press, 1954), p. 158, n. 3.

20. Locke, *Two Treatises of Government*, II, secs. 13, 124–127.

21. Hobbes, *Leviathan*, ch. 14.

22. Locke, *Treatises* II, sec. 6.

23. Ibid., secs. 12–13.

24. Ibid., sec. 12.

25. Ibid., sec. 87.

26. As Locke puts it, the individual's sovereign power is resigned "into the hands of the community in all cases that exclude him not from appealing for protection to the law established by it. And thus *all* private judgment of every particular member being excluded, the community comes to be umpire by settled standing rules...." *Treatises* II, sec. 87. Emphasis supplied.

27. *Federalist* 78.

28. *McCulloch* v. *Maryland*, 4 Wheat. 316, 407 (1819).

29. Locke, *Treatises* II, sec. 132.

30. *Ibid.*, secs. 96–97.

31. *Federalist* 9.

32. *Federalist* 84.

33. *Federalist* 10.

34. *Federalist* 9.

35. *Federalist* 10.

36. James D. Richardson, *Messages and Papers of the Presidents* (New York: ureau of National Literature, 1897), 3, p. 1395.

37. See Walter Berns, *The First Amendment and the Future of American Democracy* (New York: Basic Books, 1976), pp. 119-128.

38. Walter Berns, "The Constitution and the Migration of Slaves," *Yale Law Journal*, 78 (December 1968), pp. 226–228. (Reprinted as ch. 14, below.)

39. Walter Berns, *The First Amendment and the Future of American Democracy*, p. 26ff.

40. *Federalist* 10.

41. Thomas Babington Macaulay, "Francis Bacon," in *Critical and Historical Essays* (London: Everyman's Library, 1907, 1951), vol. 2, p. 373.

42. *Federalist* 78.

43. Ibid.

44. *Moore* v. *City of East Cleveland*, 431 U.S. 494, 544 (1977).

45. Ronald Dworkin, *Taking Rights Seriously* (Cambridge: Harvard University Press, 1977).

46. *Griswold* v. *Connecticut*, 381 U.S. 479 (1965); *Reynolds* v. *Sims*, 377 U.S. 533 (1964).

47. Walter Berns, "The Least Dangerous Branch but Only If. . . ." in Leonard J. Theberge (ed.), *The Judiciary in a Democratic Society* (Lexington, Mass.: Lexington Books, 1979), p. 17.

48. Michael P. Zuckert and Marshall McDonald, "The Original Meaning of the Fourteenth Amendment—Once Again"; Michael P. Zuckert, "Congressional Power under the Fourteenth Amendment—The Original Understanding of Section Five." Both unpublished.

49. Ibid.

50. "When we remember that it was the state legislatures (along with the state constitutions) that defined the substance of the Article IV provision respecting the 'privileges and immunities of citizens in the several states,' a provision deprived of its intended effect by the existence of slavery; and that the Fourteenth Amendment reversed the priority of state and national citizenship; and that it went on to protect national citizens from hostile state legislation; and that it empowered Congress to 'enforce . . . the provisions of this article'; then it is reasonable to conclude that Congress was empowered to define the privileges and immunities that the states were forbidden to abridge. To say nothing more here, this reading of the clause would have permitted Congress to address the problem of the freedman with Lincolnian prudence: it would have been possible to guarantee him civil rights (of the sort enumerated in the Civil Rights Act of 1866) without immediately attempting to give him—while at the same time preparing him for—the full political rights of citizens. In due course, it would have been possible to grant him the 'privilege' of attending non-segregated schools. As it turned out, the freedman got constitutional guarantees but, in practice, neither civil nor political rights until, in our own time, the Supreme Court intervened. That intervention led to our judicial explosion, just as the Court's action in *Slaughterhouse* was the condition of the *Lochner* explosion." Walter Berns, "Judicial Review and the Rights and Laws of Nature," in Philip B. Kurland, Gerhard Casper, and Dennis J. Hutchinson (eds.), *The Supreme Court Review, 1982* (Chicago: The University of Chicago Press, 1983), pp. 49-83. (Reprinted as Ch. 2, below.)

51. J. Skelly Wright, "Professor Bickel, the Scholarly Tradition, and the Supreme Court," *Harvard Law Review* 84, no. 4 (February 1971), p. 804.

52. *Frontiero v. Richardson*, 411 U.S. 677 (1973).

53. Bob Woodward and Scott Armstrong, *The Brethren: Inside the Supreme Court* (New York: Simon and Schuster, 1979), p. 254.

54. Dworkin, p. 149.

55. See Thomas Pangle, "Rediscovering Rights," *The Public Interest*, No. 50 (Winter 1978), pp. 157-160.

56. *Reynolds v. Sims*, 377 U.S. 533, 565 (1964).

57. *Cohen v. California*, 403 U.S. 15 (1971).

58. *Rosenfeld v. New Jersey*, 408 U.S. 901 (1972).

59. *Papish v. Board of Curators*, 410 U.S. 667 (1973).

60. *Spence v. Washington*, 418 U.S. 405 (1974).

61. *Smith v. Goguen*, 415 U.S. 566 (1974).

62. *Street v. New York*, 394 U.S. 576 (1969).

63. See Harvey C. Mansfield, Jr., "The American Election: Towards Constitutional Democracy?" *Government and Opposition* 16, no. 1 (Winter 1981),

pp. 6, 13.

64. *Wisconsin v. Yoder*, 406 U.S. 205 (1972). See Walter Berns, "The Importance of Being Amish," *Harper's* (March 1973), pp. 36–42. (Reprinted as Ch. 18, below.)

65. *United States v. Seeger*, 380 U.S. 163 (1965).

66. *Roe v. Wade*, 410 U.S. 113, 153 (1973).

CHAPTER 2

1. Wechsler, *Toward Neutral Principles of Constitutional Law*, 73 Harv. L. Rev. 1, 15 (1959).

2. Bickel, *The Supreme Court and the Idea of Progress* 175 and passim (1970); Kurland, *Politics, The Constitution, and the Warren Court* esp. xx ff. (1970).

3. Wright, *Professor Bickel, the Scholarly Tradition, and the Supreme Court*, 84 Harv. L. Rev. 769, 777 (1971).

4. Winter, *The Growth of Judicial Power*, in *The Judiciary in a Democratic Society* 29 (Theberge ed. 1979).

5. Id. at 49 and passim.

6. Grey, *Do We Have an Unwritten Constitution?* 27 Stan. L. Rev. 703, 710-714 (1975).

7. The case has been made by Professor Michael Zuckert of Carleton College in two as yet unpublished papers (one of them coauthored by Marshall McDonald) that, rather than being vaguely written, the three troublesome clauses of the Fourteenth Amendment are precisely drafted. Each one is addressed, as it were, to a different branch of the state governments.

8. Berger, *Government by Judiciary: The Transformation of the Fourteenth Amendment*, (Cambridge: Harvard University Press, 1977), ch. 7.

9. One example of such absurdities: aliens, according to Kenneth L. Karst, are covered by the "principle of equal citizenship," even though they "lack citizenship in the narrow sense," Karst, *The Supreme Court, 1976 Term—Foreword: Equal Citizenship under the Fourteenth Amendment*, 91 Harv. L. Rev. 1, 45 (1977). This is like saying a definition of cat that excludes dog is a narrow definition of cat.

10. Ely, *The Supreme Court, 1977 Term—Foreword: On Discovering Fundamental Values*, 92 Harv. L. Rev. 5-55 (1978).

11. Compton, *Los Angeles Times*, February 20, 1977. As quoted in Pritchett, *Living with a Living Constitution: 200 Minus 10 and Counting*, a paper prepared for delivery at the 1977 Annual Meeting of the American Politial Science Association, p. 13.

12. Karst, *Invidious Discrimination: Justice Douglas and the Return of the "Natural-Law-Due-Process Formula,"* 16 U.C.L.A. L. Rev. 716, 720 (1969).

13. Pritchett, *Living with a Living Constitution*, note 11 supra, at 1.

14. *Marbury v. Madison*, 1 Cranch 137, 176, 177 (1803).

15. *McCulloch v. Maryland*, 4 Wheat. 316, 407 (1819).

16. Id. at 415.

17. Marshall, *A Friend of the Constitution*, in *John Marshall's Defense of McCulloch v. Maryland* 185 (Gunther ed. 1969).

18. Choper, *Judicial Review and the National Political Process: A Functional Reconsideration of the Role of the Supreme Court* 4 (1980).

19. *The Federalist Papers*, No. 10 at 84 (Mentor ed. 1961).

20. Choper, note 18 supra, at 64.

21. Id. at 76.

22. Id. at 79.

23. Ely, *Democracy and Distrust: A Theory of Judicial Review* 87 (1980).

24. Tribe, *The Puzzling Persistence of Process-based Constitutional Theories*, 89 Yale L.J. 1063, 1065 (1980).

25. Ely, note 23 supra, at 49.

26. See, e.g., Berns, *The Constitution as Bill of Rights*, in *How Does the Constitution Secure Rights?* (Goldwin & Schambra, eds., forthcoming 1984). (Reprinted as Ch. 1, above.)

27. Tribe, note 24 supra, at 1072-77.

28. For a more extensive critique of the Ely book, see Barber, *The Constitutionalism of John Hart Ely*, a paper prepared for delivery at the 1981 Annual Meeting of the American Political Science Association.

29. Grey, note 6 supra, at 714.

30. Id. at 715-716.

31. Grey, *Origins of the Unwritten Constitution: Fundamental Law in American Revolutionary Thought*, 30 Stan. L. Rev. 843-893 (1978).

32. For a comprehensive treatment of modern natural right, see Strauss, *Natural Right and History*, ch. 5 (1953).

33. Grey, *Origins of the Unwritten Constitution*, note 31 supra, at 891.

34. Calvin's Case, 77 Eng. Rep. 377, 392 (K.B. 1609). As quoted in Corwin, *The "Higher Law" Background of American Constitutional Law* 45-46 (1955). First published in 42 Harv. L. Rev. 149-85; 365-409 (1928-29).

35. Grey, *Origins of the Unwritten Constitution*, note 31 supra, at 892.

36. Corwin, note 34 supra.

37. Hobbes, *Leviathan*, ch. 13.

38. Id., ch. 14.

39. Locke, *Treatises I*, secs. 86, 88; *Treatises II*, secs. 12, 13, 87.

40. Hobbes, *Leviathan*, ch. 14.

41. Id., ch. 13.

42. Id., ch. 14.

43. Id., ch. 15.

44. Hobbes, *De Cive*, ch. III, #32 (Lamprecht ed. 1949) 58.

45. Hobbes, *Leviathan*, ch. 15.

46. Mansfield, *Hobbes and the Science of Indirect Government*, 65 Am. Pol. Sci. Rev. 107 (1971).

47. Id. at 102.

48. Hobbes, *De Cive*, Preface to the Reader.

49. The Ayatollah Khomeini is a perfect example of the sort of man Hobbes

had in mind.

50. Hobbes, *A Dialogue Between a Philosopher and a Student of the Common Laws of England* (Cropsey ed. 1971).

51. Mansfield, note 46 supra, at 108.

52. Karst, *Invidious Discrimination*, note 12 supra, at 720.

53. Corwin, note 34 supra, at 66.

54. Locke, *Treatises* II, sec. 19.

55. Goldwin, *John Locke*, in *History of Political Philosophy* 453–460 (Strauss & Cropsey eds. 1972).

56. Locke, *Treatises* II, sec. 87.

57. Id., sec. 3.

58. Id., secs. 134, 151.

59. Id., sec. 143.

60. Id., ch. 14 ("Of Prerogative").

61. Grey, *Do We Have an Unwritten Constitution?* note 6 supra, at 716.

62. Locke, *Treatises* II, sec. 37-43. See Goldwin, note 55 supra, at 451–486.

63. *The Federalist Papers* No. 84, note 19 supra, at 515. My colleague Robert A. Goldwin has pointed out that in the unamended Constitution the word "right" or "rights" appears only once, namely, in the Article I, sec. 8, clause 8 provision respecting the "exclusive right [of authors and inventors] to their respective writings and discoveries," and even here the "right" is seen as a means of enabling Congress to exercise its "power . . . to promote the progress of science and useful arts."

64. Grey, *Origins of the Unwritten Constitution*, note 31 supra, at 853.

65. Grey, *Do We Have an Unwritten Constitution?* note 6 supra, at 714.

66. Grey, *Origins of the Unwritten Constitution*, note 31 supra, at 892.

67. Id. at 860.

68. Considerations of space require me to limit my discussion to Pufendorf's *De Jure Naturae et Gentium*, first published in 1672 and first translated into English in 1703. I shall refer to the 1934 translation used by Grey.

69. Pufendorf, *Of the Law of Nature and Nations*, Book II, ch. 3, #5 at 185 (Oldfather & Oldfather trans. 1934).

70. Id., Book II, ch. 3, #13-15 at 202-8.

71. Id., Book VIII, ch. 1, #1 at 1131 (emphasis added).

72. Hobbes, *De Cive*, ch. VI, sec. 16; ch. XIV, secs. 9–10.

73. Pufendorf, note 69 supra, Book VIII, ch. 1, #3 at 1134.

74. Id., Book II, ch. 3, #5 at 185.

75. Id., Book I, ch. 2, #6 at 27; Book II, ch. 3, #4 at 184.

76. Id., Book II, ch. 3, #19 at 216.

77. Id., Book VII, ch. 2, #4 at 971.

78. Id., Book VII, ch. 1, #4, 7, 10, 11; ch. 8, #1 at 1103; see also Book VII, ch. 3, #1 and ch. 4, #3.

79. Id., Book VII, ch. 2, #6, 7, 8 at 974-77.

80. Id., Book VII, ch. 6, #2, 3 at 1055, 1056.

81. Id., Book VII, ch. 6, #9 at 1066.

82. Grey, *Origins of the Unwritten Constitution*, note 31 supra, at 861.

83. Pufendorf, note 69 supra, Book VII, ch. 6, #10 at 1070 (emphasis added).

84. Id., Book VII, ch. 6, #13 at 1077.

85. Id., Book VII, ch. 2, #14 at 985.

86. Id., Book VII, ch. 2, #5 at 972.

87. Fortescue, *De Laudibus Legum Angliae*, ch. 8. As quoted in Corwin, note 34, supra, at 37.

88. Id., at 38.

89. Burlamaqui agrees that the sovereign authority may be limited by "fundamental laws" and that these laws are set down in a "formal engagement." They are, he says, "nothing else but the means" by which powers are limited. Examples are the requirements that the sovereign "consult the people themselves or their representatives" or that there be a formal separation of powers. Burlamaqui, *The Principles of Natural and Political Laws* (trans. Nugent), Part I, ch. 1, sec. xlvi, xlii, xlvii, at 48–49 and passim. This is the chapter cited by Grey, but clearly it does not support his point about unwritten fundamental laws.

Grey is of course correct in saying that Vattel teaches that the sovereign is limited by fundamental laws, but he is, again, incorrect with respect to the source of these laws. Vattel says the people "ought to determine them and make them known with plainness and precision." Vattel, *The Law of Nations, or Principles of the Law of Nature* (trans. Chitty), Book I, ch. 3, at 9. This is the chapter cited by Grey.

Rutherford's work is interesting only insofar as it demonstrates the extent to which, within a century, even Protestant "Divines" were speaking the language of Thomas Hobbes. Man lives originally in a "state of nature," which has a law of nature that forbids injury to others but of which each man is himself the executor: he has the right to use force against anyone who puts him "in danger of suffering an injury." Because of the miseries of the state of nature men contract to form "civil society," agreeing to give up their natural rights. Grey notes that Rutherford teaches that men are not obliged always to obey the sovereign, but fails to note that this disobedience takes the form of rebellion. He also notes that Rutherford speaks of "unwritten laws," but fails to note that these laws may be repealed by simple legislation. In short, Rutherford offers no support to Grey's thesis. Rutherford, *Institutes of Natural Law*, 255, 257, 396–397, 453–455 (2d American ed., Baltimore 1832).

90. Wills, *Inventing America: Jefferson's Declaration of Independence*, esp. xxiii–xxvi (1978).

91. Pole, *The Pursuit of Equality in American History* 11 (1978), as quoted in Ely, note 10 supra, at 24.

92. Id. at 31–32.

93. I *The Public Statutes at Large of the United States of America* 1–3 (1854); *Revised Statutes of the United States* 3-6 (1878); I *United States Code* xix–xxi (1940); I *The Federal and State Constitutions, Colonial Charters, and Other Organic Laws of the United States* 3–6 (1877). I am indebted for this information to an unpublished paper, Jaffa, "Inventing the Past: Garry Wills's *Inventing America*, and the Pathology of Ideological Scholarship."

94. Lincoln, speech at Springfield, Ill., June 26, 1857, in II *The Collected Works of Abraham Lincoln* 406 (Basler ed. 1953).

95. Ely, note 10 *supra*, at 22–32.

96. I *Annals of Congress* 421–22. See Berns, *The First Amendment and the Future of American Democracy* 16–18 (1976).

97. I *Annals of Congress* 451, 790.

98. The English judiciary described by Montesquieu had achieved a good deal of independence by the Act of Settlement of 1701. By this Act, the tenure of judges was made independent of the monarch. According to Hamilton, the independent judiciary is one of the discoveries of the new "science of politics." See *The Federalist Papers* No. 9, note 19 supra, at 72.

99. *The Federalist Papers*, Nos. 47, 78, note 19 supra, at 301 and 466.

100. Berns, note 4 supra, at 5.

101. Montesquieu, *The Spirit of the Laws*, Book XI, ch. 6 at 156 (Nugent trans. 1949).

102. Berns, note 4 supra, at 6.

103. Id. at 8. The quoted statement is from *The Federalist Papers*, No. 78, note 19 supra, at 466.

104. *The Federalist Papers*, No. 78, note 19 supra, at 470.

105. *Marbury v. Madison*, note 14 supra, at 180.

106. Berns, note 95 supra, ch. 1.

107. *Sexton v. Wheaton*, 8 Wheat, 229, 239 (1823). Cf. *Roe v. Wade*, 410 U.S. 113 (1973), and *Planned Parenthood of Central Missouri v. Danforth*, 428 U.S. 52 (1976).

108. Locke, *Treatises* II, ch. 6.

109. Tocqueville, II *Democracy in America*, Book III, chs. 8–11.

110. I *The Records of the Federal Convention of 1787*, 152 (Farrand ed. 1937) (emphasis added).

111. *The Federalist Papers*, No. 78, note 19 supra, at 471.

112. Id. at 470.

113. Id.

114. See note 14 supra.

115. See note 12 supra.

116. Dworkin, *Taking Rights Seriously* (1977). As one critic says, "Dworkin seems to provide no way of arguing that judicial opinions (at least in regard to 'fundamental personal or political rights') have greater legitimacy than our own, assuming that we too have sincerely weighed the relevant materials." Levinson, *Taking Law Seriously: Reflections on "Thinking Like a Lawyer,"* 30 Stan. L. Rev. 1071, 1106–7 (1978). Another reviewer points out that when "he is being most candid, Dworkin shows that what he aims at is no more than a systematic account of his personal conception of fairness and his own policy preferences as a conforming liberal professor of the 1970s. [He] surely has as much right as anyone else to offer the public his own opinions on these important matters. One might expect, however, that he would not so cavalierly dress up his own opinions as 'natural

rights,' or call the culture-bound process by which he arrives at them 'philosophy.' "
Pangle, *Rediscovering Rights*, 50 *Pub. Interest* 157, 160 (1978).

CHAPTER 8

1. ©1969 by The New York Times Company. Reprinted by permission.

2. The *New York Times*, January 5, 1970, p. 32. Whatever Ernst now says he used to say, or meant all along, what we remember from him is on the printed page, and there he said that "censorship of the theater is truly an anomaly"; and there he scoffed at the idea that a book, any book, could be "corrupting (whatever that may mean)"; and there he insisted that censorship could be justified only if it could be demonstrated that a "causal relationship" existed "between word or picture and human behavior," and that such a relationship had never been demonstrated "in the field of obscenity"! In fact, he added, "the indications seem to be to the contrary." Morris L. Ernst and Alan U. Schwartz, *Censorship: The Search for the Obscene* (New York: The Macmillan Company, 1964), pp. 142, 200, 250–251.

3. "LONG BEACH, Calif. Jan 13 [1970] (AP)—Four nude models—two male, two female—postured before the coeducational sociology class of 250 persons.

"On movie screens, lesbian and heterosexual couples went through acts of lovemaking.

"Sound systems blared recordings by the Beatles and from the rock musical 'Hair.'

"Two hours after the class ended yesterday, California State College suspended its teachers, Marion Steele, 31 years old, and Dr. Donald Robertson, 29, for thirty days without pay. Further action was threatened.

"Mr. Steele and Dr. Robertson said they had staged the show to ridicule what they called America's prudishness about sex as contrasted with its toleration of what they considered such 'glaring obscenities' as the Vietnam war, violence on television and pollution of air and water.

"This produces hangups and keeps millions from enjoying genuine sexual pleasure and makes our entire world obscene,' Dr. Robertson told the class." The *New York Times*, January 14, 1970, p. 11.

4. In *Ginzburg v. United States*, 383 U.S. 463 (1966), the Supreme Court upheld the conviction because Ginzburg had employed "pandering" in the advertising of his obscene wares, a rule never applied in the past and inapplicable in the future. The next year it resumed its habit of reversing obscenity convictions, although the publications involved were at least as offensive as anything Ginzburg published. *Redrup v. New York*, 386 U.S. 767 (1967). States have been permitted to prohibit the sale of obscenity to minors, *Ginsburg v. New York*, 390 U.S. 629 (1968), but, on the other hand, not to classify films with a view to protecting minors—not, at least, with a "vague" ordinance. *Interstate Circuit, Inc. v. Dallas*, 390 U.S. 676 (1968). Mr. Justice Douglas would not prohibit the sale of obscenity even to children; he says, and he ought to know, that most juvenile delinquents are over 50.

5. *Laocoön* (New York: Noonday Press), ch. 1, p. 10.

6. *Che!* and *Hair*, for example, are political plays. See also note 3, this chapter.

7. Erwin W. Straus, *Phenomenological Psychology* (New York: Basic Books, 1966), p. 219. I have no doubt that it is possible to want to observe sexual acts for

reasons unrelated to voyeurism. Just as a physician has a clinical interest in the parts of the body, philosophers will have an interest in the parts of the soul, or in the varieties of human things which are manifestations of the body and the soul. Such a "looking" would not be voyeurism and would be unaccompanied by shame; or the desire to see and to understand would require the "seer" to overcome shame. (Plato, *Republic*, 439e.) In any event, the case of the philosopher is politically irrelevant, and aesthetically irrelevant as well.

8. Straus, p. 221.

9. It is easy to prove that shamefulness is not the only principle governing the question of what may properly be presented on the stage; shamefulness would not, for example, govern the case of a scene showing the copulating of a married couple who love each other very much. That is not intrinsically shameful—on the contrary—yet it ought not to be shown. The principle here is, I think, an aesthetic one: such a scene is dramatically weak because the response of the audience would be characterized by prurience and not by a sympathy with what the scene is intended to portray, a beautiful love. This statement can be tested by joining a collegetown movie audience; it is confirmed unintentionally by a defender of nudity on the stage; see note 12, this chapter.

10. The modern tyrant does not encourage passivity among his subjects; on the contrary, they are expected by him to be public-spirited: to work for the State, to exceed production schedules, to be citizen soldiers in the huge armies, and to love Big Brother. Indeed, in Nazi Germany and the Soviet Union alike, the private life was and is discouraged, and with it erotic love and the private attachments it fosters. Censorship in a modern tyrannical state is designed to abolish the private life to the extent that this is possible. George Orwell understood this perfectly. This severe censorship that characterizes modern tyranny, and distinguishes it sharply from pre-modern tyranny, derives from the basis of modern tyrannical rule: both Nazism and Communism have roots in theory, and more precisely, a kind of utopian theory. The modern tyrant parades as a political philosopher, the heir of Nietzsche or Marx, with a historical mission to perform. He cannot leave his subjects alone.

11. *Ginzburg* v. *United States* 383 U.S. 463, 489–490 (1966). Dissenting opinion.

12. The *New York Times*, January 18, 1970. The author of this piece, Martin Gottfried, a man of "sophisticated critical judgment" presumably—after all, the *Times* printed him—defends *Che!* and the others, and ends up with a very sophisticated defense of a homosexual rape scene from a production entitled *Fortune and Men's Eyes*, done, of course, in the nude and apparently leaving nothing to the imagination. His principle is that "no climactic scene, in any play, should happen offstage...."

13. Allan Bloom, "The Democratization of the University," in Robert A. Goldwin ed., *How Democratic Is America?* (Chicago: Rand McNally, 1971), p. 110.

14. That this is not merely the product of English or American "puritanism" is proved by, for example, the French *faire l'amour* and the Italian *fare-all' amore*, as well as the fastidious German *mit einem liebeln*.

15. In a number of universities, students are permitted to receive course credit for "courses" taught by themselves to themselves. Not surprisingly, it was left to Cornell to carry this to its absurd extreme. In May, 1970, the Educational Policy Committee of the College of Arts and Sciences voted 5–2 to grant "three credit

hours to ten students who had 'taught' themselves a course in children's literature"—including not only *Alice in Wonderland*, but *Pinocchio, Where the Wild Things Are*, and *Now We Are Six*. "The students claimed that they had not read the books before taking their course." This implies that it is one of the jobs of a university to remedy deficiencies in kindergarten education. In any case, as one of the two dissenters later reported to the full faculty, "whether the books had ever been read to them remains unclear." *Cornell Chronicle*, June 4, 1970.

16. Aristotle, *Poetics*, 1449a–35.

17. See the chapter on "The Merchant of Venice" in Allan Bloom with Harry V. Jaffa, *Shakespeare's Politics* (New York: Basic Books, 1964).

CHAPTER 13

1. Barbara A. Brown, Thomas I. Emerson, Gail Falk, and Ann E. Freedman, "The Equal Rights Amendment: A Constitutional Basis for Equal Rights for Women," *Yale Law Journal* 80 (April 1971), pp. 871–985.

2. *Ibid.*, p. 894.

3. *Ibid.*, p. 901.

4. According to *Planned Parenthood of Central Missouri* v. *Danforth*, 428 U.S. 52 (1976), a husband may have a "deep and proper concern and interest . . . in his wife's pregnancy and in the growth and development of the fetus she is carrying," but, in the event of a conflict, his interest must give way to a wife's right to have an abortion. Read literally, the ERA would convert his interest into a right, a right equal to the wife's.

5. Kenneth L. Karst, "Invidious Discrimination: Justice Douglas and the Return of the 'Natural-Law-Due-Process Formula,'" *U.C.L.A. Law Review*, 16 (June 1969), p. 720.

CHAPTER 14

1. C. Warren, *The Supreme Court in United States History* 87–88 (1st ed. 1922).

2. Id.

3. That James Madison lent his authoritative voice to this interpretation may account for Joseph Story's adoption of the Southern reading of the clause in his influential *Commentaries on the Constitution*. J. Story, *Commentaries on the Constitution of the United States* sec. 223 (1847). Chancellor Kent's *Commentaries on American Law* had earlier taken the same position. 1 J. Kent, *Commentaries on American Law* 196 n. (1830).

4. Although the clause was discussed in dicta in a handful of cases, the Supreme Court was never called upon to interpret it directly. Marshall mentioned the clause in his opinion for the Court in *Gibbons* v. *Ogden*, 22 U.S. (9 Wheat.) 1, 216–217 (1824), where he accepted the Southern version of it; Taney, on the other hand, used it in *Dred Scott* v. *Sandford*, 60 U.S. (19 How.) 393, 411 (1857), to argue that "neither the description of persons therein referred to, nor their descendants," were embraced within the terms "citizens" or "the people of the United States." He thus assumed that the term "such persons" referred only to Negro slaves; either that or his argument would also exclude white immigrants from citizenship!

5. 2 M. Farrand, *The Records of the Federal Convention of 1787*, at 183 (rev. ed. 1937) [hereinafter cited as Farrand].

6. Id. 374.

7. Id. 396, 408.

8. This aspect of the bargain was explained succinctly to Jefferson by George Mason in 1792. He could have agreed to the Constitution, he said, if various changes had not been made during the last two weeks of the convention. One of the changes to which he objected was the deletion of the two-thirds provision. Georgia and South Carolina, he then explained, knew that, with the power to regulate commerce, Congress, unless restrained in the Constitution, "would immediately suppress the importn. of slaves." They "therefore struck up a bargain with the 3 N. Engld. states, if they would join to admit slaves for some years, the 2 Southernmost states wd join in changing the clause which required 2/3 of the legislature in any vote." 3 Farrand 367.

9. 2 id. 415.

10. At times, however, it was not at all clear just what *was* being assumed. James Wilson, speaking in 1787 to the Pennsylvania ratifying convention, argued that

> ... by this article, after the year 1808, the Congress will have power to prohibit such importation, notwithstanding the disposition of any state to the contrary. I consider this as laying the foundation for banishing slavery out of this country ... and in the mean time, the *new* states which are to be formed will be under *the control* of Congress in this particular, and slaves will never be introduced amongst them.

2 J. Elliot, *Debates on the Federal Constitution* 452 (1836 [hereinafter cited as Elliot]; 3 Farrand 161. Wilson may have had nothing more than the commerce power in mind, but it is possible that he was thinking in terms of an independent power to prohibit slavery itself. Farrand goes on to quote him as saying that within a few years "Congress will have power to *exterminate* slavery within our borders." 3 Farrand, 437, note.

11. 2 Elliott 203.

12. Letter from James Madison to Robert Walsh, Nov. 27, 1819. 3 Farrand 436.

13. Id. 437.

14. Id. 436.

15. Id. 210.

16. Id. 436.

17. Id. 346.

18. Id. 210-211 (emphasis in original).

19. 2 Elliot 452–453. In the same speech, however, Wilson also expressed the view that after 1808 "Congress will have power to *exterminate* slavery within our borders," 3 Farrand 437, which seems to imply congressional power over the domestic as well as the foreign slave trade.

20. 4 Elliot 102. "The word *migration* refers to free persons; but the word *importation* refers to slaves because free people cannot be said to be imported." Iredell was replying to James Galloway who, explaining that he wanted "this abominable trade put an end to," did not, however, want the tax on importation "extended to all persons whatsoever." The situation of North Carolina, he

continued, required additional citizens; so instead of "laying a tax, we ought to give a bounty to encourage foreigners to come among us." 4 Elliot 101.

21. Letter from Benjamin Rush to Jeremy Belknap, Feb. 28, 1788. 3 *Belknap Papers*, 397 (Massachusetts Historical Society).

22. J. McMaster & F. Stone, *Pennsylvania and the Federal Constitution* 278 (Historical Society of Pennsylvania 1888). Statements such as McKean's may have accounted for the votes of the Quakers and for the failure of the antislavery anti-Federalists to mention Article I, Section 9 in their statement of reasons for opposing the Constitution. See *Dissent of the Minority* in *Pennsylvania Packet*, issue of December 12, 1787. This dissent was signed by 21 of the 23 who voted against ratification.

23. Letter from Moses Brown to James Pendleton, Oct. 27, 1787. *Pendleton Papers* (Historical Society of Pennsylvania) (emphasis added).

24. A Citizen of the U.S., *Examination into the Leading Principles of the Federal Constitution* 40 (1787).

25. 1788 *Debates and Proceedings in the Convention of the Commonwealth of Massachusetts* 302–303 (1856) (minutes of Judge Theophilus Parsons). This language was quoted several times in the course of the Massachusetts debates.

Not all Massachusetts delegates were opposed to slavery. Benjamin Randall responded to Dawes by saying that he was "sorry to hear it said that after 1808 negroes would be free." Id. 303.

26. 3 Elliot 648.

27. Id. 269-273.

28. Id. 452-453.

29. Id. 454-456.

30. Id. 456 (emphasis added).

31. Id. 464 (emphasis added).

32. 4 Elliot 272–309.

33. Elliot prints only a few speeches from the South Carolina convention. I used xeroxed copies of the accounts in the South Carolina newspapers, the *City Gazette* and the *State Gazette*, and of the official Journal in the possession of the National Historical Publications Commission of the National Archives (Project: *Documentary History of the Ratification of the Constitution and the First Ten Amendments*). The first volume under this title will be published in 1969. I am grateful to the project's director, Professor Robert Cushman, my distinguished predecessor in constitutional law at Cornell, and to his associate, Leonard Rapport, for allowing me to consult their files of documents.

34. See p. 204, supra.

35. 2 Farrand 417.

36. Id. Mason's defense of the provision, with its reference to convicts as being among the "such persons" the migration or importation of which Congress is forbidden to prohibit prior to 1808, is altogether confusing. How does the "provision . . . prevent the introduction" of convicts? As it stands, Congress is forbidden to prevent the introduction of them prior to 1808. Did Mason mean that the tax or duty would prevent their introduction? But no one looked upon the tax or duty as being capable of preventing the introduction of slaves. Why, then, would it

have this effect on the introduction of convicts? And if the Convention was determined to exclude convicts, why wait until 1808 to do so, and why rely on a tax to be the means of discouraging their "migration" prior to 1808? If we are to believe that the word migration refers to convicts, as Mason might be understood to imply, furthermore, then the clause as finally adopted, with Mason's approval, provides no means whatever, prior to 1808, of preventing their "introduction."

One possible explanation of Mason's confusing statement would go as follows: (1) it is not clear whether Congress can prohibit convicts and slaves from entering the country; (2) this clause, by placing a temporary limitation on Congress's commerce power, does make it clear that such a power exists, or will exist after 1808; (3) such a commerce power is necessary to enable Congress to prohibit excessive "migration" of convicts, although such "migration" should be permitted for a while in view of the need in certain areas for manpower. The trouble with this interpretation is that it assumes that by "provision" Mason was referring to the commerce clause, whereas the context indicates Article I, Section 9.

37. Id. The supporters of the usual view that "migration" refers to white aliens sometimes point to the fact that the tax or duty is allowed only on the "importation" (of slaves) and not on the "migration" (of white aliens). This proves nothing at all. Congress is forbidden by the fifth clause of the same Article I, Section 9 to lay any "Tax or Duty . . . on Articles exported from any State"—including, we suggest, slaves who migrate as articles of the interstate slave trade. Thus, in accordance with this policy or principle, the tax or duty could only be laid on importation from abroad.

38. It was not unusual, however, to use the word "migration" to mean internal movement. For example, Rawlins Lowndes so used it in the South Carolina ratification debates: "With respect to migration from the Eastern States to the Southern ones, [I] do not believe that people [will] ever flock here in such considerable numbers." 4 Elliot 309. Indeed, Taney uses the word in that sense in *Dred Scott v. Sandford*, 60 U.S. (19 How.) 393, 422 (1857).

39. As has been suggested above, the absence from the record of any statement to the effect that Congress's power over the domestic slave trade was as extensive as its power over the foreign slave trade need not be taken as evidence for the contrary proposition. Everyone saw the importation and migration clause as a limitation on Congress's commerce powers. It was obvious. Was it not equally obvious that Congress's regulatory powers extended to commerce "among the several states" as well as the commerce "with foreign nations"? If the power to prohibit the "importation" of slaves was admitted by everyone to be a regulation of commerce with foreign nations, what argument was needed to show that the power to prohibit the "migration" of slaves from state to state was a regulation of commerce among the several states? It was intended to restrict this power for twenty years, and are not the words used well-adapted to that end: the temporary restriction on laws prohibiting "importation" expressing the exception to Congress's power to regulate foreign commerce, and the temporary restriction on laws prohibiting "migration" expressing the exception to Congress's power to regulate commerce among the states? As George Nicholas said in the Virginia debates, after 1808 Congress would have a "general superintendency of trade." 3 Elliot 456. And it was probably out of a concern for this employment of the commerce power that the later Madison, the states' rights Madison, argued that Congress's power to regulate commerce among

the states was of less extent than its power to regulate foreign commerce. Discussing the interstate commerce power in a letter to Joseph C. Cabell on February 13, 1829, he wrote: "Being in the same terms with the power over foreign commerce, the same extent, if taken literally, would belong to it. Yet it is very certain that it grew out of the abuse of the power by the importing states in taxing the non-importing, and was intended as a negative and preventive provision against injustice among the States themselves, rather than as a power to be used for the positive purposes of the General Government, in which alone, however, the remedial power could be lodged. And it will be safer to leave the power with this key to it, than to extend it all the qualities and incidental means belonging to the power over foreign commerce...." 4 *Letters and Other Writings of James Madison* 14-15 (1867).

40. Indeed, James Madison himself, contrary to what he was to say later, hinted as much in the First Congress during the debate on the first of the antislavery petitions presented by the Quakers:

> He admitted, that Congress is restricted by the Constitution from taking measures to abolish the slave trade; yet there are a variety of ways by which it could countenance the abolition, and regulations might be made in relation to the introduction of them into the new States to be formed out of the Western Territory.

1 *Annals of Cong.* 1246 (1790) [1789-1824]. The version of this speech printed in 4 Elliot 408 is even more suggestive:

> He [Mr. Madison] entered into a critical review of the circumstances respecting the adoption of the Constitution; the ideas upon the limitation of the powers of Congress to interfere in the *regulation of the commerce in slaves,* and showing that they undeniably were not precluded from interposing in their importation; and generally, to regulate the *mode in which every species of business shall be transacted.* He adverted to the western country and the cession of Georgia, in which Congress have certainly the power to regulate the subject of slavery; which shows gentlemen are mistaken in supposing that Congress cannot constitutionally interfere in the business in any degree whatever. [Emphasis added.]

41. 2 *Annals of Cong.* 1465 (1790) [1789-1824].

42. Id. 1504, 1517.

43. Id. 1524 (emphasis added).

44. Id. 1523. The vote was largely along North-South lines, 23 of the 29 members of the majority coming from the North, and five of the remaining six being Virginians, led by Madison.

45. 8 *Annals of Cong.* 1963 (1798) [1789-1824].

46. 8 *Annals of Cong.* 1968-1969 (1798) [1789-1824]; 3 Farrand 376.

47. 8 *Annals of Cong.* 1993 (1798) [1789-1824]; 3 Farrand 377-378.

48. P. 209, supra.

49. 36 *Annals of Cong.* 1316 (1820) [1789-1824]; 3 Farrand 443 (emphasis added).

50. Including, in one of its voices, a majority of the first House of Representatives. See p. 210, supra.

51. See note 58, infra.

52. It should be remembered that at the time of the Constitutional Convention nearly everyone viewed slavery as an evil which must and would be abolished as soon as practicable. The general aversion on the part of the Convention to speaking or thinking of slavery as a permanent and viable institution was clearly illustrated by the delegates' refusal to permit the word "slave" to appear in the Constitution.

53. Letter from James Madison to Robert Walsh. Nov. 27, 1819. 3 Farrand 436.

54. *The Federalist* No. 42, at 272–273 (Mod. Lib. ed. 1937) (Madison) (emphasis added).

55. Letter from Madison to Walsh, Jan. 11, 1820. 3 *Letters and Other Writings of James Madison* 163–164 (1876); 3 Farrand 438.

56. 3 Elliot 349–365.

57. 2 Elliot 115.

58. Act of Aug. 7, 1789, ch. 8; I Stat. 50. The actual form of action taken was stated as a law "to adapt the [Ordinance] to the [new] Constitution of the United States."

59. Act of March 26, 1804, ch. 38; 2 Stat. 283, 286. Unfortunately the *Annals of Congress* do not record the debate, either in the House or the Senate, on this provision. It was adopted by a vote of 21–7. 13 *Annals of Cong.* 242 (1804) [1789–1824]. A similar prohibition ("inhibiting" the admission of all slaves into Louisiana) was adopted by the House by a vote of 40-36. Id. 1186.

60. U.S. Const. art. IV, sec. 3.

61. Letter to Robert Walsh, Nov. 27, 1819. 9 Madison, *Writings* 5 (G. Hunt ed. 1910).

62. P. 219, supra.

63. Letter from James Madison to Robert Walsh, supra, note 61, at 9–10.

64. W.E.B. DuBois, *The Suppression of the African Slave Trade to the United States of America*, 1638–1870, at 70–93 (1896).

65. The words of praise are from 17 *Niles' Register* 307 (Jan. 8, 1820), noting the publication of the work. *The Dictionary of American Biography*, although it contains a sizeable article on Walsh, does not mention the monograph.

66. R. Walsh, *On the Spirit of the Federal Constitution, the Practice of the Federal Government, and the Obligations of the Union, Respecting the Exclusion of Slavery from the Territories and New States* 17–18 (1819).

67. Id. 20.

68. *Dred Scott* v. *Sandford*, 60 U.S. (19 How.) 393 (1857).

69. Harry V. Jaffa shows, contrary to some historians, that Lincoln was altogether correct in his reading of the *Dred Scott* opinions on this issue. See H. Jaffa, *Crisis of the House Divided* 441–444 (1959). Until the *Dred Scott* case the right to hold property in a slave was understood to derive from the laws of the states permitting slavery. In *Dred Scott*, however, the Court solemnly declared that "the right of property in a slave is distinctly and expressly affirmed in the *Constitution*"— a change of tremendous magnitude. *Dred Scott* v. *Sandford*, 60 U.S. (19 How.) 393, 451 (1857) (emphasis added).

70. T. Jefferson, *Works* (Ford ed. 1899) 157, 158, 162 (letters to John Holmes, April 22, 1820 and Charles Pinckney, Sept. 30, 1820).

71. *New York v. Miln*, 36 U.S. (11 Pet.) 102 (1837); *Groves v. Slaughter*, 40 U.S. (15 Pet.) 449, 507 (1841) (Taney, C.J., concurring); *The Passenger Cases*, 48 U.S. (7 How.) 283, 464 (Taney, C.J. dissenting).

72. Act of April 30, 1802, sec. 5, ch. 40; 2 Stat. 173.

73. 6 *The Papers of Thomas Jefferson* 582 (J. Boyd ed. 1957).

74. Six states of the nine present voted in favor of it, one short of the requirement for passage. Of the 23 members voting, 16 voted in its favor. 26 *Journal of the Continental Congress* 247 (G. Hunt ed. 1928).

75. Letter from James Madison to Robert Walsh, Nov. 27, 1819. 3 Farrand 436.

76. 6 *The Papers of Thomas Jefferson, supra* note 73, at 588. As to how the antislavery provision, deleted from the 1784 Ordinance was put back into the 1787 Ordinance, see J. Barrett, *Evolution of the Ordinance of 1787,* at 69, 76 (1891).

77. This is the version of Jefferson's plan as it appears in the Report of the Committee (March 1, 1784). 6 *The Papers of Thomas Jefferson* 605 (J. Boyd ed. 1957). Jefferson, along with Jeremiah Townley Chase and David Howell, was a member of this committee. The language in the Report was altered slightly on final passage. Id. 615. It appears, after further alteration, as Section 14 of the 1787 Ordinance.

78. In *Strader v. Graham*, 51 U.S. (10 How.) 82, 96 (1850), Chief Justice Taney went out of his way to say that the six articles of the Northwest Ordinance, "said to be perpetual as a compact, are not made a part of the new Constitution." He cited *Pollard v. Hagan*, 44 U.S. (3 How.) 212 (1845), and *Permoli v. The First Municipality*, 44 U.S. (3 How.) 588 (1845), but in none of the three cases was this question squarely before the Court.

79. Act of Aug. 7, 1789, ch. 8; 1 Stat. 50. See p. 219 supra. In addition to the amorphous compact theory of the Continental Congress, of course, the First Congress had Article IV, Section 3 (the power to make rules and regulations respecting the territories) and Article I, Section 8 (the commerce power) to rely on.

80. *The Federalist* No. 10, at 60–61 (Mod. Lib. ed. 1937) (Madison).

81. Id. 55.

82. Furthermore, as Madison asserts in *Federalist* 10, the representatives in Congress will be abler and more disinterested men; and precisely because of the great number and variety of interests they will be called upon to reconcile, they will be freer to ignore the demands of factions and to follow the rules of justice.

83. See p. 211, supra.

84. See note 40 supra.

85. *The Federalist* No. 53, at 351 (Mod. Lib. ed. 1937) (Madison).

86. 2 J. Richardson, *Messages and Papers of the Presidents* 584–585 (1900). The date of the veto was March 3, 1817.

CHAPTER 15

1. Message to Congress, February 28, 1963.

2. Herbert Wechsler, "Toward Neutral Principles of Constitutional Law," 73 *Harvard Law Review* 29 (1959).

3. *Screws v. United States*, 325 U.S. 91, 92 (1945).

4. "The Congress shall have Power . . . To regulate Commerce with Foreign Nations, and among the several States, and with the Indian Tribes." Article I, Sec. 8 (3).

5. Thomas Reed Powell, *Vagaries and Varieties in Constitutional Interpretation* (New York: Columbia University Press, 1956), p. 14.

6. 333 U.S. 28 (1948).

7. *Morgan v. Virginia*, 328 U.S. 373 (1946).

8. *Shelton v. Tucker*, 364 U.S. 479, 485, 487–488 (1960).

9. Alexander M. Bickel, *The Least Dangerous Branch* (Indianapolis and New York: Bobbs-Merrill Company, 1962), p. 53.

10. William W. Van Alstyne and Kenneth L. Karst, "State Action," 14 *Stanford Law Review* 58 (Dec., 1961).

11. *Hannah v. Larche*, 363 U.S. 420, 494 (1960).

12. Ibid. at 497, 498, 499.

13. *Wood v. Georgia*, 370 U.S. 375, 380 (1962).

14. 18 USCA 1504.

15. *Patterson v. Colorado*, 205 U.S. 454, 462 (1907).

16. The power of a federal judge summarily to punish such comments is governed by a federal statute which has given rise to a distinct body of law. This statute is in addition to the one quoted in the text above regarding communications sent to jurors.

17. *Wood v. Georgia* at 400.

18. Ibid. at 401–402.

19. *Irvin v. Dowd*, 366 U.S. 717, 729–730 (1961).

20. *Shepherd v. Florida*, 341 U.S. 50, 51 (1951).

21. Ibid. at 55.

22. Richard C. Donnelly and Ronald Goldfarb, "Contempt by Publication in the United States," 29 *Modern Law Review* 254 (1961).

23. As quoted in Alpheus Thomas Mason, *The Supreme Court from Taft to Warren* (Baton Rouge: Louisiana State University Press, 1958), p. 106.

24. Justice Frankfurter dissenting in *Terminiello v. Chicago*, 337 U.S. 1, 11 (1949).

25. Wechsler, p. 23.

26. *Hammer v. Dagenhart*, 247 U.S. 251 (1918).

27. 109 U.S. 3 (1883).

28. *Strauder v. West Virginia*, 100 U.S. 303 (1880).

29. *Ex parte Virginia*, 100 U.S. 339; 25 L.Ed. 676, 679 (1880).

30. *Guinn v. United States*, 238 U.S. 347 (1915).

31. *Lane* v. *Wilson*, 307 U.S. 268, 275 (1939).

32. *Grovey* v. *Townsend*, 295 U.S. 45 (1935).

33. *Smith* v. *Allwright*, 321 U.S. 649 (1944).

34. *Rice* v. *Elmore*, 165 F(2d) 387 (1947); certiorari denied, 333 U.S. 875 (1948).

35. *Terry* v. *Adams*, 345 U.S. 461 (1953).

36. The first section of the Fifteenth Amendment reads as follows: "The right of citizens of the United States to vote shall not be denied or abridged by the United States or by any State on account of race, color, or previous condition of servitude."

37. *Terry* v. *Adams*, p. 469.

38. Wechsler, p. 29.

39. *Shelley* v. *Kraemer*, 334 U.S. I, 20 (1948).

40. *Barrows* v. *Jackson*, 346 U.S. 249 (1953).

41. *Shelley* v. *Kraemer*, at 11.

42. *Peterson* v. *City of Greenville*, 373 U.S. 244 (1963).

43. *Lombard* v. *Louisiana*, 373 U.S. 267, 273 (1963).

44. On June 10, 1963, the Court agreed to review three new sit-in cases. *Barr* v. *City of Columbia*, *Bouie and Neal* v. *City of Columbia*, 374 U.S. 804, 805; *Bell* v. *Maryland*, 374 U.S. 805; and noted probable jurisdiction in another: *Robinson* v. *Florida*, 374 U.S. 803.

45. John P. Frank, *Cases on Constitutional Law* (Chicago: Callaghan & Co., 1952), p. 1032.

46. "Whoever, under color of any law, statute, ordinance, regulation, or custom, willfully subjects any inhabitant of any State ... to the deprivation of any rights, privileges, or immunities secured or protected by the Constitution or laws of the United States ... shall be fined not more than $1000 or imprisoned not more than one year, or both." 18 U.S.C. 242 (1950 ed.).

47. 42 U.S.C. 1983 (1950 ed.).

48. The conspiracy provision, 18 U.S.C. 241, protects a citizen in the enjoyment of a federal right, but the federal right here is a right only against those acting under color of law.

49. *Buck* v. *Bell*, 274 U.S. 200, 208 (1927).

50. "Judicial enforcement is of course state action, but this is not the end of the inquiry. The ultimate substantive question is whether there has been '[S]tate action of a particular character' (*Civil Rights Cases*, 3 S.Ct. at 21)—whether the character of the State's involvement in an arbitrary discrimination is such that it should be held *responsible* for the discrimination.

"This limitation on the scope of the prohibitions of the Fourteenth Amendment serves several vital functions in our system. Underlying the cases involving an alleged denial of equal protection by ostensibly private action is a clash of competing constitutional claims of a high order; liberty and equality. Freedom of the individual to choose his associates or his neighbors, to use and dispose of his property as he sees fit, to be irrational, arbitrary, capricious, even unjust in his personal relations are things all entitled to a large measure of protection from governmental interference. This liberty would be overridden, in the name of equality, if the strictures of the Amendment were applied to governmental and private action without distinction. Also inherent in the concept of state action are values of federalism, a recognition that there are areas of private rights upon which federal power should not lay a heavy hand and which should properly be left to the more precise instruments of local authority." Mr. Justice Harlan concurring in the result of the *Peterson* case and dissenting in whole or in part in the other sit-in cases decided May 20, 1963. 373 U.S. 244, 249–250.

51. Louis H. Pollak, "Racial Discrimination and Judicial Integrity: A Reply to Professor Wechsler," 108 *University of Pennsylvania Law Review* 13 (1959).

52. See *Gordon v. Gordon*, 332 Mass. 197; 124 N.E.2d 228 (1955).

53. Pollak, pp. 12–13.

54. It can be regarded as coercion, of course, only if we assume that the son's attachment to his father's money is such as to overcome his attachment to the woman he would make his bride and to principle.

55. Pollak, p. 14. Pollak's article was written before he was of counsel in the sit-in cases, where he joined in the argument urging the reversal of the trespass convictions.

56. *Zorach v. Clauson*, 343 U.S. 306, 313 (1952).

57. It is estimated that charitable trusts value tens of billions of dollars, and that each year sees the addition of trusts worth $4 billion. See Elias Clark, "Charitable Trusts, the Fourteenth Amendment and the Will of Stephen Girard," 66 *Yale Law Journal* 1010 (1957).

58. 357 U.S. 570 (1958). The first time the case came up, the Court held that it was a denial of the Fourteenth Amendment for officials of the City of Philadelphia to serve as trustees and administer the school set up under the will of Stephen Girard while excluding Negroes from the school, 353 U.S. 230 (1957). But when the Orphans Court substituted "private" individuals as trustees, the Supreme Court refused to review the case.

59. Van Alstyne and Karst, p. 57.

60. 365 U.S. 715, 722 (1961).

61. Ibid., at 727.

62. Jean-Jacques Rousseau, *Politics and the Arts: Letter to M. d'Alembert on the Theatre.* trans. Allan Bloom (Glencoe, Ill.: The Free Press, 1960), p. 66.

63. It is not suggested that these are the only possible rules available to the Court. Nor is it altogether inconceivable that the Court will decide against the Negroes.

64. Robert Horn, "National Constitutional Rights and the Desegregation Crisis," 10 *Western Political Quarterly* 463 (June, 1957).

65. Jack Greenberg, *Race Relations and American Law* (New York: Columbia University Press, 1959), pp. 2, 26.

66. Morton Grodzins, "Metropolitan Segregation," 197 *Scientific American* 38, 40 (October, 1957).

67. Not counted within this figure are students in those 26 (out of the total of 130) Washington schools that have no white students at all. Of the remaining 104 public schools where Negroes attend with whites, 22 have fewer than 5 white

students, and 41 have fewer than 10 white students. The statistics are taken from the *Statistical Summary* published by the Southern Education Reporting Service (November, 1962). One year later the number of Negroes in schools with whites had risen to 9.3 per cent, but the situation was essentially unchanged. For example, Negro enrollment in the schools in Washington, D.C., had risen by 7,156 and the number in schools with whites by 12,249; but the white enrollment in District schools had fallen by 2,338. Negroes, about 57 per cent of the general population of the District in 1963, now constitute 85.7 per cent of the public school enrollment (*Southern School News*, December, 1963). In Louisville, Kentucky, to cite one more example, 73 per cent (1,478) of the Negro high school students attend Central High School. In 1961–62, there was *one* white student in the school (The United States Commission on Civil Rights, *Civil Rights U.S.A./Public Schools Southern States 1962*, pp. 30, 55).

68. Grodzins, p. 37.

69. Greenberg, p. 310. The other information comes from the Census Tracts of the cities involved and from private surveys.

70. Grodzins, p. 37.

71. The public accommodations section of the civil rights bill now (January, 1964) awaiting a rule from the House Rules Committee is grounded, uneasily, on both the Commerce Clause and the Fourteenth Amendment. To say nothing more, there is some doubt as to its constitutionality.

72. On January 11, 1964, Morrison lost again, this time to John McKeithen.

73. Louis H. Pollak, "Emancipation and Law: A Century of Process," in Robert A. Goldwin, ed., *100 Years of Emancipation* (Chicago: Rand McNally & Co., 1963, 1964), p. 181.